D1251327

Contents

TALES FROM SHAKESPEARE

In this engaging new book, writer and critic Graham Holderness shows how a classic Shakespeare play can be the source for a modern story, providing a creative 'collision' between the Shakespeare text and contemporary concerns. Using an analogy from particle physics, Holderness tests his methodology through specific examples, structured in four parts: a recreation of performances of *Hamlet* and *Richard II* aboard the East India Company ship the *Red Dragon* in 1607; an imagined encounter between Shakespeare and Ben Jonson writing the King James Bible; the creation of a contemporary folk hero based on *Coriolanus* and drawing on films such as *Skyfall* and *The Hurt Locker*; and an account of the terrorist bombing at a performance of *Twelfth Night* in Qatar in 2005. These pieces of narrative and drama are interspersed with literary criticism, each using a feature of the original Shakespeare play or its performance to illuminate the extraordinary elasticity of Shakespeare. The 'tales' provoke questions about what we understand to be Shakespeare and not-Shakespeare, making the book of vital interest to students, scholars, and enthusiasts of Shakespeare, literary criticism, and creative writing.

GRAHAM HOLDERNESS is Research Professor in English at the University of Hertfordshire. He has published extensively in early modern and modern literature, and drama. His influential publications include *Shakespeare's History* (1985), *The Shakespeare Myth* (1988), the trilogy *Cultural Shakespeare: Essays in the Shakespeare Myth* (2001), *Visual Shakespeare: Essays in Film and Television* (2002), and *Textual Shakespeare: Writing and the Word* (2003), the innovative biography *Nine Lives of William Shakespeare* (2011), and the novel *The Prince of Denmark* (2001). He is also a dramatist and poet, and his poetry collection *Craeft* received a Poetry Book Society award in 2002.

TALES FROM SHAKESPEARE

Creative Collisions

GRAHAM HOLDERNESS

CAMBRIDGE
UNIVERSITY PRESS

CAMBRIDGE
UNIVERSITY PRESS

University Printing House, Cambridge CB2 8BS, United Kingdom

Cambridge University Press is part of the University of Cambridge.

It furthers the University's mission by disseminating knowledge in the pursuit of
education, learning, and research at the highest international levels of excellence.

www.cambridge.org
Information on this title: www.cambridge.org/9781107071292

First published 2014

Printed in the United Kingdom by Clays, St Ives plc

A catalogue record for this publication is available from the British Library

Library of Congress Cataloguing in Publication data
Holderness, Graham.
Tales from Shakespeare : Creative Collisions / Graham Holderness.
pages cm
Includes bibliographical references and index.
ISBN 978-1-107-07129-2 (hardback)
1. Shakespeare, William, 1564–1616–Adaptations–History and criticism.   2. Shakespeare,
William, 1564–1616–Criticism and interpretation.   3. Shakespeare, William,
1564–1616–Influence.   I. Title.
PR2880.A1H65 2014
822.3′3–dc23
2014002312

ISBN 978-1-107-07129-2 hardback

To my parents
Who bought me Tales from Shakespeare

Preface

I CREATIVE COLLISIONS

Ideas rose in clouds: I felt them collide until pairs interlocked, so to speak, making a stable combination. (*Henri Poincaré*)

When I first read Shakespeare at school, the plays were firmly located within a set of contingent discourses clearly marking out what was Shakespeare from what was not.

These contexts formed the infrastructure of Shakespeare studies: Tudor history; the arts and manners of the Elizabethan court; the history of the theatre, mediaeval to early modern; the literary world, with its as yet un-dissociated Renaissance sensibility. The critical context was provided by T. S. Eliot, F. R. Leavis, G. Wilson Knight.

Though deeply embedded in this culture, I was also aware that Shakespeare had an unnerving tendency to pop up everywhere around me. I heard his words in pop songs ('You know someone said, the world's a stage'); saw his plays travestied in comedy sketches by Tony Hancock, and Morecombe and Wise ('What d'ye think of it so far?'); found his image in advertisements, and his face on beer-mats. But there seemed to be no bridges linking the Shakespeare of the academy with the Shakespeare of that popular culture my critical mentors despised and ignored; no meaningful connection between Shakespeare and not-Shakespeare.

Thirty years later, it was possible to document these interactions, and to discuss Shakespeare in relation to popular culture, tourism, and advertising; to the general fields of theatre, education, and television; and to social contexts such as politics, media, and gender that had been made visible by critical theory. My edited collection

The Shakespeare Myth (1988) pioneered, in the teeth of no little resistance, many such approaches that have, in the meantime, become much more familiar. But the wounds of controversy quickly heal, and academic institutions adjust and rebalance themselves. Though the geography has changed, there are still clear-cut borders between what is acknowledged to be Shakespeare, and what is not. Or rather, it is accepted that Shakespeare permeates everything, but there is no corresponding recognition that everything permeates Shakespeare.

This book readdresses this problem via a methodology derived from an analogy with contemporary particle physics. The concept of 'collision', signifying the impact of a number of forces and objects upon one another, is a useful analogy for describing and accounting for what sometimes happens to produce the phenomenon we know as 'Shakespeare'. A collision may be violent and destructive, as in a car crash, or it may be harmless and hardly noticeable, as when two people bump into one another. But in every case the collision makes a difference, alters the trajectory of the objects themselves, and creates new energy that did not exist before. The examples of Shakespearean 'collision' I have written on below vary, from the extreme violence of the 9/11 terrorist attacks, to the more 'normal' interaction between a classical text and a contemporary process of adaptation or appropriation. But in every case the collision can be seen to release new 'available energy' and to modify both objects and the forces that move them.

My introduction explores various methodologies based on analogies from the natural sciences, which are widely (if unconsciously) deployed in Shakespeare studies, using *Hamlet* as a test-case. All these approaches concur in proving the extraordinary elasticity of the Shakespearean text, which can undergo protean changes without ever completely losing its identity. Once this position is accepted, it becomes easier to perceive that some encounters between Shakespeare and not-Shakespeare are not at all the random and accidental collisions they at first sight appear to be. Such encounters release new energies and create new particles, generating new meanings and modifying both parties to the collision.

Four chapters of the book test this methodology through specific examples: the performances of *Hamlet* and *Richard II* aboard the East India Company ship the *Red Dragon* off the coast of Africa in 1607; the brief encounter between Shakespeare and the King James Bible in the latter's anniversary year of 2011; the cinematic adaptation of *Coriolanus* by Ralph Fiennes, which links Shakespeare's play with a modern folk-hero who can also be found in films such as *Skyfall* and *The Hurt Locker*; and lastly the terrorist suicide-bombing of a performance of *Twelfth Night* in Qatar in March 2005, which in turn illuminates the impact on Shakespeare of the terrorist attacks of 9/11. In each case, the 'collision' is fully documented and described, contextualised and interpreted, then explained and expounded in terms of the reciprocal impact between 'Shakespeare' and what was 'not-Shakespeare' until the collision itself brought them productively together.

II TALES FROM SHAKESPEARE

'That little poem you wrote in Mrs Matuschek's guest-book; did you make that up yourself?'

'Well, that was half and half.'

'Half and half? What do you mean?'

'Half Shakespeare and half me. You see I just turn the lines around to suit the occasion.' (*The Shop Around the Corner* (1948))

A major thrust of my argument is that the basic primary activities constituting Shakespeare studies – scholarly editing; historical context-ualisation and analysis; critical and theoretical interpretation; theatrical or cinematic production; creative adaptation – exist in a continuum, and when compared, prove to be remarkably similar to one another. My view, which I developed previously in the book *Textual Shakespeare* (2003), is that all these activities resemble one another more than they differ. They are all, in fact, 'appropriations', and there is no other way of approaching Shakespeare but by appropriation of one kind or another. As I wrote:

The ultimate question ... concerns the relations between these various activities that go on with, and around, literary texts – reading, textual scholarship, editorial processing, critical interpretation, textual theory. Are these quite different activities that need to be understood in terms of their interaction with one another, or are they are all aspects of a common search for understanding through writing? Do they represent different ways of interpreting the process of reading; or are they all rather extensions of the single fundamental act of reading – reading, as it were, at a more advanced level? If the latter, then we move from a model in which reading is the primary activity, and all other critical and scholarly functions become secondary, ancillary to the originating act of decoding; to one in which the processes of remaking the text are shared in common between textual study, editing, critical interpretation, indeed all our various 'reading' practices; where 'a real reader is a writer'.[1]

All readings of Shakespeare are appropriations. So are all scholarly texts, and critical discussions, and theatrical productions, and creative adaptations of Shakespeare, appropriations. The 'collisions' I have studied here will bear out these assertions. But the final test for such a view rests with the creative rewriting or reworking of Shakespeare: is it still 'Shakespeare'? Or something else? The position I argue is that expressed by Hélène Cixous in the maxim quoted above: 'The real reader is a writer.' In *Textual Shakespeare* I took this exhortation literally, and made the quantum leap from 'reading' to 'writing' as a proper critical activity. If our processes of reading involve a continual remaking of Shakespeare, then our writing should also entail rewriting. Criticism must involve the creative deployment of literary conventions, as well as the discursive prosecution of rational argument. *Textual Shakespeare* included, between its chapters of academic analysis, short creative pieces – poems and translations, rewritten Shakespeare scenes, extracts from a novel – that comment on, and pursue, the intellectual arguments by creative reworkings of language.

In a more recent work, *Nine Lives of William Shakespeare* (2011), I took this approach much further, balancing scholarly and critical argument around the Shakespeare biography with specimens of creative writing that parallel the academic discussion.

This book therefore ruptures some of the boundaries that normally corral academic and scholarly discourses separately from creative and imaginative writing. What this means is that the book operates on two discrete 'tracks', running in parallel and intersecting, but operating by different sets of rules or signals. In the creative works, the historical facts and traditions are implicit, but the normal disciplines of scholarly writing do not apply. Here some of the facts are invented; traditions are offered as facts; speculation is presented as manifest knowledge.[2]

'Criticism' and 'creativity' are generally thought of, both in theory and practice, as alternatives. Their pairing even sets them up in binary opposition, one against the other. And when we look at the ways in which we construct critical writing, in the curriculum and in everyday pedagogic practice, this is understandable. It is almost de rigueur to open a discussion of these issues with parallel columns of descriptive terms that we apply respectively to critical and creative writing. On the one hand, criticism is discursive, analytical, logical, clear, argumentative, impersonal, objective. On the other hand, creativity is intuitive, evocative, expressive, performative, personal, subjective. And so on.

And yet criticism, or at least literary criticism, is surely nothing more than an effort to explain and account for creativity, as it is manifested in writing. There is, at the very least, continuity between the two, since the one is a means to knowledge of the other. Typically the critical incorporates the creative into itself, by the device of quotation. At the very best, one might claim that criticism is the precursor of creativity, criticism's John the Baptist to creativity's Christ, announcing its imminent advent. Like John the Baptist, criticism is 'not itself that light', but is 'sent to bear witness of that light'. The best criticism ushers creativity into human knowledge, so that the light need not shine in darkness; but then eclipses itself in favour of a greater one who is to come. As creativity waxes, so criticism wanes. Having prophesied creativity's imminence and its own demise, criticism faces a kenotic evacuation of meaning as it renders the creative intelligible and accessible in its own right.

However, in reality, things are not that simple. Notwithstanding his deference and deferral to Jesus, John claimed considerable authority in his own right too, not least the authority of tradition, of the Old Testament prophets; and many people (including Herod Antipas) could not tell the difference between Jesus and John. A few Christians still follow John, believing him to be the true Messiah. And some have argued for a systematic replacement of literature by literary theory.

I want to suggest a different relationship between criticism and creativity: to suggest that the best criticism is actually creative writing, and that the two are not really binary opposites at all, but more like non-identical twins (as Jesus and John are often represented). Criticism that separates itself off from literature, linguistically and discursively, is producing something else, philosophy or critical theory. The most perfect harmony between criticism and creativity is where they become almost indistinguishable. And possibly the best criticism of all is that which succeeds in using language in the way it is used by creative writers.

'Creative criticism' mingles criticism and creativity together in a promiscuously hybrid discourse. Its arguments operate, as do the creative works it studies, as much by metaphor as by logical argument. And it penetrates into areas where criticism normally dares not go, deep into the subjectivity of the critic and reader. It proposes, in short, a new and fundamentally reorientated relationship between criticism and creativity.

The function of such rewriting in *Tales from Shakespeare* was to formally convert Shakespeare into not-Shakespeare, in order to determine how much of 'Shakespeare' remains. The fictional excursions that follow arise in each case from the particular collision under investigation: they represent examples of new particles and new energies released by the impact. Chapter 2 invents a shipboard journal that provides an imaginary eyewitness account of *Richard II* being performed off the coast of Sierra Leone. Chapter 4 supplements the convergence of Shakespeare and the King James Bible with a dramatic extension of two short stories, by Rudyard Kipling and Anthony Burgess, which imagine Shakespeare becoming involved in the production of the Authorized Version. Chapter 6 pursues the case that Ralph Fiennes's adaptation of *Coriolanus* produces a generic twentieth-century folk-hero, by locating Shakespeare's Roman character inside a spy thriller. Chapter 8 provides a critical-creative commentary on Shakespeare and terrorism, by weaving together an analysis of an event, the bombing of the Doha Players Theatre in 2005, with an imagined narrative of the suicide bomber's own encounter with Shakespeare.

Many things collide in the pages below: ships and plays, Southwark and Africa; theatre and pulpit, the Globe and St Paul's; Rome and Belgrade, Coriolanus and James Bond; Al-Quaeda and amateur dramatics, car bombs and poetry. It is a book about many different things.

But it remains, in the end, a book about Shakespeare.

Acknowledgements

Parts of the Introduction were previously published in '"Dressing old words new": Shakespeare, Science and Appropriation', *Borrowers and Lenders: The Journal of Shakespeare and Appropriation*, 1:2 (University of Georgia, October 2005), n.p. Earlier versions of the two chapters of Part IV appeared as 'Shakespeare and Terror', *Shakespeare After 9/11*, special issue of *Shakespeare Yearbook*, edited by Matthew Biberman, Julia Reinhard Lupton, and Graham Holderness (Lewiston, NY: Edwin Mellen Press, 2011), and '"Rudely interrupted": Shakespeare and Terrorism' (with Bryan Loughrey) *Critical Survey*, 19:3 (December 2007). Material is reproduced by kind permission of the editors.

The play *Wholly Writ* was performed at Shakespeare's Globe in June 2011 and at the Shakespeare Birthplace Trust, Stratford-upon-Avon, in July 2011. The Globe cast comprised: James Wallace as William Shakespeare, Kevin Quarmby as Ben Jonson, Frances Marshall as Ann Shakespeare, and Rachel Winters as Judith Shakespeare. The Stratford cast comprised: Sam Lesser as William Shakespeare, John Heffernan as Ben Jonson, and Penny Downie as Ann and Judith Shakespeare.

Introduction: from appropriation to collision

Why is my verse so barren of new pride?
So far from variation or quicke change?
Why with the time do I not glance aside
To new-found methods and to compounds strange?
Why write I still all one, ever the same,
And keepe invention in a noted weed,
That every word doth almost tell my name,
Shewing their birth, and where they did proceed?
O know sweet love, I alwaies write of you,
And you and love are still my argument:
So all my best is dressing old words new,
Spending againe what is already spent:
For as the Sun is daily new and old,
So is my love still telling what is told.[1]

Shakespeare's Sonnet 76 laments the fact that the poet's writing is continually restating the same experience, his love, without ever changing the subject, or generating anything new. His lyric poetry seems to be stuck in the same confessional rut, obsessively personal, just reiterating the same emotional condition; and his poetic language is limply and limpidly transparent, so that no reader could possibly doubt its authorial source: 'every word doth almost tell my name, / Shewing their birth, and where they did proceed'.

How ironic. Today Shakespeare's sonnets are just as likely to be interpreted as an impersonal poetic drama that bears only a tangential relationship to the life of their author, as a direct expression of the poet's biography. One of the most vexing questions about

Shakespeare's life, a life that has in itself become a field of great controversy, is precisely that relationship between the authenticity of the poetic voice and the real biographical roots of the poetry. If every word in poetry really did suggest, 'tell'[2] the author's name, unmistakably revealing its nativity and provenance, how much simpler life would be. In fact the printed text of Sonnet 76 fails to deliver this required clarity of exposition. In the 1609 edition the very word 'tel' that should denote confessional transparency reads, presumably by printer's error, as 'fel.' By substituting 'tell' we are accepting an uncontroversial Capell emendation, but we are also already allowing someone else to speak on behalf of the allegedly self-revelatory name of Shakespeare.

Modern literary scholarship would not in any case expect to find, in literature, any such limpid textual transparency as that invoked by this sonnet. In the last decades of the twentieth century, textual theory experienced what D. C. Greetham calls an 'inversion' comparable to Marx's inversion of Hegel.[3] Just as Marx insisted that matter, not spirit, is the real substance of the world, so modern bibliographers have looked to the 'material text' rather than to the original authorial utterance or 'idea' as the 'real foundation' of textuality, 'making the very post-lapsarian contingencies of the text, its negotiations with its own history, as the *base* of textual operations, and therefore making authoriality, and especially authorial intention, into merely a "function" (or the *superstructure*) of this history rather than its *raison-d'être*.[4] Instead of seeking to emulate a text-that-never-was, the authorial text imagined as original, complete and perfect in itself, bibliography now accepts textuality as a history of change:

The textual condition's only law is the law of change. It is a law, however, like all laws, that operates within certain limits. Every text enters the world under determinate sociohistorical conditions, and while these conditions may and should be variously defined and imagined, they establish the horizon within which the life histories of different texts can play themselves out. The law of change declares that these histories will exhibit a ceaseless process of textual development and mutation – a process which can only be arrested if all the textual transformations of a particular work fall into nonexistence. To study texts and textualities, then, we have to study these complex (and open-ended) histories of textual change and variance.[5]

The first casualty of this process is of course the author, whose metaphorical 'death' is also entailed in the birth of writing. The death of the author is the birth of 'appropriation', as Foucault put it in his foundational essay 'What is an Author?': 'discourses are objects of appropriation'.[6] If the author is no longer the guarantor of meaning, then meaning derives from the interaction of reader with text, and the reader has taken control from the author. The reader is an appropriator, not a subject, of the writing. As such, writing can no longer ever claim to be homogeneous and permanent, 'all one, ever the same'. It survives only in appropriation, only by its capacity for mutability, for 'variation or quick change'.

II

Just how ceaseless and open-ended are these processes of 'textual development and mutation?' If a 'work' can undergo an almost infinite process of textual transformation, how can we be sure it's the same 'work'? At what point does textual variance produce not a mutation, but a new text? When dealing with 'appropriations' of Shakespeare, since many are the work of other writers, are we still dealing with Shakespeare? Can we keep on 'dressing old words new', and simultaneously regarding them as the same old words?

In a landmark text, Jean I. Marsden argued that to focus on 'appropriations' is to produce 'a view of Shakespeare embedded not only in his own culture but in ours, forcing us to consider both the impact we have on the plays and the impact they have on us'.[7] Appropriation studies are more likely, by definition, to be concerned with the impact we have on the plays, than with the impact they have on us. Appropriation for Marsden is a unilateral seizure, as in the *OED* definition 'To appropriate: to take possession of for one's own; to take to oneself'. To take is also to take away: appropriation is simultaneously expropriation, forfeiture by the taken of intrinsic meaning and value.

Associated with abduction, adoption and theft, appropriation's central tenet is the desire for possession. It comprehends both the commandeering of the desired object and the process of making this object one's own, controlling it by possessing it. Appropriation is neither dispassionate nor disinterested; it has connotations of usurpation, of seizure for one's own uses ...
(Marsden, *Appropriation*, p. 1)

The forcefulness of this language shows the critic perceiving appropriation as violence, and reacting with liberal outrage against an act of cultural colonisation. But increasingly we have become convinced that there is no other way of engaging with the canonical literature of the past. In Terence Hawkes's famous phrase, 'human actions, activities, the "things of this world", don't themselves "mean". It is *we* who mean *by* them.'[8] Or as Gary Taylor puts it, 'We find in Shakespeare only what we bring to him or what others have left behind; he gives us back our own values.'[9] So there is nothing other than appropriation. Marsden's view is predicated on the post-structuralist truism, *verum factum*,[10] the world is what we make of it. Or as the occasionally Cartesian Hamlet puts it, 'There is nothing either good or bad but thinking makes it so.'[11]

> Every act of interpretation can be seen as an act of appropriation – making sense of a literary artefact by fitting it into our own parameters. The literary work thus becomes ours; we possess it by reinventing it as surely as if we had secured its physical presence by force. (Marsden, *Appropriation*, p. 1)

But is reinvention, as this rhetoric hotly asserts, tantamount to kidnapping, if there is no kid to nap? Martial is said to have invented the term 'plagiarism' from *plagiarius*, a kidnapper; but this was to describe writers who stole his work and misrepresented it as their own.[12] If we can only make sense of a literary artefact by fitting it into our own parameters, then it's a case of *mutatis mutandis*. Why characterise this natural process as hostage-taking violence? How do we define the entity we are taking over? If it remains undefined, how do we know whether we're hacking off its limbs, or breathing new life into a lifeless body? Is the work being laid on a Bed of Procrustes, or on an operating table for resuscitation? Marsden raises this question herself, but then retorts only with another question: 'One impulse when faced with this plethora of conflicting images may be to ask where the real Shakespeare lies. But is this question answerable or even relevant?' (*Appropriation*, pp. 8–9).

Appropriation studies of Shakespeare thus begin with a contradiction. We can only know the work by reinventing it, by appropriation. But such reinvention is conceived as a violent assault on the work's original identity, expropriation. Yet the work has no original identity. Or rather this 'identity' is alternately denied and assumed,

erased and recuperated. Writing has no meaning other than what
we make of it. Yet we believe that the meanings ascribed by
our appropriations are different from other meanings of the work.
'Different from' predicates a comparator; there can be no difference
without another. But we find ourselves no longer able with any
confidence to relocate that elusive and inscrutable stranger.

III

Revisiting the same territory a decade later, Christy Desmet develops
Jean Marsden's approach by acknowledging both positive and negative connotations of 'appropriation'.

The word 'appropriation' implies an exchange, either the theft of something
valuable (such as property or ideas) or a gift, the allocation of resources for a
worthy cause (such as the legislative appropriation of funds for a new
school).[13]

This redefinition (which works better in American than British
English) is then applied to Shakespeare by dividing 'appropriations'
into 'big time' and 'small time' initiatives.[14] On the one hand there
are the large-scale colonisations of Shakespeare by some dominant
ideology; on the other more local, individual, particular acts of
rewriting that share a common revisionist agenda: 'individual acts
of "re-vision" that arise from love, or rage, or simply a desire to play
with Shakespeare' (Desmet and Sawyer, *Shakespeare and Appropriation*, p. 2). In some ways this distinction recuperates, in a less
reductive way, the distinctions attempted in cultural materialist work
of the 1980s between conservative and radical appropriations. But
Desmet's approach offers a much more positive view of the interaction between the 'work' and its meanings, by acknowledging a
constitutive reciprocity, accepting that the work does have its impact
on us, as well as vice versa. Or as John Joughin puts it, 'Insofar as we
continue to appropriate Shakespeare, it's worth remembering that
Shakespeare also continues to appropriate us.'[15]
   But this approach encounters the same difficulty in defining
exactly what the driver of that counter-appropriation is, and what
of the work exists beyond its multiple appropriations. Both Marsden
(*Appropriation*, pp. 8–9; see above) and Hawkes raise this question,

only to deflect it towards another enquiry: 'Serious conundrums remain. If we abandon the notion either of an absolute "truth" about Shakespeare the dramatist, or of a "truth" that his plays embody or entail, what can we make of the concept of an "alternative" to that truth?' (Hawkes, *Alternative Shakespeares*, vol. II, p. 15). Desmet closes her introduction to *Shakespeare and Appropriation* by seeking a way through this impasse. Revisiting Terence Hawkes's 'mean *by*' slogan, she suggests that the work is not reducible to its appropriations, but rather is a fertile source for the proliferation of new meanings.

Terrence Hawkes, in a much misunderstood phrase, says that Shakespeare does not mean; rather '*we* mean *by* Shakespeare'. The point is not that Shakespeare has no meaning, but that because meaning changes with context, he has, if anything, more meanings than we can yet imagine. (p. 12)[16]

Despite the caveat, the formulation 'more meanings than we can yet imagine' is in one sense entirely consistent with the post-structuralist principle that Shakespeare has no intrinsic meaning, or at least none that is accessible. There is no immanent or permanent meaning; all meaning is generated anew by acts of the imagination. All acts of the imagination are local, context-specific, always different and always changing. Human beings, their society and culture, will go on changing in ways as yet unimaginable; and they will go on attaching new and different meanings to Shakespeare. Therefore, the future meanings of Shakespeare are as yet unimaginable.

What interests me about this phrase however is the way in which it chimes with, perhaps even recuperates, a language of infinity, the unknowable, the unimaginable, that we would naturally associate with traditional Bardolatry, or with its contemporary reaffirmations.[17] As we undertake each reimagining of Shakespeare, we own and understand the product of the activity. Yet when we contemplate Shakespeare's future potentiality for reimaginings, we are faced with something alien, inconceivable, unknowable. This formulation echoes the language we find in Matthew Arnold:

> Others abide our question. Thou art free.
> We ask and ask – Thou smilest and art still
> Out-topping knowledge.[18]

Or Ralph Waldo Emerson:

[Shakespeare] wrote the text of modern life . . . he is inconceivably wise; the others, conceivably. A good reader can, in a sort, nestle into Plato's brain and think from thence; but not into Shakespeare's. We are still out of doors. For executive faculty, for creation, Shakespeare is unique. No man can imagine it better.[19]

Or Henry James:

The secret that baffles us being the secret of the Man, we know, as I have granted, that we shall never touch the man directly in the Artist. We stake our hopes thus on indirectness, which may contain possibilities; we take that very truth for our counsel of despair, try to look at it as helpful for the Criticism of the future.[20]

Clearly all these nineteenth-century thinkers assume Shakespeare as an originator of meaning. But they also recognise that our only access to that plenitudinous source is through something similar to what we now call appropriation: 'indirectness' (James), 'question' (Arnold), or in Emerson's wonderful phrase, by peering into Shakespeare's brain from an *unheimlich* position irrevocably external to it, 'out of doors'.

It is interesting that so many contemporary critics have begun to pay new attention to these old voices.[21] Although we would not wish to share their Bardolatry, and we are now finally convinced that Shakespeare's work is changeable, multiple, unfixed, and unstable, we still nonetheless find ourselves seeking an origin for that work in the indefinable, the invisible, the limitless. And after all, even Terry Eagleton once suggested that Shakespeare remains somehow ahead of us, and 'we have yet to catch up with him'.[22]

IV

Shakespeare now exists in an environment of textual multiplicity. The text is multiple, iterable, subject to an inevitable law of change. It is never original, always copied. The grounds on which a priori assumptions could be made about the automatic superiority of one text over another have disappeared: so texts remain to us as plural, relative to one another, not severed into separation by some absolute judgement, but embedded in a network of differences. The text gives us no direct access to any pure space of authorial intention, for someone has always already got there before us.

When Descartes addressed this same problem, he deployed the figure of beeswax, an example lying easily to hand in the form of the stick of sealing wax in his desk. At first glimpse wax is a piece of solid matter with definable properties – density, temperature, acousticity. It bears sensory traces of its own history, being redolent of honey and pollen.[23]

Let us take, for example, this piece of wax which has just been taken from the hive; it has not yet lost the sweetness of the honey it contained; it still retains something of the smell of the flowers from which it was gathered; its colour, shape and size, are apparent; it is hard, cold, it is tangible; and if you tap it, it will emit a sound. So, all the things by which a body can be known distinctly are to be found together in this one. (p. 108)

But when heated, the wax changes shape, colour, taste, smell, transmutes from one state of matter, solid, to another, liquid. All the empirical evidence suggests that in terms of physical properties perceivable by the senses, this object has undergone several radical changes of state and condition.

But, as I am speaking, let it be placed near a flame: what remained of its taste is dispelled, the smell disappears, the colour changes, it grows bigger, becomes liquid, warms up, one can hardly touch it, and although one taps it, it will no longer make any sound. Does the same wax remain after this change? One must admit that it does remain, and no one can deny it. What, then, was it I that knew in this piece of wax with such distinctness? (p. 108)

Since to the senses 'wax' is a discontinuous and incommensurable sequence of changes, and yet the observer continues to know it as wax, the identity of the object is not in itself, but in 'an intuition of the mind': 'Certainly it could be nothing of all the things that I observed by means of the senses, for everything which fell under taste, smell, sight, touch or hearing, is changed, and yet the same wax remains' (p. 109). Descartes goes on of course from these observations to prove that he himself exists; since although he can doubt anything about wax, he cannot doubt his knowledge of it: for 'it cannot be that when I see or ... think I see, I, who think, am nothing' (p. 111).

A modern scientist would simply say that Descartes's methods of observation were too limited and superficial to understand the changes undergone by this substance. But if he had known enough biochemistry to understand how wax is manufactured by the worker bee's digestive system, and secreted on to its abdominal plates; or its chemical composition of fatty acids, hydrocarbons, and the propolis resin and pigments that give it colour and scent; or even its atomic structure of carboxylic acids and monohydroxy alcohols, which can be quantified and graphically depicted – then his conclusion would surely have been the same. 'Wax' is not a singular lexical unit that corresponds to a singular object. It is a summary or shorthand term that covers and subsumes all this information. The word can just as easily denote 'wax' to be a sequence of chemical changes and altered physical states, as it can point to 'wax' as a stable and solid object.

Descartes's meditation provides one possible model for understanding a play like Shakespeare's *Hamlet*. Like his stick of sealing wax, *Hamlet* lies to hand as a solid object, the text on my desk. Observation deduces a list of obvious properties: singularity, completeness, coherence, identity, stability, continuity. Closer observation discloses traces of origin and development: the shapes of narrative sources, the lineaments of an ur-*Hamlet*, the distinguishing marks of a vexed theatrical history. Once I begin to read the text, to interpret it, to write about it, to prepare it for a theatrical performance, to rewrite it – in a word to appropriate it, then I am applying Descartes's flame, and discovering that *Hamlet* is indeed a 'ceaseless process of textual development and mutation'. But just as Descartes was content to call all that 'wax', so I am reconciled to calling all this by the composite yet univocal name, *Hamlet*.

v

Descartes has taken us via philosophy into the biosciences. But modern critics with their focus on the material text seem to prefer models and metaphors from the apparently more solid science of chemistry. In this discourse we can find *Hamlet*, and Shakespeare himself, represented as a solid object such as a metal. Martin Scofield in his book on appropriations of *Hamlet*[24] speaks of the plays as a 'ductile' medium (the ductility of a metal is its capacity to be drawn out into thin rods or wires). Similarly Stephen Greenblatt speaks of Shakespeare's work as being enduring because flexible: 'The fantastic diffusion and long life of Shakespeare's works depends on their extraordinary malleability.'[25]

The secret of Shakespeare's longevity and plurality lies in the 'malleability' of the works. The word is common in contemporary Shakespeare studies, and is used to indicate the fact that the text is responsive to actions upon it, co-operates with adaptation, offers itself up for conversion and transformation. Though used generally to denote plasticity in any material substance, the 'malleability' belongs properly to metallurgy (as its derivation from *malleus*, hammer, indicates). The malleability of metals derives from their peculiar atomic structure, which consists of tightly packed groups of positive ions that are held in place by a strongly attractive but relatively mobile sea of free electrons. Force applied to the surface of a metal allows atoms to 'slip' over one another without loss of density. So you can hammer iron into different shapes without changing the structure or properties of its crystals. 'Ductility' also represents a change of shape that entails no change in the internal structure of atoms and molecules.

The metaphor provides an explanation of textual mutability diametrically opposed to the post-structuralist inflections of 'appropriation'. If *Hamlet* is like a metal, then the changes it undergoes entail no fundamental chemical change, and are produced by an interaction of internal properties and external forces. Iron hammered into rods, or copper into wire, remain unmistakably, elementally, iron and copper. *Hamlet*, hammered, squeezed, bent, wire-drawn – re-edited, interpreted, performed, adapted, travestied, rewritten – remains elementally *Hamlet*.[26]

There is no particular reason, other than an instinctive preference for solidity as a guarantor of 'materiality', why *Hamlet* should be compared to a solid rather than to one of the other states of matter, liquids and gases. Language in a play or poem does not behave with the random arbitrary motion of atoms in a gas. Liquids, on the other hand, with their peculiar couplings of atoms, their combinations of density and fluidity, their capacity to hold together through extensive motion, could possibly serve as a better model. But these parallels may well in any case be too generic to be sustained, since the states of matter correspond more accurately to primary categories such as language and narrative, and a play is more like an artefact constructed from metal than like metal itself; more like an ornamental fountain than like water.

VI

But given the dependence of poetry and drama on human activity, is a play not more like a living than an elemental thing, somewhere in the midst of Aristotle's distinction between natural and artificial beings? In the same sentence as his 'malleability' reference, Greenblatt uses another figure which sends us back towards biology again: 'The fantastic diffusion and long life of Shakespeare's works depends on their extraordinary malleability, their protean capacity to elude definition and escape secure possession' ('General Introduction', p. 1).

Greenblatt's other metaphor, 'protean', seems quite different, but is remarkably similar, in its implications. In place of a solid body which can be reshaped by the application of external force, Proteus is a divinity who can change at will into a variety of quite different forms. A sea-god of Greek mythology, he is capable of 'all sorts of transformations', can 'change himself not only into every beast on earth, but into water and blazing fire'.[27] Proteus is Poseidon's shepherd, responsible for the care of his 'flocks' of seals. He is also a sage who knows everything of the past, the present, and the future. But like Hamlet himself, he is 'niggard of question' (3.1.13), and hates giving information. He must be captured and firmly bound, held through all his shape-shifting mutations, and only then will he consent to disclose the truth. In the *Odyssey* Menelaus recounts to Telemachus the story of how he managed to hold Proteus long enough to learn of his past mistakes and his future destiny.

At midday the old man himself emerged, found his fat seals already there, and went the rounds to make his count … When he had done, he too lay down to sleep. Then with a shout, we leapt upon him and flung our arms round his back. But the old man's skill and cunning had not deserted him. He began by turning himself into a bearded lion and then into a snake, and after that a panther and a giant boar. He changed into running water and a great tree in leaf. But we set our teeth and held him like a vice. (p. 76)

Bacon saw Proteus as a model for matter itself. In *De Sapientia Veterum* (*The Wisdom of the Ancients*), he proposes that the 'fable' of Proteus unlocks the secrets of Nature, and explains the states of matter.[28]

For under the person of Proteus, *the first Matter (which next to God is the auncientest thing) may bee represented: for Matter dwells in the concavity of heaven as in a Cave. He is* Neptunes *bond-man, because the operations and dispensations of Matter are chiefly exercised in liquid bodies.*

His flocke or hearde seemes to be nothing but the ordinarie *Species* of sensible creatures, plants, and mettals in which Matter seemes to diffuse and as it were spend it selfe ... (p. 67)

Reflecting the ancient idea that the universe consisted of one common material substance shaped by divine power into all the varied phenomena of life, Bacon uses the Proteus myth to explain the paradox of unity in diversity. Though the universe is varied and plural, it was initially formed from one fundamental substance, 'matter', which is associated with water and the 'liquid' state of aquatic life. This is of course exactly how creation is described in the Book of Genesis chapter 1 verse 2.

And the earth was without form, and void; and darkness was upon the face of the deep ... And God said, Let there be a firmament in the midst of the waters, and let it divide the waters from the waters.

According to Bacon, 'by the power of that divine word (*Producat*) Matter at the Creators command did congregate it selfe (not by ambages or turnings, but instantly) to the production of its worke into an act and constitution of Species' (*Sapientia Veterum*, p. 68). The creatures include Man: 'And the Lord God formed Man of the dust of the ground' (Genesis 1.7), or as we would now say from the billions-of-years-old cosmic dust from which the universe is constituted. Matter is both one and many.

For Bacon, the hero who captures Proteus and extracts his secrets is the scientist. But there is no docile and obedient yielding up of Nature's secrets to the analytical method. On the contrary, matter, like Proteus, will transform itself into many elusive shapes rather than accept subjugation.

If any experte Minister of Nature shall encounter Matter by main force, vexing and urging her with intent and purpose to reduce her to nothing; she

contrariwise (seeing annihilation and absolute destruction cannot bee effected but by the omnipotence of God) being thus caught in the straites of necessitie, doth change and turne her selfe into divers strange formes and shapes of thinges. (*Sapientia Veterum*, p. 69)

Linked by a common derivation from *protos* (primary or fundamental), in Bacon's interpretation the myth Proteus parallels the substance 'protein'. Biochemists call proteins 'the building blocks of life', since they are fundamental to all biological change and development. Long chain molecules of amino acids, proteins are the basis of biological activity. As enzymes, they drive all biochemical reactions. As antibodies they recognise invasive elements and prompt the immune system to confront them. As structural elements, they are the main constituents of bones, muscle, skin, and blood vessels.[29] This insight takes us back to Descartes. The various substances that make up the body seem to perception very different, not manifestly made of the same stuff. Yet they are all constituted from proteins, a common primary matter undergoing continual self-transformation.

Protein may take many forms, but it's still protein. However broad the range of his permutations, Proteus remains Proteus. Like an elemental metal, the changes he undergoes are changes only of shape, not of identity or internal structure. If Shakespeare is like Proteus, then all his manifold and plural forms remain permutations of the same singular entity. All these permutations should of course carry, if this conceit holds, a DNA code that can be traced back to the biological parent. Just as the Human Genome Project has specified the sequence of amino acid beads along a protein chain, so it should be possible to identify even remote and dissimilar products of Shakespeare as nonetheless Shakespearean.

In an essay exploring similar ideas, Linda Charnes gives the example of a striking biological discovery.[30] Observing that DNA samples of tree moulds taken from different parts of a forest in Michigan were all essentially the same, 'clones of the same genetic being', scientists postulated that beneath the forest there must be living and growing a gigantic subterranean fungus, weighing more than 100 tons. On the surface, a widespread and varied collection of fungi growing on rotting wood; underneath, 'the world's oldest and biggest living organism'. Charnes deploys this phenomenon as a figure for Shakespeare. Contemporary culture is a decomposing forest. The various 'Shakespearean fragments and texts which are popping up all over its surface' may appear to be new forms, *sui generis*. In fact they are outcrops of that massive subterranean growth, Shakespeare, on which their very existence is predicated: 'Their presence reassuringly enables us to "infer" that underneath all of the historical "debris", behind the fragmenting claims and postures of "postmodernity", there is still "a there there"; something … that we cannot actually see but whose presence must nevertheless be posited' (p. 66).

VII

Each of these models, philosophical and scientific, reinforce our intuitive sense that *Hamlet*, and Shakespeare, are both one and many, formed but still forming, 'still and moving'.[31] Physics, chemistry, and biology, even at this elementary level, present us with ideal types of a primary 'matter', divisible into elements, but with common atomic and molecular structures that can both maintain stability and produce unique combinations. Matter can undergo transformation without destruction. These models allow for continual and radical change without any loss of identity

But there is one thing missing from this discussion; and this is the hardest point of all to reach. Chemical elements exhibit changes of state in response to physical conditions. Carbon appears as one of its allotropes, graphite, coal, or diamond, depending on the circumambient context in which it forms.[32] Carbon itself possesses the potentiality for change as an intrinsic capability. But how did carbon acquire this protean talent? By an act or process of creation. Proteins also have an innate organic capacity for self-transformation. They transform themselves in obedience to instructions in the genetic DNA code. But whence do they acquire those instructions? From an act of creation.

In another interesting comparison Gary Taylor compares Shakespearean 'genius' in its uniqueness, its singularity, to ideas from astrophysics about the black hole:

A singularity (represented by the symbol *) is the centre of a black hole; it is a mathematical point in space having no length, breadth or depth, a point at the centre of a once vast, now collapsing star where matter is crushed by its own irresistible gravity into literally zero volume. Even light cannot escape from a black hole; time itself stops.

If Shakespeare has a singularity, it is because he has become a black hole. Light, insight, intelligence, matter – all pour ceaselessly into him, as critics are drawn into the densening vortex of his reputation; they add their own weight to his increasing mass. The light from other stars – other poets, other dramatists – is wrenched and bent as it passes by him on its way to us. He warps cultural space-time; he distorts our view of the universe around him . . . But Shakespeare himself no longer transmits visible light: his stellar energies have been trapped within the gravity-well of his own reputation. (*Reinventing Shakespeare*, p. 411)

Like the 'cease of majesty' in *Hamlet*, the black hole 'Dies not alone, but like a gulf doth draw / What's near with it' (3.3.15–17). Barely escaped from the black hole himself, Gary Taylor pleads for 'available cultural space for other writers, such as . . . Thomas Middleton'.[33] Of course not everything disappears into black holes: if a stellar body has sufficient mass it can resist even that enormous gravitational pull. Taylor should take comfort from the example of Cygnus X-1, a massive hot star which is apparently towed around by an aptly named 'dark companion', a kind of stellar Thomas Middleton, a black hole against whose attractive force it has managed to stabilise itself.

But the mathematical concept of 'singularity' has a much larger import even than this, since it also represents the originating moment of creation itself, the single point of infinite density in 'Big Bang' theory. Stephen Hawking took a phrase from *Hamlet* as the title of his third book, *The Universe in a Nutshell*.[34] 'I could be bounded in a nutshell, and count myself a king of infinite space':

the behaviour of the vast universe can be understood in terms of its history in imagined time, which is a tiny, slightly flattened sphere. It is like Hamlet's nutshell, yet this nut encodes everything that happens in real time. So Hamlet was quite right. We could be bounded in a nutshell and still count ourselves kings of infinite space. (p. 99)

Similarly the 'vast universe' had its origin in an immeasurably small but inconceivably powerful point. This singularity has been described in language, defined in mathematical calculations, and explained in cosmological theories. But it is a point where language and mathematics and theory all break down. It cannot be explained. Astrophysicists cannot for example understand why the singularity that produced the universe didn't just produce a black hole. Or what stops the universe from disappearing into another one . . .

VIII

I derive my concept of 'collision' from the popular understanding of particle physics. As a term, 'collision' is widely and casually used in Shakespeare criticism, to describe the interaction of characters and forces in a play, especially a tragedy, or to explain the impact of contextual factors on Shakespearean drama. My use of the word is predicated on an analogy with recent discoveries in the behaviour of subatomic particles in experiments such as those conducted in the Large Hadron Collider in Switzerland.

For centuries atoms were thought of as the basic building blocks of matter: but advances in nuclear physics revealed that subatomic particles, electrons surrounding atomic nuclei and held in place by electrical forces, are as much forms of material architecture as the more easily observable atoms themselves. Ever since the atom was theoretically broken down into smaller constituent parts, physicists have tried to make sense of their diversity and behaviour. By the early 1970s these particles were much better understood as complexities built from smaller particles (quarks, antiquarks, gluons). This new understanding brought with it an apparently insoluble problem: what holds it all together? The architecture that scientists could 'see' and calculate theoretically, should not on the available evidence work at all. Something else had to be there, pervading the universe, a 'non-zero field' (named 'Higgs' after the physicist Peter Higgs) that works to alter the properties of many of the particles of nature.

Understanding what this field is, and how it works, is one of the central projects of particle physicists today, and the main justification for building the Large Hadron Collider. Within this vast machine, subatomic particles are directed towards one another by electromagnetic fields to cause high-energy particle collisions (hence the popular though incorrect term 'atom-smasher'). The process has been explained by analogies such as dropping a television set out of a window, or smashing a watch, in order to deduce, from the fragments, how the system worked. But this is to emphasise only the destructive facet of the experiment. Far more important is the remarkable property of nature, that when sufficient energy is crammed into a sufficiently small space, particles that were not previously present can sometimes be created out of that energy. The extremely compressed energy technique is the only one we know that can allow us to create heavy or exceedingly rare particles, 'compounds strange' that humans have never previously observed. The recent discovery of a particle that to some extent matches the expected form of the 'Higgs' particle is an extraordinary example of the success of these experiments. These particles have never been 'known' by any kind of scientific observation, though their existence has been predicated, by calculations and theoretical hypotheses in quantum physics. Now we can not only 'find' them, but actually create them in an experimental context. Particle collision between two objects can produce a new object that did not previously exist.

It is my general argument that the concept of 'collision', signifying the impact of a number of forces and objects upon one another, is a useful analogy for describing and accounting for what sometimes happens to produce the phenomenon we know as 'Shakespeare'. Such an approach can be thought of by some people as destructive, since the 'Shakespeare' generated from such collisions does not necessarily resemble what they think of as 'Shakespeare' at all. How much significance can be attached to the documentary record, taken from the papers of the East India Company, indicating that plays called *Hamlet* and *Richard II* were apparently performed on board the ship the *Red Dragon* off the coast of Africa in 1607? The record has been disputed as a possible forgery, and in any case the context is so unexpected that it does not answer readily to any conventional method of analysis. But if we think, accepting the record for the sake of argument as true, of the rapprochement between Shakespeare and the East India Company's presence in West Africa as a 'collision', then it becomes possible to understand what may have happened, and what new meanings have been, and can be, generated from that historical event.

What happens when a Shakespeare comedy comes into contact with a terrorist suicide bomb (which is exactly what happened when the Doha Players Theatre in Qatar was attacked during a production of *Twelfth Night* in March 2005)? Clearly this incident can be understood as a 'collision', but was it essentially a random and fortuitous accident, comparable to a car crash (which tells us nothing about Shakespeare, and only something about terrorism)? Or is it possible to extrapolate from the event, using both analytical and imaginative methods of deduction and intuition, a range of new meanings that did not previously exist?

The case I am making is designed to prove that these things actually happen in culture, as particle collision happens in nature. But the very fact that I am making an argument to explain a reality makes the case itself an artifice, an experimental model, a linguistic machine built to both produce and account for specific manifestations of creativity. This book should be thought of, to speak analogically, not as a verbal description of a historical object, or as a linguistic analysis of a cultural process, but rather as the Large Hadron Collider of Shakespeare studies, designed to drive objects towards one another in high-impact collisions. And as in the commonplace watch-smashing metaphor that tries to explain particle acceleration, I do believe we need to destroy 'Shakespeare' in order to understand what 'Shakespeare' really is. I believe we need to observe Shakespeare colliding with objects that are not Shakespeare, where both are driven by forces that can appear to be random but in their mutual impact generate an observable and meaningful pattern. Of course we will then want to put the pieces back together again, since we hold Shakespeare to be unique and irreplaceable, not substitutable like a watch or a television. But is the Shakespeare we reassemble the same as the Shakespeare we observed fragmenting under the impact of collision? Or are we actually seeing new particles and patterns of new energy radiating outwards from the point of collision, in an unpredictable but purposeful and meaningful way?

IX

When I consider every thing that growes
Holds in perfection but a little moment.
That this huge stage presenteth nought but showes
Whereon the stars in secret influence comment.
When I perceive that men as plants increase,

Cheared and checkt even by the selfe-same skie:
Vaunt in their youthfull sap, at height decrease,
And were their brave state out of memory.
Then the conceit of this inconstant stay
Sets you most rich in youth before my sight,
Where wastfull Time debateth with decay,
To change your day of youth to sullied night,
And all in war with Time for love of you,
As he takes from you, I engraft you new.[35]

All the scientific models discussed above converge on the fundamental truth that preoccupied Shakespeare and animated his sonnets: that while nothing is constant in nature but change, human beings continue to quest for the abiding and eternal, not in the abstract immortality of religion, but in the very processes of change and decay that seem to threaten all life with assured destruction. Acknowledging the law of 'variation', the poet notwithstanding seeks, in love and in language, the point of fixity that gives definition and meaning to life. This project runs the risk of mere repetition, a nostalgic adherence to a vanishing convention. But poetry, like science, can temporarily stabilise the constantly collapsing and mutating energies of the universe into an evanescent but beautiful coherence.

> For as the Sun is daily new and old,
> So is my love still telling what is told.
> Sonnet 76

Shakespeare was thinking quite simply here of the sun's daily recession and return, the apparently eternal alternation of sunrise and sunset. In the light of modern astrophysics this figure seems extraordinarily prescient. The immense process of nuclear fission that powers the sun depends absolutely on 'variation' and the continual production of 'compounds strange'. The atomic structure of the sun is in a constant state of mutability, and yet its structure remains constant, as it produces new energy and converts it to mass: it is indeed at every moment 'new' and 'old'. Shakespeare's own love poetry shares the same paradoxical combination of rest and inconstancy, fixity and change. It seems to keep saying the same thing, but can only do so by employing new combinations of words and music.

How, then, to retain identity and meaning in an environment of continual and inexorable change, where the only choices seem to be: surrender to 'variation'; or just keep on 'telling what is told'? Here mutability is viewed elegiacally as a continual process of loss. The world we love is growing and dying, our place in it no more than an 'inconstant stay'. As in many of the sonnets, reflections on mutability focus with unusual force an image of changeless beauty, always about to change. In love with the lover, but in war with Time, the poet will preserve beauty, not by trying to hold on to it, but by 'engrafting' it into a new synergy. In doing so, he has both accepted the destruction of the loved object, and affirmed its potentiality for creative development. Human life is both 'cheared' and 'check't', both stimulated and inhibited, by the same restlessly mutating energies. The DNA blueprint of beauty will survive into a new efflorescence, but only when it is synergised with something other in a new combination of matter and spirit. Change and permanence, as G. M. Hopkins insisted, are one; and many:

> Flesh fade, and mortal trash
> Fall to the residuary worm; world's wildfire, leave but ash ...
> This Jack, joke, poor potsherd, patch, matchwood, immortal diamond,
> Is immortal diamond.
>
> *Poetry and Prose*, ed. Gardner, p. 66

PART I

CHAPTER I

The voyage of the Red Dragon

I

At the end of March 1607 the crew of the *Red Dragon* weighed anchor off the coast of southern England on a voyage to the East Indies. The *Dragon* was accompanied by the *Hector* under the command of William Hawkins and – nominally at least – by the *Consent*, although her commander, David Middleton, had for unexplained reasons left ahead of his companions and later rendezvous proved elusive.

The 'General' in supreme command of this Third Voyage of the East India Company was William Keeling. Keeling's instructions were to lead his fleet to Bantam (the first English trading 'factory' to be established by the Company in the Far East at Java) by way of Socotra, Aden, and Surat, the principal port of the largely landlocked Mughal Empire. The purpose of the voyage was threefold. To identify additional potential markets for English broadcloth (the Company was perennially optimistic that the inhabitants of the tropics could be persuaded to wear woollen clothes). To explore the prospect of short-circuiting extended trade routes to the South China seas by obtaining spices from the entrepôts of Aden and Surat. And, ideally, to establish a 'triangular trade': selling broadcloth for cash around the ports of the Arabian sea; purchasing with the proceeds cotton cloth in Surat and along the Coromandel coast of India for export to Java; exchanging there cotton for spices through the Company's Bantam factory, in the process boosting economic activity sufficiently to justify investment in defences against local and Dutch predation; returning finally to London laden with hopefully profitable cargoes of spices. The Third Voyage thus carried with it a vast array of woollen commodities; a second-in-command, William

Hawkins, with diplomatic credentials who was sufficiently fluent in Turkish, the lingua franca of the largely Islamic ruling classes of the region, to undertake trade negotiations; and sufficient firepower both to solace friend and deter foe.

Having missed the trade-winds, progress proved painfully slow. By August the *Dragon* and *Hector* had reached only the West Coast of Africa, where they found themselves becalmed off the coast of modern-day Sierra Leone. Keeling's enlightened concern for the welfare of his crew was remarkably demonstrated during this enforced leisure. To maintain morale and keep his men from 'idleness and unlawful games',[1] he encouraged theatrical entertainments, and in the event the crew of the *Dragon* gave a landmark performance of *Hamlet* before an audience that included not only officers but a visiting African dignitary. Nor was the repertoire of the *Dragon* limited to a single text: a little later the crew provided a command performance of *Richard II* while Keeling entertained his second-in-command Hawkins to dinner.[2] As far as we are aware, this was the first performance of a Shakespeare play outside of Europe; the first performance of a Shakespeare play on board a ship; the first amateur performance of a Shakespeare play; and presumably (given that the visiting dignitary understood Portuguese but not English) the first performance of a Shakespeare play to be translated.

After further frustratingly slow progress, in late April 1608 the *Dragon* arrived off the shores of Socotra, a safe haven commanding entry to the Gulf of Aden. Then a desolate island noted principally for its strategic position (which had led to its brief occupation by the Portuguese in the early 1500s) and as a source of aloes, Socotra is now an integral part of the Arab Republic of Yemen, and a thriving eco-tourism destination. Here, during an extended stay, Keeling learnt rudimentary Arabic and the theatrical talents of the *Dragon*'s crew were again exercised with a reprise performance of *Hamlet*. Shakespeare thus entered the Arab world through performance enacted by servants of a nascent nautical empire, directed by officers of a capitalist enterprise engaged in bitter trade rivalry with European competitors, and for the entertainment of an audience combining company staff and officers with representatives of the local peoples.

The members of the Third Voyage took various paths from Socotra. The *Dragon* loaded nearly a ton of aloes and sailed direct to Bantam, encountering strong opposition from Dutch forces intent on preserving their trade monopoly. Keeling's perseverance however earned the respect of the Company's directors and in 1615 he was reappointed as commander of its Fifth Voyage with plenipotentiary authority to implement far-reaching reforms to the Company's by then extensive organisational presence in the Far East, establishing an administrative regime that subsequently underpinned an indirect colonial rule. To the very end of his life Keeling retained his Shakespearean connections, retiring in 1617 to become captain of Cowes Castle, a sinecure almost certainly in the gift of the governor of the Isle of Wight, Shakespeare's patron the Earl of Southampton.

Middleton had, by the time Keeling set sail from Socotra, already begun his return journey from Java, having purchased a cargo of cloves for £3,000 that would be sold on the London market for £36,000. The stupendous profit margin was critical in persuading the largely risk-averse directors of the East India Company to invest heavily in developing the Far East market. Middleton became one of their most influential officers in the venture.

After his departure from Socotra, Hawkins followed his specific commission, setting sail for Surat in order to 'proceed to the Court of the Great Mogul at Agra, and there to present his credentials' to the Emperor Akbar as agent of the Company in the hope that trading privileges in western India might be secured (Strachan and Penrose, *Journals*, p. 22). The negotiations proved tortuous in the extreme but eventually led to a successful treaty. The Battle of Plessy, which effectively established de facto English rule in India, was ostensibly fought to protect the terms of Hawkins's treaty. The East India Company returned to Socotra in 1834, annexing the island in order to protect trade routes to India, the jewel in the imperial crown. The Third Voyage of the East India Company thus delineates in miniature the expansion of the British Empire. And Shakespeare's work appears to have played a part in the story.

II

The factual narrative set out above is based on a number of historical documents, primarily the journals of the voyage kept by the captain and members of the company. For most of their existence these documents have been housed in libraries and archives, accessible to the general reader only through edited extracts, but they have recently been published in full by Richmond Barbour. Barbour's splendid critical edition prints five journals from the voyage, three produced on the sister ship *Hector*, and two from the *Dragon*, 'The *Red Dragon* Journal of John Hearne and William Finch', and the surviving summary of Keeling's own journal.[3]

These journals, whose authenticity is in general unchallenged, and whose accuracy of observation and report is beyond question, naturally corroborate one another (which is the very reason they were kept in the first place), despite their stylistic and narrative variations. Except, that is, in one significant particular: there is only one account of the performances of Shakespeare on board the *Dragon*, and that is in the journal of the captain himself, William Keeling. Other details from the same entries (such as the shooting of an elephant) recur in the other narratives. But no one else thought it worthwhile to record the first known performance of Shakespeare's *Hamlet*.

There is a further difficulty. While the other journals of the voyage are extant in original documents, Keeling's journal disappeared sometime in the nineteenth century. A condensed version of it was published by Samuel Purchas in 1625, though the extracts reproduced make no mention of Shakespeare.[4] We possess the accounts of the Shakespeare performances only because, before the document itself was lost, the references to Shakespeare were copied, twice, in 1825 and 1849. The two copies are slightly different from one another.[5] This is the earlier version, published by Ambrose Gunthio in the *European Magazine* in 1825.

Sept. 5, 1607. I sent the Portuguese interpreter, according to his desire, aboard the Hector, where he broke fast, and after came aboard to me, where we had the TRAGEDY OF HAMLET; and in the afternoon we went altogether ashore, to see if we could shoot an elephant.

Sept. 29, 1607. Captaine Hawkins dined with me, when my company acted KINGE RICHARD THE SECOND.

Now in fact this citation was not discovered until 1951. So the initial impact of the story on Shakespeare scholarship was effected through the later reference, which was included as an appendix in an edited collection of *Voyages Towards the North-West, in search of a passage from Cathay to India, 1496–1631* (1849), by Thomas Rundall, a clerk of the East India Company.

1607.

September 5. I sent the interpreter, according to his desier, abord the Hector, whear he brooke fast, and after came abord me, where *we gave the tragedie of Hamlett.*

[*September*] 30. Captain Hawkins dined with me, wher *my companions acted Kinge Richard the Second.*

[*September*] 31. I invited Captain Hawkins to a ffishe dinner, and had *Hamlet acted* abord me, which I permit to keepe my people from idelenss and unlawfull games, or sleepe.

Though published in 1849, this source seems to have remained unnoticed by Shakespeare scholars until 1865, when it was cited by historian William B. Rye in his *England as seen by Foreigners in the Days of Elizabeth and James I*.[6] Even before the story of Shakespeare and the *Red Dragon* had entered the scholarly literature on Shakespeare, another historian had cast doubt on the authenticity of the narrative. Clements Markham in *The Voyages of Sir James Lancaster* (1877) alludes to it, notes discrepancies in dates, and observes that the primary source, Keeling's journal, was missing from the archive.[7] Thus scepticism and belief about the story of Shakespeare on the *Red Dragon* were twinned from an early age.

The natural history of a forgery is to be initially believed, subsequently doubted, and ultimately exposed. The trajectory of the Shakespeare and the *Red Dragon* story is quite different, in that it was both doubted and believed almost at the same historical moment, and has ever since enlisted both sceptics and believers on either side of its case. In his *Life of William Shakespeare* (1898), Sir Sidney Lee included the extract from Keeling's journal among Shakespeare forgeries.[8] But shortly afterwards the Keeling record was vigorously defended by F. S. Boas, who argued for its authenticity on the grounds that Rundall had cited the extract 'merely to illustrate a feature of discipline on board ship' and appears to have had no interest at all in securing a Shakespeare 'scoop' of the first ever recorded performance of *Hamlet*.[9] Probably the most influential positive endorsement of the Keeling record was its acceptance by the great E. K. Chambers in his *William Shakespeare: A Study of*

Facts and Problems (1930).[10] From that point on, the majority opinion accepted that the entries in the Keeling journal were genuine, and that in 1607 *Hamlet* and *Richard II* were indeed performed on board the *Red Dragon* off the coast of what is now Sierra Leone. When in 1951 Earl R. Wasserman found the 1825 variant copy of the same journal entries, his discovery seemed to confirm, once for all, that the historical record of the performances was genuine and credible.[11]

III

Today those shipboard productions of 1607 are widely accepted by scholars and editors as part of the history of Shakespeare's plays in performance. Editors of both *Hamlet* and *Richard II* cite the performances as accepted historical fact.[12] Gary Taylor, a prominent modern supporter of the Third Voyage records, published extracts from both Keeling's journal and the journal of Finch and Hearne.[13] Richmond Barbour's work, mentioned above, enables the contemporary reader to survey the whole suite of journals covering the voyage, and thus to see the Shakespeare allusions in their immediate historical context. It is worth considering why this historical episode, despite its remoteness from the more customary location of Shakespeare's work in the Elizabethan and Jacobean professional theatre, and what some have regarded as its questionable veracity, should have become such an important and common point of reference for Shakespeare scholarship, criticism, and performance history.

When, at the end of the nineteenth century, Sidney Lee condemned the *Red Dragon* story as a hoax, he was seeking to purify the authentic Shakespearean record from the contamination of forgery. It scarcely mattered to him that the story provided an unusual, exciting, and immensely suggestive opening on to the history of Shakespeare in performance. His critic F. S. Boas however, responding in 1923, grasped the full potential of the anecdote as a significant episode in a much larger narrative, the story of the British Empire.

At a time when our mercantile marine has been covering itself with glory on every sea, it is an act of *pietas* to reclaim for it the proud distinction of having been the pioneer in carrying Shakespearean drama into the uttermost ends of the earth.[14]

Patriotically invoking the British victory of 1918, Boas presents the ships of the East India Company as pioneers of both cultural and economic imperialism, since they were not only paving the roads of empire, but bearing with them the dramatic literature that became recognised as among Britain's foremost cultural achievements. Regarded in this light, these amateur productions, which took place on board a ship anchored off the coast of Africa and played before a mixed audience of Britons and foreigners, seem more strongly indicative of the imperial and Shakespearean future than a local national drama, parochially rooted on Tudor London's Bankside.

Gary Taylor also celebrates the *Red Dragon* performances as of great historical significance, but he does so from a post-colonial, rather than an imperialist, perspective. In their internationalism and multiculturalism, they predicted for him a future in which Shakespeare would achieve a 'global international reputation'. Taylor describes the context of the performances as an admirable example of 'civilized multicultural exchange' (Taylor in Kamps and Singh, *Travel Knowledge*, p. 242) that contrasts strongly with many subsequent colonial interventions and foreshadows the co-operation and reciprocity of our contemporary global traffic in world Shakespeare.

Editors who cite the *Red Dragon* performances as the beginning of a stage history for *Hamlet* or *Richard II* are also locating them at the beginning of the long process that eventually made Shakespeare a completely globalised, international, and multicultural author, performed in many different languages, admired in many different cultures. The imperialist and the post-colonial narratives are fundamentally divergent in terms of ideology, but in remarkable agreement about the status of the *Red Dragon* productions of Shakespeare as the starting-point for understanding the Shakespeare of the present: the Shakespeare who belongs not to London, but to the world; not to Little England, but to the globe, and to the myriad peoples of the globe. The natural point of origin for this contemporary world Shakespeare was on the planks of the *Red Dragon*, rather than the boards of the Globe Theatre.

One of the problems arising from these incorporations of the *Red Dragon* productions into various master narratives of Shakespearean history, is that they tend to naturalise and domesticate the inherent strangeness of the episode by tracing a linear continuity from the shipboard performances to accepted orthodoxies of the present day. For surely, given the national and professional theatrical context in which Shakespeare's works came to be performed and published, nothing could be more peripheral than the amateur, maritime, foreign, and translated locale that witnessed these plays? This strangeness is not lost on any of those who have endorsed the significance of the *Red Dragon* story.

Has there ever been a stranger episode in stage-history than this shipboard performance of *Hamlet*? ... it is incredible that anyone should have invented such an incident, if it had not taken place. (Boas, *Shakespeare and the Universities*, p. 93)

Gary Taylor suggests that *Hamlet* now being so universally familiar, we can only recover the sense of 'astonishment' that must have greeted its first performances by imaginatively reconstructing and observing that production in the 'extraordinary setting' of a ship anchored off Sierra Leone (Taylor in Kamps and Singh, *Travel Knowledge*, p. 224). But the common purpose of both the colonialist and anti-colonialist critic is to argue that this apparent 'strangeness' should in fact be discounted, since what we are really observing here is the true point of origin for our contemporary globalised Shakespeare. Like many other examples of historical anachronism, the cosmopolitan present looks back to an alien past, minimises historical difference, privileges the detail that most nearly concurs with its own ideology, and normalises what must at the time have been, and should still be recognisable now, as unusual, extraordinary, and strange.

It is my argument that we should aim to recover this strangeness. A huge accumulation of irrefutable historical evidence places Shakespeare and his plays in an established historical context, which is that of the professional metropolitan theatre of late Tudor and early Stuart England. This is where the plays were written, performed, published, seen and read, spoken and written about. The parameters of the Shakespearean drama are drawn around the city, the court, and the London entertainment industry. So when *Hamlet* and *Richard II* were played on the deck of a ship off the coast of Sierra Leone, they should not really have been there. They simply did not belong to that locale. They could not possibly have been written and dramatised with any conceivable thought of such a production venue. As Ania Loomba puts it: 'It is curiously appropriate that these initial Shakespearian travels should have to contend with a debate about "authenticity", for the export of Shakespeare necessarily inaugurated a history of "inauthentic" performances. The plays were performed abroad by English people who were not quite proper players.'[15] It was no part of the East India Company's policy to export examples of contemporary popular drama, which is presumably why scholars have encountered difficulty in finding other comparable examples of the same sort of thing from the same period.[16] We can cleverly draw analogies between the planks of a ship and the boards of a theatre, but that does not make it any easier to imagine how these plays can in practice have been put on by such men, in such conditions, and before such an audience. In other words the encounter between Shakespeare and Africa should not, in my view, be regarded as a natural embodiment of Shakespeare's future global destiny, and a precursor of things to come; it should be regarded as a bizarre, outlandish freak of theatrical history, occasioned most probably by the accidental penchant of the captain for the drama, and a personal attachment to the work of Shakespeare. It was a collision between objects and forces that met one another in an unpredictable concatenation of random and arbitrary conditions. Once the collision had occurred, it manifestly began to generate both new particles and new energies, forging a link that had not previously existed between Shakespeare and the peripheral, forbidding, offshore world of the incipient colonial subject.

IV

The sheer inexplicable and irreducible oddity of the record is the real reason why it has been continuously doubted and attacked as fraudulent and inauthentic. Recently Bernice Kliman in an article in *Shakespeare Quarterly* restated Sidney Lee's view of the Keeling record as a forgery perpetrated by John Payne Collier.[17] Kliman enumerates the sceptical observations of previous critics, posing all the questions that call the genuineness of the record into doubt. Why did it go unnoticed when it was first published? Why is Keeling's original journal missing? Why is there no record of any other similar performances by English sailors on board ship?[18] Why is it that historians have been generally sceptical about the entries, while literary critics have embraced them with enthusiasm? Why do the two published versions of the incident differ from one another, in detail and in dates? Why, in the last instance, is it so hard to believe that this ever really happened at all?

Kliman's purpose in the article is twofold: to 'settle the account's status' as a text, and to expose the 'unconscious political motives of earlier scholars who argued for the Keeling account's authenticity' (p. 202). She admits she is unable to finally prove the first of these objectives, and that her case is built up from 'circumstantial evidence' (p. 180). She pursues the second objective by observing that imperialist and post-colonial critics have all wanted, for their own ideological purposes, to believe the entries, since they so strongly confirm the veracity of their colonial or post-colonial interpretations of Shakespeare and empire. Without exactly accusing these critics of complicity with a hoax, Kliman suggests that interpretative desire can lead to a minimising of concerns about textual authenticity.

Arguments that depend on allegations of ideological bias in the interpretation of texts require two conditions in order to be effective. If the scholar is accusing her predecessor of textual inaccuracy, then she needs to be able to present evidence bearing on the true original state of the text. But this cannot be done in this instance. The other is that the scholar should acknowledge that ideological bias pertains to *all* acts of interpretation, not only to those of one's opponents, and subject her own a priori assumptions to the same scrutiny. Kliman's argument falls short on both these points:

> If we can detach the supposed performances from the need to either boost or bash Shakespeare and England, and even from the admirable aim of trying to understand the role of race in travel accounts, we can now agree that the entry recording performances is at least partially forged and that we can construct a conjectural narrative around the known original data. (p. 202)

But in the absence of positive evidence of the original text, the charge of forgery cannot be proven; and it is hard to see why Kliman's admittedly 'conjectural narrative' is any more valid than the conjectures of Gary Taylor or Ania Loomba or F. S. Boas. Though concerned to expose the unconscious bias of empire boosters and empire bashers, Kliman acknowledges no ideological interest on the part of her own case. And yet her argument clearly springs from that widespread commitment to undermining traditional assumptions, and exposing cherished beliefs which we find active throughout contemporary culture, from the scientific atheism of Richard Dawkins to the popular Gnosticism of Dan Brown, and is particularly strong among journalists and media commentators. These are not ideology-free intellectual positions. The difficulty attendant upon them is that they need to claim a basis in irrefutable evidence and absolute certainty. Where compelling evidence is lacking, certainty of conviction must needs take its place.

Kliman's argument about the authenticity of the Keeling testimony has re-divided an already bifurcated academic constituency. Contemporary scholars of reputation and gravitas can be found on both sides of the question, as has been the case since the record surfaced in the nineteenth century. Some agree that the entry is a forgery; others find no reason to suspect it as anything other than genuine.

One critic whose work I have quoted, Ania Loomba, aligns herself with neither of these positions, and discovers common ideological ground between the supporters and detractors of the *Red Dragon* theatre, and between the positive and negative narratives of empire. Looking back to the nineteenth-century dispute, she shows that those alleging forgery poured scorn on the idea that a ship's crew of 1607 could perform two Shakespeare plays. But those who accept the entries as genuine are equally condescending in their assessment of the crew, since they pass over without comment the fact that Keeling, if he did use Shakespeare's plays on board the ship, did so explicitly to keep his men in a condition of docility and obedience. Thus Loomba finds, between both parties, a shared ideological elitism.

> I am not interested in examining the 'truth' status of Keeling's journal entries. Rather, my point in pursuing these elusive first records of a travelling Shakespeare is to indicate how archival differences can be submerged in a common understanding that lowly sailors cannot perform the real Shakespeare. (Loomba, 'Transformations', p. 113)

v

Here then are three approaches to the story of Shakespeare and the *Red Dragon*. Those who regard the text as genuine use it to locate Shakespeare within divergent narratives of empire. Those who deny its historical authenticity turn the event into a story about nineteenth-century forgery. Loomba adopts a more sceptical position, and uses the story as a case-study in ideological appropriations of historical evidence.

There is another way, a path between scepticism and imagination. The authenticity or otherwise of this supposed event remains, in my view, impossible to prove or disprove. A cautious and judicious scholar might well prefer to steer clear of so dubious and contested a historical example, and draw no conclusions either way. But the indisputable fact remains, that forgery or not, the enacting of Shakespeare on the deck of the *Red Dragon* has become part of scholarly controversy, historical narrative, and critical debate. We can pay court to the contemporary Gnostic fashion for debunking myths, uncovering conspiracies, and exposing hoaxes.[19] But if in doing so, we forget that our primary material here is not the East India Company, but Shakespeare – not history, but fiction – then we are in danger of being left holding nothing but a handful of dust.

Aye, I talk of dreams, the children of an idle brain, begot of nothing but vain fantasy. It might even be possible to argue that *it makes no difference at all* whether the Keeling record is a forgery or not. It is a gripping and interesting story, that in due course became incorporated into larger stories about the growth of empire, the relations between colonial powers and their subjects, the morality of colonialism, the role of culture in the quest for global economic and political hegemony.

If the 'truth' claims of the record cannot finally be adjudicated, what difference does it make? It is manifest that the historical narratives into which these shipboard performances of Shakespeare have been incorporated do not in any way depend upon its authenticity for their validity and power. The British Empire assumed control of a very large share of the globe, whether or not *Hamlet* was played on the deck of the *Red Dragon*. British language and culture, including particularly Shakespeare, certainly later became an important element in the apparatus of empire-building, if not in this very early pre-imperial stage. Shakespeare has become a global dramatist, largely as a consequence of earlier colonisation, and of the empire and its dissolution. Global Shakespeare is a hybrid product of imperial dissemination and post-colonial cultural struggle.

Proving Keeling's record inauthentic, if this could be done, would not in any way invalidate any part of these powerful and truthful historical narratives.

The anxiety underpinning Kliman's essay can be readily understood. As scholars approaching Keeling's record, we are presented with a text that exists only in later copies by other hands, and for which there is no authentic original source. The variant copies differ from one another in ways that are hard to understand. We are surrounded by interpretations that can only take, as their point of departure, textual evidence we know to be far removed from the writer's own recording hand. Some interpreters invoke the lost original, others work from the transmitted copy, and all accuse one another of drawing on inauthentic material, and reconciling it with ideological bias. I am speaking of course of Captain William Keeling's account of the first recorded performance of *Hamlet*. I might as well, though, have been talking about the play *Hamlet* itself.

VI

There are stories that become part of other stories, generate counter-stories, and disseminate their influence, often invisibly, throughout a culture. My response to the story of *Richard II* on the *Red Dragon* is not to seek proof of its authenticity, or to expose it as a fraud, or even to deploy it in an anti-colonialist critique of ideology. It is to make it into another story. There follows an imaginative fiction, 'Shooting an elephant', based on the account of Shakespeare performed on the *Red Dragon* and offering a 'critical-creative' commentary on the narrative, and on its possible subsequent meanings. This 'tale' also draws on the other journals of the Third Voyage for stylistic models, as well as for content.

The story invents an imaginary journal, kept by a young merchant of the company, sailing with the *Red Dragon*. Almost all the existing critical discussions of this topic focus on the performance of *Hamlet*. 'Shooting an elephant' looks instead at the performance of *Richard II*, and meditates imaginatively on the possible reasons for that play's presence in this outlandish context, and the potential implications of its mediation to Africa in the context of subsequent European imperialism.

The story operates as a historical mystery narrative that follows the trajectory of the real voyage, but plays with a 'conspiracy theory' connecting the company's intervention into West Africa, backwards to the Essex rebellion, and forwards to subsequent colonial adventures. In 1601 *Richard II* was deployed by Essex's supporters as a model for unconstitutional 'regime change'. A number of other historical threads are brought together in that shipboard performance: the fact that Sir Thomas Smith, first governor of the East India Company and still governor in 1607, was arrested and imprisoned on suspicion of assisting the Earl of Essex; the fact that the Earl of Southampton was both Shakespeare's patron and possibly Keeling's (Keeling retired to the Isle of Wight, of which Southampton was governor), as well as involved in the East India Company and a ringleader of the Essex revolt; and the fact that Nicholas Ling, who published *Richard II*, was one of the founding members of the East India Company.

In the tale Keeling shows *Richard II* to a group of African dignitaries in order to persuade them to overthrow their ruler, King Burre, who is hostile to the Company, and to English interests, and replace him with a friendly ruler. The anachronistic term 'regime change' (America's declared objective in relation to Saddam Hussein's Iraq) is used deliberately to anticipate future events, thus imagining the ultimate destiny of empire as enfolded within its earliest origins. The tale thus plays (some will say creatively, others irresponsibly) with these intriguing facts, to construct a fictional mystery story in which *Richard II* is used for its propaganda capability of facilitating a bloodless *coup d'état* in Sierra Leone. What happens in the tale is not what happened in history, but it might have, and if it did, it would have provided a paradigm for what has happened many times over in the subsequent history of English imperialism, and American foreign intervention.

CHAPTER 2

'Shooting an elephant'

5 September 1607

Fair weather. After dinner our General and Captain Hawkins went ashore, where we understood by the Negroes of an elephant which was not far off. So our General caused four good shot with their muskets to go along with the Negro to see if they could shoot him; which they did, all four being at once close by him. Yet he made way from them so violently that they were not able to follow him; but they espied that he bled very much all the way as he went. But they could do no good upon him, so they returned.

> Journal of John Hearne and William Finch, merchants of the *Red Dragon* (British Library MS L/MAR/A/v)

MARCH THE 4TH, 1607

In the government of commonwealths it is customary to make great use of matters long ago performed, and to compare them with things present. In so momentous an enterprise as that upon which we are now embarked, which is nothing less than a passage from the Western to the Eastern ends of the earth, many noteworthy matters offer occasion of record, and should on no account be buried in oblivion. Just as travellers of the past have left their reminiscences for the benefit of later ages, so may my modest records assist those of the future to make better sense of their own world.

And though I am in no way qualified to maintain a proper record of this voyage, being myself a stranger to sea affairs, and a sojourner only in my own native soil, I yet hope that my observations as a simple merchant on this great undertaking may prove to be of some value.

For this Third Voyage of the East India Company, trading to the Indies, is intended as a new kind of expedition. The governors of the Company have determined that we should not only return home with success, but establish trading routes and factories in the East, and in the course of that activity spread the name of the Company, and the reputation of English commerce, as a peaceable and profitable enterprise. Some of our earlier voyages being little less than privateering, conducted for the main part in the pursuit of wealth, and having scant regard for the interests of the native peoples to be met on the way, the name of English trade has become besmirched with the reputation of piracy, and this not only in the scandalous mouths of our competitors the Dutch and the Portuguese, but also in the minds of many wise and cultivated rulers of those distant parts. Indeed this very ship the *Red Dragon* began its career in the service of a privateer, the Earl of Cumberland, who sold it to the Company when he joined as a partner.

We are enjoined to treat the peoples we meet, not as subjects to be robbed or enslaved, their goods to be seized and their villages burned, but as partners in a mutually profitable trade. For even had we the power, in men and arms, to subdue the natives of Africa and India, to leave behind us a trail of hatred and recrimination would be but a poor legacy to those who follow in our wake. Even the meanest of the dwellers on these coasts have what we need to succeed in our expedition – food and water – and we have the capacity to secure these provisions by peaceful exchange. Our men are severely warned, under threat of harsh punishment, that in these encounters they must offer no harm to the Africans and Arabs, but to behave themselves peaceably and civilly towards them at all times. All gentleness is to be used towards these peoples, to help recover the scandal of our reputation as nothing more than colonists, and little better than pirates.

The purpose of our voyage is to proceed with our fleet to Java by way of Socotra, Aden, and Surat, the principal port of the Mughal Empire; to find markets for our English broadcloth; to seek for spices nearer home in Aden and Surat; to obtain cotton cloth in Java, and exchange it for spices in India. To this end we are loaded with a cargo of woollen cloth. Our expedition will take us on the long voyage around the *Cap Bonsperanza* at the southernmost tip of Africa, into the Indian Ocean and thus towards the East Indies. We will need prosperous winds and fair weather, as well as continual supplies of food and water from the shores, if we are to arrive at our destination in good health, and fit for the prosecution of our business.

MARCH THE 21ST, 1607

Our little fleet of three ships, the *Dragon*, the *Hector*, and the *Consent*, is already reduced to two, since the *Consent* has sailed from Tilbury before us. We hope to reunite en route. We are to weigh anchor and depart on the morrow. I have already made the acquaintance of my fellow merchants, most of whom are older than me by some years, and effected a passing introduction to our captain Master Hippon, who is always too busy and distracted to engage in conversation.

It was at this time that I became aware of the presence on board the ship of a small group of men who seemed to have no specific function in the vessel's little kingdom. I had occasionally glimpsed one of them moving about the ship, intent on some errand, talking to no one. These men were neither sailors nor merchants. They were handsome men, their clothes were of a finer cloth than the ordinary seamen, and their hands white and unroughened by sea-going labours. I traced one of them to a small cabin close to the General's quarters, within which the little company stayed secluded. Assuming their mysterious presence in some way concerned the General, I put them from my mind.

I have yet to catch a glimpse of that same General, Mister Keeling, who has overall command of the fleet, but who so far keeps to his cabin, and is yet to be seen on deck. On merchant voyages such as this, the supreme commander is an agent of the Company more than a seaman, so the management of an individual vessel is left to the Master. The General bears the responsibilities of navigation, as well as authority in discipline, and office in the management of trade. The Master commands the ship, but the General commands the expedition.

Already some curiosity about the character of General Keeling begins to be whispered around the ship. I have stood and gazed at the opaque portholes of his cabin for hours together, wondering what preoccupies him and keeps him secluded. I imagine him poring over charts, consulting almanacs, studying company accounts. But for all I know he could be engaged in some clandestine activity unknown to any of us. Seeing me standing staring at the General's cabin, an old seaman tapped me on the shoulder and beckoned me toward the ship's side. On my asking him if he knew General Keeling, he stole a sidelong glance back towards the cabin, as if to ensure we were not observed, and gave a brief nod. What is he like, I asked? The sailor would only gesture towards the sea, running green and high below us, by which I took him to mean the General was very deep. I long to see him.

MAY THE 7TH, 1607

Today having passed the Canary Islands to port, we brought the ship in to anchor at Maio in the Cape Verde islands. One of our crewmen, a Portuguese, who had sailed that way, promised us a safe harbour, water, and meat. We found no water, and a few half-starved goats. Tonight we steer westward towards Brazil to catch the trade-winds that will take us around the tip of Africa. Already our food and water are running low. And still there is no sign of our General, who takes all his meals in his cabin, and talks only with Master Hippon.

Conversing with my fellow merchants, I tried to draw from them such knowledge as they might possess about General Keeling. None knew him personally, though he had commanded a ship the *Susan* on the Company's Second Voyage, and was known as one of the corporation's chief merchants and factors. The seamen respected and feared him in equal measure. His reputation for discipline was that of a man capable of harshness, but strict in the execution of justice: hard but fair. The Company, I was told, spoke of his good command, attributed to the love and respect his men returned to him for his kind usage of them. Yet though he was known in the boardroom for kindness and compassion, on deck his name was more feared than loved. His justice was swift, sudden, and cruel. Some of the merchants on board had had occasion, one of my fellows confided in me, to remonstrate with the General over the harshness of some punishment, a man's ducking at the yard-arm, for a trivial offence. The merchants soon retired from that confrontation, when the General made it obvious that any challenge to his authority before the men could result in a similar punishment meted out to the challenger.

He was also thought to have very high connections in the English nobility, and even to have been entrusted with some kind of mysterious government service abroad. Such fragmentary information only deepened my curiosity concerning this inscrutable man. What was he first and foremost: admiral, merchant, diplomat, politician, secret agent? And if he carried secrets with him, to whom did they belong, and for whom were they intended? We all served him, as our General. But whom did our General serve?

JUNE THE 15TH, 1607

This day we sighted the main coast of Brazil at Cap San Augustin, which sighting proved, I gathered from my fellows, that we had sailed too far to the west, and ought to be turning eastwards towards Africa. But continually we were beset by calms and contrary winds, and found ourselves drifting haplessly to and fro across that infinite featureless ocean. Many of the sailors were beset by scurvy, and some afflicted with a flux. The Master looked worried, and his visits to the General's cabin became more frequent. The merchants talked amongst themselves, and some were for abandoning the voyage, and returning to England. We seemed to be sailing, like some ghost ship of legend, towards the unknown edge of the world, with bad luck our constant companion, and spectres for our crew. In the hot darkness of the equatorial night, as the great southern moon silvered our motionless rigging, whispers of mutiny echoed around the silent decks.

JULY THE 30TH, 1607

And now it was at last, in our hour of greatest need, that our General showed himself, and in the course of one day revealed the force of his mettle, and the strength of his spirit. I was leaning idly over the taffrail as the sun rose, watching the quiet overlapping waves that served us for a wake, when I became aware of a new presence on deck. The few hands that were about turned their heads towards the door of the captain's cabin, and suddenly fell silent and still in their labours. I looked in the direction of their gaze, and for the first time saw Mister Keeling himself, emerged from his cabin, standing to look around the ship, and to take his bearings of wind and weather. It was probably but the accident of the rising sun falling full upon him, and my being placed at the ship's stern as we drifted slowly eastwards, but to my wondering eyes his black-clothed figure seemed not an object, but a source of illumination, as if I were beholding with my own eyes one of the emissaries of light from heaven descending, or seeing a man whose body formed the epicentre of some great conflagration. Then the tropical sun swung swiftly above the horizon, its rays levelling a shining path across the surface of the sea, and gone was that creature of brightness and flame. In its place stood Mister Keeling our General, a welcome apparition indeed, looking about him cheerfully enough, and already, it seemed to my innocent senses, beginning to spread a new air of confidence around the stricken ship.

That day marked the turning-point of our fortunes as well as of our course. It was as if Mister Keeling took hold of his little fleet between his hands, and in doing so seized control of all our destinies. His first concern, I observed, or at least the first object of his attentions, was not the ships or the charts, but the men. He visited the sick on board both the *Dragon* and the *Hector*, addressing as best he could their comfort between decks, and ensuring their supply of food and water. He took count of the numbers of men afflicted with the scurvy. He spoke to the two Captains, Mr Hawkins and Mr Hippon, and the more senior mariners, in their own language, of winds and waves and tides, treating them as equals, and listening carefully to their concerns. Lastly he called his officers, together with Masters Hawkins and Hippon, to a meeting to discuss our predicament. This conference was held, not secluded in the General's cabin, but under an awning slung across the fo'c'sle, in the full sight and hearing of the common sailors before the *Dragon*'s mast. Here General Keeling heard representations from all sections of the crew, the complaints of the men of their sickness; the concerns of the officers regarding our want of fresh food and water; and the perplexity of the Masters as to how their ships, given the adverse conditions of wind and tides, could be delivered safely to our destination on the other side of the world.

I observed the face of the General throughout this colloquy. He listened with attention and impassivity, exhibiting no reaction to these various complaints, even though some came near to touching upon the manner of his command. After each member of the council had had his say, he reflected for a space in silence, as if absorbing all he had heard before coming to a judgement. At last he looked up, his countenance expressing both authority and resolve, and uttered to the open ears of both passenger and crew what all of us equally wanted to hear.

He accepted that, enfeebled as we were, and subjected as we remained to adverse weather, we could not continue our voyage without first finding some haven of succour and solace, which would provide us with the opportunity of rest, supply, and medical comforts for the stricken mariners. This reassured us much that the General did not intend to press on recklessly with a voyage that showed no promise of success. As to the sentiment that we should return to England, this he dismissed as a counsel of despair. Moreover, he affirmed, it was his belief that help lay much closer to hand than home. He then produced a book, Mr Hakluyt's book of voyages or *Principal Navigations*, from which he read to the assembled company of a country that lay on our present latitude, and would provide us with the sanctuary we desperately needed. This land was known as Sierra Leone, and lay on the western coast of Africa. The General assured us from his observations, and with the seamanship of his captain, we would be able to reach this haven within a matter of days. Here we would find a safe harbour for our ship, people friendly and hospitable, plentiful supplies of fresh water and food, and opportunity for our sick and weary of rest and recreation. The meeting broke up with smiles and a cheerful resolve. As if to endorse our General's wisdom, a freshening westerly breeze began to stir our rigging, and with cheers from the men, we hoisted sail for Africa.

AUGUST THE 6TH, 1607

This day we sighted land, a broad harbour, a foreshore thickly clumped with green vegetation, and beyond the tawny bulk of a mountain range. This place was named by a Portuguese *Sierra Lyone*, otherwise the *Mountains of the Lion*, after these peaks, which may look from the sea like the mane of a lion, or the shape of a lion's flank. Some say the name was given by other travellers who had found their encampments stalked by lions. Though we saw none, it was easy to imagine such fierce creatures secretly haunting the undergrowth, their golden eyes glaring at us through the green. We approached the shore slowly, the *Dragon* first followed by the *Hector* astern, not knowing how quickly the depths shallowed, or how friendly the inhabitants might prove to be. The shore was wreathed in a fog that now hid the land, now cleared to reveal its contours. Through the mist a fine hot rain hissed continually on to our decks.

After half an hour we came to an anchor, and watched for signs of life. They were not long in appearing, for presently we saw people running down to the beach, and waving to us a white flag, signifying that we should land. The General ordered that our pinnace be manned, and rowed ashore. There our people met with the natives, though none could understand their speech, and relied on signs. Presently however the pinnace returned, leaving two of our men, as was the custom, as hostage, and carrying four Negroes from the coast. These men were entertained by the General in his cabin, and treated with all courtesy. In the evening they were returned to the shore, with a good understanding of our needs, for the next morning came many Negroes to the ship in their canoas, bearing limes, and lemons, and hens, which we exchanged for beads and knives. The fruit was of good service for the refreshment of our sick men, and the fresh meat most welcome to seamen fed for months on little but salt pork. Meanwhile some of our men cast nets into the water, and caught good store of fish. Knowing that such goods were to be had from this coast, and that the people were friendly and ready to trade, we settled in for a protracted stay in Sierra Leone.

AUGUST THE 16TH, 1607

On this day our General ordered that pinnaces from both ships be manned with a good number of men, and he himself went aboard with Captain Hawkins of the *Hector*. Knowing that some of us merchants were eager to be ashore, he invited a few of us to join the expedition. Once on land, we marched up the country to one of their towns, as they signified it to us, though in truth it was but a mean collection of shabby huts. Here we were met by a man of much consequence among them, one Lucas Fernandez, who spoke

Portuguese very well, and was interpreter to their king, his name being Boree, or Burré. Our General conversed with this Fernandez in fluent Portuguese, which I understood imperfectly. But with the assistance of one of my fellows who had better command of the tongue, I was able to follow their conversation. They spoke of King Burré, and the General voiced much desire to meet with him. Fernandez explained that the King dwelt in another town some leagues away, and rarely visited the coast. He welcomed the General to travel up into the country to meet with him. This Mr Keeling seemed loath to do, to depart so far from our ship and her guns, too far into an unknown territory. In turn the General sent an invitation by Fernandez to the King to come aboard the *Dragon* to be entertained. Fernandez said he would bear this message, and so we parted in friendship and with exchange of gifts. The Negroes gave the General some pieces of gold and the tooth of an elephant, for these goods they had aplenty, in return for some knives and other tools, for which they had no means of manufacture.

I know not why, but there seemed to me to be some depth of meaning in their discourse that I could not fathom. This was more than their shared understanding of a language I knew but partially. There was some understanding between Mr Keeling and this Fernandez, beyond accustomed courtesy. When Fernandez spoke of the King, there seemed in his tone an insincerity that puzzled me. And when the General declined the King's invitation, and in his turn extended his own welcome, it appeared to me that they shared some complicity beyond language, some secret knowledge that could not be spoken in the hearing of others. I said nothing to anyone else about my suspicions, thinking it better to keep my own counsel. What was it to me if, here in Sierra Leone, the King's interpreter enjoyed a compact with the emissary of a foreign power? It was none of my business.

AUGUST THE 30TH, 1607

Thereafter these matters became my business, and indeed that of all of us numbered in the enterprise. I woke this morning early to the noise of shouting from landward, and mounting the deck observed a tumult raised amongst the Negroes on shore. There were some forty of them on the beach, all presenting a most warlike appearance,

brandishing aloft their long spears and raffia shields, uttering the
most chilling of war-cries, and signalling some message which,
though unintelligible, plainly bode ill towards us. The master was
for taking the pinnace directly to shore to discover the matter, not
thinking there could be any real danger from people who had offered
us such friendship, and imagining some misunderstanding to be the
cause of such violence. But the General counselled patience. It
seemed he was right in his judgement, for very soon these forty
men were joined by as many again, equally well appointed as to their
weapons and armour, and the whole assembly began to offer us
unmistakable signs of hostility, pointing their spears in our direction
and loudly howling their battle-cries. There was no sign of Lucas
Fernandez, or of the King. We knew not what to think.

Presently the General gave order that the *Dragon* should be turned
at anchor so her guns pointed shorewards, and pinnaces from both
ships filled forthwith with our own men, fully armed with muskets,
pistols, and swords. I watched the three boats surging manfully
towards the shore, our General and the two Captains standing firmly
aft, the long muskets of the crewmen pointing towards the waiting
spears of the enemy, the oars beating time to the noise of a drum that
all but drowned out the shouting from shore. Before the boats
beached on the shelving sand, the company of Negroes had melted
away into the forest. Warrior-like though their appearance may have
been, they had no stomach for standing that day against an armed
detachment of the East India Company.

Then I saw emerging from the trees, in another direction, Lucas
Fernandez himself, with some of his fellows, bearing a white flag in
sign of peace. I saw the General stride up to him and guessed that he
was questioning him as to the meaning of this late display of arms, as
he pointed towards the trees in the direction the other Negroes had
gone, as if asking what was amiss with them. I saw Lucas stretch out
his hands as if in obeisance or apology. Then all heads turned
towards the forest, as a noise from beyond the trees seemed to
indicate the chance of another sally from the armed band, Lucas
was swiftly brought into a boat, and all turned and rowed back
towards the ships. I saw Lucas being brought aboard, his face
showing much consternation, and that of the General displaying as
much anger as I had ever seen cross his countenance, usually so

peaceable and unperturbed. Lucas was soon safe in the General's cabin, the pistols and muskets back in the store, and the ship restored to quietness once again.

AUGUST THE 31ST, 1607

I confess that this night my curiosity to know what was passing between the General and Lucas Fernandez got the better of me, and I risked myself in a reckless shift to overhear their conversation. Having gazed for an hour's space at the lighted windows of the General's cabin, wondering what could be passing within, my anxiety for knowledge at last overcame me, and under cover of darkness I clambered up the rigging to the upper deck, and finding there a large barrel that stood next to the General's window, slipped off the top and climbed within. The barrel fortunately being empty save for a few apples, I was easily able to ensconce myself inside. The hoops of the cask being loose, and the General's window standing open for the heat, I was able through cracks between the staves to hear their conversation, and even from time to time to catch a glimpse of what was passing within the cabin.

To my surprise the General and Lucas were conversing in English, a language I had not known the latter understood. The story I heard astonished me, and left me baffled in my own mind as to whether our General's intentions were to be considered right or wrong. Certainly they seemed to run counter to the Company's policy of non-interference in the affairs of another nation, at least as I understood it. But I knew only too well that I was but a very junior, inexperienced agent of the Company, and in need of a deeper education in the covert wisdom of international trade. That few hours in the apple barrel gave me an entirely different understanding of the long and crooked roads that lead to empire.

As I arrived at my look-out post, I heard Lucas Fernandez completing in a broken voice his explanation to how it was that the General had suffered the inconvenience of this show of arms. It appeared that King Burré, who was a very old man, and had ruled for many years, had enjoyed good relations with Portuguese traders for many years past. From these men he had been taught to favour the Portuguese nation above all others, and to despise both the

Dutch and the English tradesmen who followed this way after the
Portuguese had moved on. The men we had seen were sent by King
Burré as an earnest of his intention that no Englishman should set
foot on his land. The voice of Lucas Fernandez broke with emotion
as he laid these matters before the General, since he, Lucas, felt only
affection towards the English, who had shown him many favours.
Many times he had tried to persuade the King that the English
should be regarded as friends and partners in trade. But the King
remained adamant that his people would never trade with the
English, who would always be unwelcome to the shores of his
kingdom. Catching a glimpse of Lucas's face, I saw that tears stood
in his eyes, as he expressed his sorrow that his own power was strictly
subservient to that of the King, and that King Burré's enmity would
make it impossible for us to remain any longer, or to further enjoy
the benefits of their hospitality.

I heard the General reply to this speech, and though I could not
see his face, I could imagine its expression of composure and natural
authority, as he sought to reassure Lucas that nothing but friendship
still subsisted between the two of them. Mister Keeling made it plain
that he doubted nothing of Lucas's loyalty, and regretted much that
King Burré was of a different mind. But he was forced to acknowledge that a sovereign ruler of any kingdom might choose his own
friends and enemies. He assured Lucas that if the Company's ships
were not wanted in this kingdom, they would sail away on the
morrow without a backward glance. Yet it remained a matter of
much chagrin to him, that so much advantage could come to the
people of Sierra Leone from an amicable partnership with England,
and that so much promise should be sacrificed to one man's enmity.

It seemed to me, as I knelt in the apple barrel, that the General
was going too far in speaking thus of King Burré, since it was none of
our business to question a foreign ruler's authority, or to set a subject
against a king in any country in the world. Such talk would be
treasonable at home, and seditious abroad. The General seemed to
agree with my opinion, since he turned the conversation to other
topics. But after some words of solicitude to calm the feelings of his
distraught companion, he crept insidiously back to the same point,
asking Lucas question after question about the politics of the kingdom, and the safety of King Burré's throne. How old was the King?

How long had he ruled? Did he succeed his father? Who were his chief officers and supporters? Who were the rich and powerful men of the kingdom? How did they view him? Did any of them feel he was mistaken in his partiality for one foreign nation over another? Had there ever been any signs of rebellion among his people, any attempts to kill or depose him? Was there an heir apparent who would replace him when he should chance to die? Or some popular candidate to the throne, who could replace him and command the loyalty and service of the nation?

All this time Lucas remained quiet and, as I caught glimpses of his face, clearly thinking very carefully about the General's words. I could barely hear his replies, since at that moment a wind sprang up and began to rattle the window shutter. He seemed to be confiding in the General that there was in the kingdom a company of men close to the King who felt he had ruled long enough, and that his judgement was become poor. These men believed, said Lucas, that it was in the best interests of the kingdom to persuade King Burré to resign, so a younger and more able man could assume his sceptre, to rule the kingdom wisely and well. But the King himself . . . I could barely hear how this speech continued, but I guessed that the King was unwilling to abdicate, and his courtiers loath to use force to remove him. I am sure there was more to be heard here, but it was at this crucial point in the conversation that I had reason to fear discovery, for the General, finding his swinging porthole an annoyance, came to the window to secure it. His face was inches from mine, and my blood froze at the thought of discovery. But fortunately I proved invisible inside the barrel. Fearful of the consequences if I were caught, and unable in any case to hear more through the firmly shut casement, I lifted the lid of the barrel and made my escape.

SEPTEMBER THE 26TH, 1607

I thought no more of these matters for some days, being only too happy to escape without discovery from my eavesdropping adventure in the apple barrel. Business on board the ship was brisk and time-consuming, as we began the long process of taking in stores to prepare for the next stage of our voyage. The task was rendered all the more difficult by the hostility demonstrated towards us by

King Burré's men, which involved us in longer forays up and down the coast to find and fetch what we needed. Though we merchants were not involved in the heavy work of transporting and stowing supplies, with the still depleted crew at full stretch, there was always some task to be undertaken.

It was at this time that I became more aware of the strange and unusual presence on board of those mariners I have mentioned before, who seemed most unlike common seamen, with their finer clothes, white un-workmanlike hands, and cultivated manner of speaking. Most of the time they remained secluded in their quarters astern, but now they seemed more in evidence, as one man would emerge to pick up some store of wood, or an unwanted end of rope, before disappearing once more into their fastness below decks. Passing by the door of their cabin, I heard the sounds of sawing and hammering, as if someone were building something. I also heard voices raised, as if in anger or pleading, and even the sounds of scuffling and the clink of swords. But when I reported these odd and disconcerting observations to one of my fellows, a veteran of earlier voyages, he smiled and indicated that I should mind my own business. No harm would arise from these mysteries, he said. Perhaps even some pleasantry.

SEPTEMBER THE 29TH, 1607

This last night most of my questions have been answered, and many of the mysteries on board ship resolved. Not that I am any clearer in my mind about the darker purpose of our voyage, but at least I now know who the mysterious supernumerary mariners are, and what was the true import of the General's business with Lucas Fernandez.

All day the ship was being prepared for a great feast to entertain a party from the shore. Food and drink were made ready, and a space cleared for the provision of some form of entertainment. Seats were arranged for the guests to view this show, whatever it might prove to be. So much care was taken over these preparations, suggesting so lavish and spectacular an entertainment, that some of us believed King Burré himself must have been persuaded to come aboard to join the General in a feast of amity and reconciliation.

As it fell out, no such matter. About 6 o' clock we saw a number of canoas leave the shore and paddle towards the ship. As the guests came aboard, I observed that their leader was Lucas Fernandez himself, and concluded from this that we were not to see the King. Together with Lucas were a number of men who appeared to be the chief dignitaries of the kingdom. Their appearance startled me, since I had not seen these people dressed in their ceremonial garb. Their teeth were filed to sharp points, their eyebrows plucked. They wore gold rings not only in their ears, but their noses too. Each man's hair was braided and shaved into elegant patterns, and their bodies tattooed by means of hot irons with images of beasts and birds, monkeys and elephants, parrots and macaws. All seemed to be very proud, and received the greetings of our officers with some hauteur. But all of them, I noticed, deferred to Lucas Fernandez as if he were *primus inter pares* among them. At first I thought this was merely because he knew the Portuguese language and could communicate with their hosts. But soon I was to realise there was much more to his pre-eminence here than mere linguistic fluency.

First the General feasted them in his cabin, but then afterwards they were all led to the space on deck that had been prepared for entertainment. Here they were invited to take the seats that had been set up around the open space. Lucas Fernandez in particular assumed his seat in the largest of the chairs, in the very midst of the company, as if he were singled out for some special favour. We merchants gathered around the circle to watch, together with the crew. From where I stood I was able not only to see the action, but to observe the faces of our guests, and in addition that of the General himself, who took a chair right by the mast.

No sooner had we taken our places, than to my astonishment a man stepped forward on deck dressed in every respect like a king, with gorgeous robes and a gilded crown. He stood for a while and eyed the company with a regal stare, before stepping to the side of the circle to make way for other men who joined him in what I now realised to be a playing circle. The King spoke to one of his fellows in words I remembered having heard before:

> Old John of Gaunt, time-honour'd Lancaster,
> Hast thou, according to thy oath and band,
> Brought hither Henry Hereford thy bold son,
> Here to make good the boisterous late appeal,
> Which then our leisure would not let us hear,
> Against the Duke of Norfolk, Thomas Mowbray?

The men were actors, the deck of the *Dragon* had become a stage, and the ship herself a theatre. These were the mysterious men I had seen and heard, obviously preparing their piece for this evening's performance. The play chanced to be one I knew, the *Tragedy of Richard II* by the famous playwright Master William Shakespeare of the King's Men. I had seen it performed, I forget where, and that more than once, since for a brief time a few years previous it seemed to be playing everywhere, in streets and houses as well as in theatres.

I knew the play and its history, but our guests, other than Lucas himself, knew neither play, nor language, nor even the very idea of theatre. They stared, and questioned one another, but Lucas Fernandez spoke to them with some kind of explanation. I observed that another man sat by him and turned the play's English into Portuguese, while he himself conveyed the general sense of the action to his fellows in their own native tongue.

At first the African dignitaries were baffled by what was being presented to them, and unable to distinguish between truth and pretence. When any of the actors had occasion to draw a sword against another, they were alarmed, and had to be restrained from joining the fray on one side or the other. Soon however they began to understand that the action was truly a representation, not a reality. Their disbelief once suspended, they were spellbound by the spectacle, and intrigued by the narrative the play unfolded. King Richard seemed in this actor's interpretation to be rash and reckless, high-handed and despotic in his hereditary pride. His abrogations of his subjects' rights, such as his banishments of Mowbray and Bolingbroke, and his seizure of Gaunt's lands, were executed with arrogance and contempt. None of this was lost, I noticed, on our guests, who showed in their countenance how little they liked this style of ruling.

I said that I had seen the play more than once, and remembered it fairly well. But there came one scene in this performance that I could not recall having seen before. It showed King Richard, defeated in arms and stripped of his loyal supporters, brought before Henry Bolingbroke and asked to surrender his crown. 'To do what service am I sent for hither?' he asked the company. 'To do that office of thine own good will,' replied another, playing the Duke of York:

> Which tired majesty did make thee offer,
> The resignation of thy state and crown
> To Henry Bolingbroke.

Here King Richard, for all his pride, seemed to concede his kingly authority most readily.

> Give me the crown. Here, cousin, seize the crown;
> Here cousin:
> On this side my hand, and on that side yours.

'Are you contented to resign the crown?' asked Bolingbroke. 'Ay,' replied Richard. And then, stage by stage, he undid his own kingship.

> Now mark me, how I will undo myself;
> I give this heavy weight from off my head
> And this unwieldy sceptre from my hand,
> The pride of kingly sway from out my heart;
> With mine own tears I wash away my balm,
> With mine own hands I give away my crown,
> With mine own tongue deny my sacred state,
> With mine own breath release all duty's rites:
> All pomp and majesty I do forswear;
> My manors, rents, revenues I forego;
> My acts, decrees, and statutes I deny:
> God pardon all oaths that are broke to me!
> Long mayst thou live in Richard's seat to sit,
> And soon lie Richard in an earthly pit!
> God save King Harry, unking'd Richard says,
> And send him many years of sunshine days!

As he spoke these words the actor turned away from his fellow, and spoke directly to Lucas Fernandez, even holding out the crown towards him like a gift, as if the matter of the play in some way concerned him. I could see on the faces of Lucas's fellows that they fully understood the import of this action. Here, on this ship of the East India Company, they had been able to see, with their own eyes, the possibility of a monarch voluntarily resigning his crown; to hear the deed expressed in the poetry of our greatest playwright; and to see it performed in the speech and gesture of a most persuasive actor. I could see in their faces the realisation dawning that this was something that could be done, in earnest as in pretence. And when the player's crown was offered to Lucas, they all but nodded in approval, showing great contentment with this resolution of the action.

The remainder of the play, which I recalled being of some length, was done briefly, unceremoniously, as if the real purpose of the drama was to get Bolingbroke on the throne, and then brush quickly over any unfortunate complications. Richard disappeared from view almost as soon as he was deposed, and Henry was triumphantly crowned king in his place. There was no sign of lament for Richard's fall, no predictions of future disaster. It was a version of the play as Henry IV himself might have had it composed. It was history written from the viewpoint of the victor. Our guests of course knew no better, and were happy with the play as it was presented, wishing for nothing more. I found the performance disturbing, and resolved to understand it better. As luck would have it, helping some of the crew to clear away after our guests had returned to shore, I found hidden under a chair a copy of the play itself, left there by one of the actors, and quickly slipped it into my pocket.

SEPTEMBER THE 30TH, 1607

Perusing the play-text by the light of a lantern in my cabin, I noticed first that it was published by Nicholas Ling, whose name I remembered as a founding member of the East India Company. Then my suspicions about the performance were indeed confirmed. The play we had seen performed on the deck of the *Dragon* was not the play as Master Shakespeare had written it. The scene I had thought an interpolation, that of Richard's deposition, was indeed present in the text, though I had no memory of it forming any part of the performances I had seen. But the text was thickly marked with cuts, whole lines and phrase scored through with a broad pen. All the cuts were of the same kind: they were elements in the text that could be read as vindicating Richard's right to rule, and questioning the authority of Bolingbroke and the other nobles to remove him. They left the play as almost a kind of manifesto for the right of nobility to remove from his throne a king whose rule they disapproved. The scene of the deposition had evidently been censored in the performances I had seen, but was here reinstated to endorse the morality of regime change.

And reading that mutilated text, I realised at last why the General had brought such a play with him on this voyage, and why he chose to stage it for the enlightenment of this group of nobles from Sierra Leone. The message of the play, in this form, was clear. Its implementation in practice would lead to nothing less than a regime change, with King Burré deposed, and Lucas Fernandez chosen as the new king. And this, I now understood, was our General's darker purpose. We had neither right nor power, as emissaries of the East India Company, to effect such a change. But if the influential men of a kingdom could be persuaded to engineer such a transition for themselves, replacing an unfriendly with an amicable sovereign, then the business of the Company, and the commerce of our own nation, could only benefit.

Within a few days I understood this mission to be accomplished, with King Burré deposed and imprisoned somewhere inland, while Lucas Fernandez was proclaimed king. Our access to food and water became easy, and trade with the natives in such commodities as gold pieces and elephant's teeth became brisk and profitable. I had no opportunity to observe any of this business myself, since for reasons I was to learn only later, I was confined to my quarters and not permitted on deck. Though I was given no explanation of this detention, I was given to understand it was on the General's orders, and it was evident to me that he had received intelligence of my spying, or perhaps learned of my interest in the play-text, which had disappeared from my cabin while I was busy elsewhere. It was only when we were under way, as I knew from the sounds of raised anchor and hoisted sail, that I was ordered on deck to watch the coast of Sierra Leone begin to recede into history. I could see on the shore a party of Negroes, led by their new king Lucas Fernandez, waving farewell to us as we sailed away. They all wept, and seemed, in outward appearance at least, to be very sorrowful for our departure. I had no time to linger over this sight since I was ordered to present myself immediately in the General's cabin, and proceeded there, I must own, knowing his reputation for severity, with a cold hand of fear gripping my heart.

I had no need of such foreboding, since the General showed me nothing but kindness. He asked about my background and education, and indicated that he had learned of my interest in these late events. Since he invited confidence, I told him of everything I had observed and deduced, about the politics of Sierra Leone, about the play he had commissioned for our guests, and about the change of regime that seemed so portentously to follow it.

He was silent for a while, filling his pipe with tobacco, then sat back in his chair to speak. He talked of our present king James, of his wisdom and justice, of the peace he had sealed with Spain, and of his support for commerce. But not so long ago, he said, the kingdom had not been equally blessed. In the final years of her late majesty's reign, he confided, when Queen Elizabeth's rule seemed to have lost its way, there were many in the kingdom who wished for a better king. King James was ready to succeed, if he had been given the opportunity. But there were some whose impatience for change led them to risk everything for their country's good.

I told him that I remembered those days, and especially the fate of the noble Earl of Essex, who was much admired by my father, and who lost his head in that enterprise. Aye, said the General, and he was not alone in his endeavour. There were many among his supporters, he said, who remain alive, and are to be found among the sponsors of the East India Company. Why, our own Governor, he said, Sir Thomas Smith, lay in the Tower under a charge of assisting the Earl. I said I knew nothing of that. One of our greatest backers, he said, and one I count as a particular friend, the Earl of Southampton, stood side by side with Essex in his defence of the realm against those upstart favourites who misled the Queen.

Beginning now to spy some of the connections the General was drawing together, I asked, was not the Earl of Southampton the patron of Master Shakespeare, he who wrote the play we saw yesternight? He was, in truth, said the General, and it was that very play of his, *Richard II*, that the two earls devised as a means of showing the people their intent to remove the Queen, and replace her with a new king. Was this not treason, I asked? Why yes, replied the General, it could hardly be described otherwise. And the price was paid: Essex lies headless under the stones of St Peter in Chains. Yet Southampton is to be found well and at court; Shakespeare is a Groom of the King's Bedchamber, and his company, who staged that play for Essex, are the King's Men; and Sir Thomas Smith is yet Governor of the East India Company. Queen Elizabeth lies at peace in the Abbey, and we have a new king who is a true friend to business. Treason is a name we give to a lost cause, he said with a smile. If a cause be successful, we call it not treason.

Now this affair of King Burré and Lucas Fernandez, he went on, can be compared with that crisis in our own country's history. If it is time for a king to go, and make way for a better ruler, then the people of the realm may decide to make that change. If we can show them how this might be done, we do no wrong. If they saw in the play *Richard II* the wished-for abdication of their own king, then the play formed a mirror for their own desires. It is not something we ourselves engineered. For it is, after all, only an old play, long out of favour, dealing with long-forgotten quarrels. We raised no English arms against King Burré.

And yet I tell you this, my boy, he said. We may never pass this way again, but because of what we have done here today, those who follow us will find a very different welcome on these shores. They will find, in place of hostility, love; in place of war, peace; and in place of hatred, a free and friendly traffic of commerce and exchange. We are bringing light to some of the darkest places of the earth. Do you see it now?

I owned that I did, and resolved to do all in my power to assist the General in carrying that flaming, luminescent torch into the hot obscurity of jungle and desert. I asked the General where we were bound for next, and he told me he hoped to drop anchor on the other side of Africa, by the shores of an Arabian island kingdom called Socotra, ruled by one Ben Said. Are the natives there like to be friendly, I asked? Not yet, he said. But they soon will be. We may need to show them a play or two first.

OCTOBER THE 15TH, 1607

One other memory of our time in Sierra Leone remained with me, proving hard to shake off. Indeed it pursued me in dreams, so that long afterwards I would wake from a nightmare and believe I was back again in that hot, restless land. We had gone ashore, the weather being fair, our company led by the General and Captain Hawkins, where we understood by the Negroes of an elephant which was not far off. So our General caused four good shots with their muskets to go along with the Negro, to see if they could shoot him. We followed, as the Negro softly and silently crept though the jungle, to come upon the elephant in secrecy. At the edge of a clearing he stopped, and we all stopped with him. In the open space we beheld the elephant, a magnificent bull with huge tusks, grazing quietly with his trunk from the trees. I remember feeling the ponderous mass of that huge bulk, more like a rock or a tree than a living thing, filling that close hot space, as blood fills the heart. Then my ears were deafened, and my eyes momentarily blinded, by the volley and flash of four muskets firing at once, and as the drifting smoke cleared I saw, as if in a slow silence, the great beast, wounded, turn towards us as if in indignation, then start away from us and run crashing into the jungle, so violently that we had hard shift to pursue him. As we ran in his track, easily followed from the smashed branches and upturned roots of trees, we observed that he bled very much all the way from his wounds. And so as we could do no good upon him, and night falling, we returned to our boats.

On returning to the ship we were conscious only of disappointment at the failure to capture our prey. But night after night, as we sailed away from that lion-haunted coast, a great afflicted beast lurched through my dreams, wounded nigh unto death from our musket balls, leaving behind him a trail of green devastation vividly splashed with the bright red of his own life-blood. Thus my memories of Africa crash nightly into the kingdom of my dreams: the abiding memory of a wounded creature, huge and powerful, innocent and suffering, crippled by our carelessness. He offered us no violence, yet we killed him. In truth, in the end, we could do no good upon him.

PART II

CHAPTER 3

Shakespeare and the King James Bible

I

I indicated above that the kinds of cultural collision I am concerned with can vary in severity, analogically speaking, from a car crash, to two people accidentally bumping into one another. The topic of this chapter more closely resembles the latter than the former. In 2011, the quatercentenary year of the 'Authorized Version' of 1611, Shakespeare appears to have accidentally bumped into the King James Bible (KJV). Commentary on the KJV was universal in its anniversary year, and Shakespeare was invariably mentioned as in some way implicated by some imputed contingency. And yet as far as anyone knows, prior to 2011 they had nothing much to do with one another.

Connections between Shakespeare and the Bible are familiar, but generally fortuitous and circumstantial. Victor Hugo is quoted as having said 'England has two books; the Bible and Shakespeare. England made Shakespeare, but the Bible made England.' In this Francophile fantasy, to exclude all other English writing necessarily seals an intimate connection between the only two books we have left. Something like Hugo's highly selective reading of English literature underlies the popular and long-running BBC radio series *Desert Island Discs*, in which the invited 'castaways' are always supplied with only two books, the Bible and 'the Complete Works of Shakespeare'. A castaway is assumed to need these two books because they are foundational texts of our civilisation, twin masterpieces of English writing. Critic Louis Marder predicted that the first books to be

This chapter is based on 'Bible Babel: Shakespeare and the King James Bible', the Wanamaker Fellowship Lecture I delivered at Shakespeare's Globe on 14 June 2011.

offered to alien visitors from another planet to represent 'the fruits of our terrestrial culture' would be the Bible and Shakespeare.[1]

There are of course many versions of both these books. But the most famous are the King James Bible of 1611 and the First Folio of Shakespeare's works, published in 1623. Nominate these editions, and the Bible and Shakespeare are closely contiguous in history, products of that same post-Renaissance moment shortly before the English Civil War, and share a parallel classic status. Between them, they are said to have influenced the English language and literature in English more than any other books. But this accident of historical contiguity, sanctified by a recognition of these two books as the finest touchstones of English literature, does not satisfy a general curiosity about some deeper link between Shakespeare and the Bible. If the two books are connected, is it not natural to seek some causal relationship between them? If one represents the crown of English writing, while the other is the work of the greatest of all English writers, do they not in some more concrete way belong together?

But which is cause and which effect? In a 2011 television programme with the self-explanatory title *The King James Bible: The Book that Changed the World*, Melvyn Bragg illustrated his view that no other book has had so much influence on the English language, partly by reference to the works of Shakespeare.[2] The programme showed Bragg walking around Stratford-upon-Avon, sitting in Holy Trinity Church, hearing in voice-over a series of biblically influenced Shakespeare quotations. But there was some embarrassment about this claim, since virtually all Shakespeare's plays had been written, performed, and even published before the 1611 translation appeared. In order to connect the two, Bragg talks about Shakespeare's works being saturated with 'the Bible that for the most part became the King James Bible' – in other words, the earlier translations the KJV was explicitly undertaken to supersede. We are encouraged to conceive of the KJV doing its work of influencing the language of literature, long before it was actually produced.

Now the Bible is certainly inside Shakespeare, but not in the King James Version. Shakespeare's Bible of choice seems to have been the Calvinist Geneva Bible, published in 1560, the translation King James himself most disliked for its subversive political opinions on kingship and authority. Melvyn Bragg's desire to put Shakespeare and the KJV together outpaces the historical evidence for any such connection.

Could there be some deeper causality working in this other direction, from playwright to biblical translation? If the KJV is not inside Shakespeare, perhaps Shakespeare himself might have had a role in the KJV? This is a long-running myth. 'You know who Bill Shakespeare was, don't you sonny?' says a character in Martin Scorsese's *Gangs of New York*. 'He's the Fellah that wrote the King James Bible.' The black revolutionary leader Malcolm X asked the same question 'if Shakespeare existed' and was 'the top poet around', why was he not involved in the translation of the Bible? American college students doing their term papers plaintively post the same question on the internet: 'Did Shakespeare write the King James Bible?' And some friend trying to be helpful will reply: no, but he helped his friend King James to write it.

II

It is natural to assume that this apparently fortuitous, perhaps even arbitrary, contingency owes more to subsequent appropriations of Shakespeare for quasi-religious ideologies, than to any substantive cultural and historical connection. Theatre and reformed church were of course sworn enemies in this period: stage plays were vigorously denounced from pulpit and pamphlet, and the theatres were eventually closed during the Commonwealth. The Puritans who initiated the new translation were certainly hostile to the theatre. It was Dr John Rainolds, the president of Corpus Christi College, Oxford, who put the proposal for a new translation to the King: 'Dr Reynolds ... moved his Majesty that there might be a new translation of the Bible, because those which were allowed in the reigns of King Henry the Eighth and Edward the Sixth were corrupt, and not answerable to the truth of the original.'[3] This was the same Dr Reynolds who had delivered, in 1599, in the form of a published controversy with Dr William Gager, a particularly aggressive denunciation of the theatre (together with other sports and leisure pursuits), *Th'overthrow of Stage-Playes*.[4]

It has been argued that the strategy of linking the Bible and 'the Complete Works of Shakespeare' together, as master documents of English culture, has more to do with efforts to confer on Shakespeare's work a quasi-divine status comparable to that of the Bible. 'The telling juxtaposition of the Bible with the "Complete Works of Shakespeare"', argues John Drakakis, constitutes 'a tacit acknowledgement of Shakespeare as universal, transcendent, and eternal': '*Desert Island Discs* attributes to Shakespeare's influence ... a divine status. Shakespeare, thus removed from human history, becomes for us the "Absolute Subject" whose all-embracing "Word" takes its place alongside the Bible as our guarantee of civilisation and humanity.'[5] But the two books display other affinities beside their traditional linking in the castaway's two-volume set of the greatest stories ever told. Both were published under the aegis of royal patronage: the new translation of the Bible was a project explicitly sponsored by James at the Hampton Court Conference in 1604;[6] and the First Folio an edition, compiled by two actors of the King's Men, of works by the royal company's foremost playwright. Both carry dedications to royal or aristocratic patrons: the KJV is dedicated to 'the most High and Mighty Prince James',[7] and the Folio 'To the most noble and incomparable paire of brethren, William Earle of Pembroke, Lord Chamberlaine to the Kings most Excellent Maiesty; and Philip Earle of Montgomery, Gentleman of his Maiesties Bedchamber'.[8] Both represent canonical compilations of works initially written and published as individual texts that bore quite different relations (or even no relation at all) to one another. (There is also, it should be noted, at this point a substantive difference, in that the First Folio is the initial point of Shakespearean canon formation, whereas the canon of the biblical books had been substantially agreed and approved by the fourth century AD.)[9]

Both books were produced in the same publishing format, a bound folio text, printed in roman type with double columns; and both were aimed to some degree at a new publishing market. The contents of both the Bible and the First Folio of Shakespeare's plays had been, and remained, freely available in oral performative media. Both volumes therefore collected and circulated writings already accessible to lettered and unlettered alike, through the ear, from every church pulpit, and from the stages of the metropolitan theatre. 'The godly learned', claimed the editors of the KJV, 'provided translations into the vulgar for their countrymen, inasmuch that most nations under heaven did shortly after their conversion hear Christ speaking unto them in their mother tongue'.[10] 'These Playes' say Heminge and Condell, drawing for a parallel on the oral procedures of the law courts, 'haue had their triall alreadie, and stood out all Appeales.'[11] The writings in each case were converted by editing and publication into a form that could possibly have been used as a text for performance, but was more likely to be used for private reading. Although these are big books by modern standards, it was still to private readers, rather than to their natural performative contexts, that they seem to have appealed. The First Folio could have been used as a prompt-book, but not as a source for actors' parts; and though the Folio KJV was intended to replace the 'ordinary Bible read in the church, commonly called the Bishops' Bible',[12] it is clear that it did not automatically replace the existing Bibles that were held in churches and used by the clergy for liturgical and devotional purposes. As evidence that other and earlier editions continued to be used, after the publication of the KJV, we can find them quoted, not only in sermons by such clerics as John Donne, but even in those of Lancelot Andrewes, one of the KJV's leading translators, and in those of Miles Smith, who was both a translator and a co-author of the KJV's prefatory essay 'The Translators to the Reader'.[13]

These two books closely resemble one another in terms of cultural efficacy and function. Both were apparently published in order to supersede earlier variant versions of the same text or texts. Although, as I indicated above, the First Folio was opening and defining a canon, whereas the KJV was re-presenting a canon closed some twelve centuries earlier, both publications were aiming at what, in the modern language of marketing, we would describe as seeking a larger market share by eliminating competition. It is clear that the editors and translators presented their products to the public in the expectation that they would supplant those existing and still competitive versions. At the same time they were claiming for their new products substantial cultural power and authority: whether in presenting the words of Shakespeare, or the Word of God, they claimed to be doing so in a form authorised and approved by higher secular and ecclesiastical authorities. Both sets of editors assumed that the cultural and literary value of the material they were reproducing was not in dispute, having already been well established and authenticated; but both claimed that this particular publication had a unique value in defining and establishing the authority and value of the works in question.

Both books embodied the intention of fixing a text so that no further corruption or mistranslation could be visited upon it. The translators of the KJV said in their introduction: 'We never thought from the beginning that we should need to make a new translation, nor yet to make of a bad one a good one; but to make a good one better, or out of many good ones one principal good one, not justly to be excepted against' (p. lxv). The editors of the First Folio said in their address to 'The Great Variety of Readers':

> Before you were abus'd with diverse stolne, and surreptitious copies, maimed, and deformed by the frauds and stealthes of injurious impostors, that expos'd them: even those, are now offer'd to your view cur'd, and perfect of their limbes; and all the rest, absolute in their numbers, as he conceived them. (p. 7)

The two volumes were aimed therefore primarily at new 'market segments', divergent sections of the small but print-hungry literate reading public (they were not of course aimed at the same readers, and possibly even at two different and to some degree mutually exclusive categories of reader). Heminge and Condell, in their brief preface, address 'the great Variety of Readers', many of whom, as both the preface and some of the commendatory poems indicate, would have been expected to know the plays from performance, but are now assumed to have the inclination to 'buy', 'read', and if necessary 'censure' the scripts of those performances, collected and presented in an approved and authoritative literary text.

III

There is one other respect in which the two books reveal a quite extraordinary resemblance. People often ask how such a great piece of writing as the King James Bible could have been produced 'by a committee of people no-one has ever heard of'.[14] In 2011 several learned commentators who should have known better promulgated the misconception that the translators sat in a group and translated, line by line and word by word. In fact, as the rules of the translation make clear, the work was to be undertaken in both an individual and a collective way, with a particular translator producing a new version which would then be discussed, amended, and approved by the whole 'company'.

8. Every particular Man of each Company, to take the same Chapter, or Chapters, and having translated or amended them severally by himself, where he thinketh good, all to meet together, confer what they have done, and agree for their Parts what shall stand.[15]

We know the translators applied this method from a manuscript in the Lambeth Palace Library entitled *An English Translation of the Epistles of Paule the Apostle*, a book of about 125 pages, bound in vellum, which is nothing less than a working text of the King James Bible.[16] Each page is ruled out in red ink into double columns, with margins on both sides. It provides a version of the Epistles, with notes in the left margin. These books of the Bible were done by the 'second Westminster Company' under William Barlow. One person produced an initial version of the text, but then the manuscript went through several hands. Missing words have been supplied, letters added, spelling corrected, punctuation changed. This is a collaborative editing process done collectively by a group of people. But it began with one man's individual creative input, his personal version of St Paul. There was always one writer – 'severally [separately] by himself' – drafting the initial text for consideration and amendment by the group. The work of each individual translator was referred to the whole company for discussion and amendment. So the project entailed a combination of individual scholarly work, and collective review and approval. No one translator could have the final say in the process; but equally the committees could not embark on their work without the prior productions of individual scholarship.

This text and the writing process it adumbrates can be compared to the manuscript of *Sir Thomas More*, the single unique example of Shakespeare's handwriting on a theatrical manuscript.[17] *Sir Thomas More* is a collaborative work, probably written largely by Anthony Munday and Henry Chettle, to which Shakespeare was apparently asked to contribute after it had been critically reviewed by the censor. Shakespeare's handwriting lies on the page, together with the hands

of several others, all writing and revising in a continuous collaborative process. Some like to think of Shakespeare writing alone, putting
his quill pen to a pristine sheet of blank paper. But the evidence here
shows him writing on the pages of a text already written, and already
revised, by others. We see him not necessarily, as the classic writerly
image suggests, alone and isolated, withdrawn from the world,
communing only with the voices of his imagination. Instead, he is
working as a professional writer within a busy, noisy, and stressful
environment, where writers worked together under enormous pres-
sures of time, censorship, theatrical practicalities, to get the show on
the road.

And there is another key similarity here. These texts were not put
together by people who thought of themselves as writers in the
specialised modern sense. They were writers, but they were also
actors and priests, for whom writing had specific uses and functions.
Their approach to writing was practical and professional. The plays
were written for dramatic use in the theatre; the Bible for liturgical
application in the church. All these words were written and printed
to be spoken, to be heard. At the final review meeting, the KJV
translators sat and heard one of their number read the Bible aloud,
and gave their comments and corrections.

That part of the Bible was given to him who was most excellent in such a
tongue and then they met together, and one read the translation, the rest
holding in their hands some Bible, either of the learned tongues, or French,
Spanish, Italian etc. If they found any fault, they spoke up; if not he
read on. (quoted in Nicolson, *When God Spoke English*, p. 209)

That is a later note by John Selden, but we are sure of its accuracy
from the minutes of that meeting taken by John Bois (Nicolson,
When God Spoke English, p. 209), which show the translators reading,
listening, disputing in exactly this fashion.

IV

These are parallels and similarities, not intertextual connections. But
all this makes the two books, the KJV and the 'Complete Works of
Shakespeare', sound so similar that they must surely have emerged
from, and belonged to, a common and unified Jacobean court and

civic culture. The new translation of the Bible was produced on the specific order of the King, given at the Hampton Court conference in 1604; done by the leading bishops and academic clergy of London, Oxford, and Cambridge; and printed by the King's printer. By 1603, Shakespeare's acting company was the King's Men; they were servants of the royal household, each member granted the title 'Groom of the Chamber'; and they regularly acted at court and before the King. The whole population of the country in 1603 was only 3.75 million. The population of London was 200,000. The literate were a minority of that total. The number of people with an office at court, a sub-section of the latter, was tiny.

In Southwark Cathedral lie the graves of Lancelot Andrewes, one of the foremost leaders of the KJV project, and Philip Henslowe, and Philip Massinger, and John Fletcher, and Shakespeare's younger brother Edmund. Clergy and players, bishop and theatre manager, translator and dramatist lie peacefully together in death. Did they never encounter one another in life? Did Shakespeare, Groom of the Royal Chamber, really know nothing at all about the massive publishing project that produced the KJV? There was clearly overlap from the theatre side, since the companies performed at court as well as in the public playhouse, and the bishops must have been present on such occasions, and must have heard Shakespeare's words. Equally, on great state occasions, the King's Men were present at court, and must have heard sermons from those who were involved in the translation of the KJV. James Shapiro has suggested that Shakespeare might have heard Lancelot Andrewes preach at Richmond Palace during Lent in 1599, and that echoes of Andrewes's rhetoric can be traced in *Henry V*.[18] One of the Oxford translators was a man called Richard Edes, who preached at a state occasion in 1604 when the King's Men, Shakespeare among them, marched in the procession. Edes was also a poet and dramatist who wrote a Latin play on *Julius Caesar*, from which Shakespeare could well have picked up that strange, unhistorical phrase, spoken in Latin, in his own Caesar play; '*et tu Brute*'. Why should Shakespeare's Caesar, having spoken English throughout, suddenly lapse into Latin? And why does he use a phrase for which there is no historical justification, in Plutarch or anywhere else? Did he acquire it from one of the KJV translators?

V

There is another piece of 'evidence' that to some people at least provides conclusive proof that Shakespeare did in fact have a hand in the translation of the King James Bible. This appears in the KJV translation of Psalm 46, 'God is our refuge and strength'. If we count forty-six words from the beginning of the psalm, we reach the word 'shake'. The previous text had 'tremble', so this word was introduced by the KJV translators. Then if we count forty-six words from the end, not including the formal salutation 'Selah', we find 'Spear'. Which was previously 'sword'. Thus 'Shake' and 'spear' are, at least numerologically, connected in the text. 'Shake-spear' was born of course in 1564. How old was he, for at least part of 1611? He was 46.

This curious accident, or coincidence, has fascinated numerologists and conspiracy theorists beyond measure. Why? Because it seems to indicate that there may be some substance to that belief for which there is no evidence whatsoever, but an immense reservoir of desire: that Shakespeare made some contribution to the KJV; that the author of one of the greatest bodies of work in English had a hand in the other.

Thus far I have considered this relationship, or lack of it, historically, as a matter of fact, that might be proved or disproved by appeal to evidence. But now we enter, via that strange inexplicable cryptogram, the world of imagination and fantasy. One day at a lunch-club in Fleet Street, John Buchan, Rudyard Kipling, and others were discussing the question of how the Authorised Version of the Bible came to be written in such magnificent English. The official revisers were no doubt outstanding scholars, but what evidence was there, other than the translation standing in their names, that they were outstanding masters of the language? Surely, said John Buchan, there were hidden hands at work, the hands of the great literary geniuses of the age – Shakespeare's, Ben Jonson's. Kipling said to Buchan, 'That's an idea,' and away he went 'to turn it over'.[19]

Kipling's story 'Proofs of Holy Writ', praised by John Buchan as the best story Kipling ever wrote, imagines Shakespeare and Ben Jonson in Shakespeare's garden at New Place, Stratford. They talk theatre gossip and argue over their respective dramatic methods: Jonson defending learning, craftsmanship, and classical unity, and

Shakespeare expressing his faith in education through entertainment. Jonson criticises Shakespeare's eclecticism and populism; Shakespeare defends his work. Shakespeare interrogates Jonson's literary quarrelsomeness, stating that writers should stick together, since they have responsibility for 'the betterment of the present age'. Then a messenger arrives to collect some papers. Jonson learns that his friend has been asked to contribute to the new translation of the Bible by Miles Smith, author of 'The Translator to the Reader', and as it happens (like Shakespeare) the son of a butcher. Shakespeare tells Jonson that Smith had seen *Macbeth* at Oxford, and felt it to contain profound theological feeling. So he asks Shakespeare to take over some difficult passages from the Prophets and to give them a bit of style. 'They never called on me,' says Jonson, clearly annoyed. The two dramatists start to work together on a passage of Isaiah 60 – 'Arise, shine, for thy light is come, and the glory of the Lord is risen upon thee.' Jonson advises Shakespeare on the ancient languages (Shakespeare having of course 'small Latin and less Greek') and engages in a collation of the variant texts in preceding English translations, just as the KJV translators were required to do. Together they make the biblical passage into the wonderful poetry we find in the KJV. Shakespeare commits their joint work to the messenger, and Jonson asks: 'Who will know we had a part in it?' 'God maybe,' Shakespeare replies, 'if he ever lays ear to earth.'

Kipling's fantasy constructs a scenario for which there is no historical or literary evidence at all. And yet there is something compelling, intriguing, persuasive about what he has imagined. The idea of Shakespeare and Ben Jonson working together on a passage of Isaiah! Pooling their complementary talents, adding style to scholarship, making out of a linguist's literal translation a masterpiece of prophetic poetry. This is not what was, or even in all honesty what might have been. It is rather how it should have been, if things were different, and more like what they ought to be.

Some forty years later, Antony Burgess produced a new version of Kipling's story, though without acknowledging his source. Entitled 'Will and Testament', this story was published as a prelude to Burgess's comic novel *Enderby's Dark Lady*.[20] In this version, it is Jonson, not Shakespeare, who has been commissioned to take some of the work of translating the KJV. Burgess twists the story in other ways too. Where Kipling set his fantasy in the garden of New Place, Burgess has Shakespeare lodging in Silver Street, and the scene is an urban cesspit of a London full of criminals, prostitutes, spies, and conspirators. Ben Jonson appears to be involved in the Gunpowder Plot, but is actually a double agent spying on the plotters. Imprisoned in the Marshalsea, Jonson passes his information on to Shakespeare, who goes and tells it to Robert Cecil, who already knows about it anyway. Out of prison, Jonson explains to Shakespeare that he has been given portions of the Bible to translate, including some of the Psalms. Shakespeare is immensely annoyed that he has not been selected for this task, though in this tale it's a deliberate exclusion by James, because he had found Shakespeare impertinent. Jonson gives Shakespeare a few Psalms to work on himself, and Shakespeare returns to Stratford.

Stratford is nothing like the rural idyll of Kipling's story. New Place is overrun with Puritans, entertained by Shakespeare's wife Ann. The town has just discovered Shakespeare's *Sonnets*, which confirm them in their view of him as a dissolute libertine. His daughter mopes around, unmarried. His other daughter Susanna's husband, Dr John Hall, informs him that the town has decreed plays ungodly, and incidentally that Shakespeare displays clear symptoms of syphilis. So, surrounded by enmity and dislike in Stratford, his family against him, the local people convinced he is a dissolute bohemian, and facing terminal syphilis, as an act of defiance Shakespeare puts his name into Psalm 46, and reads it aloud in church the following Sunday. Where Kipling's Shakespeare is self-effacing and content with anonymity, Burgess's Shakespeare is embattled and self-assertive. Back in London, Ben and Will meet again, and Shakespeare tells Jonson about his version of Psalm 46. He's worried about repercussions. Apparently, Ben tells him, one of the translators has said he liked the reading and saw no particular ulterior meaning in it. 'He had never, you see, said Ben sweetly, heard of the name Shakespeare' (p. 34).

He had never heard of the name Shakespeare. Right at the end of the story, then, Burgess wakes us up from the dream-world of his fantasy and reminds us of the sober truth that, as far as the evidence of history is concerned, there seems to have been an impenetrable Berlin Wall separating the 'Complete Works of Shakespeare' from the King James Bible. When we link them together, we do so for our own purposes. We join these books together for our own ideological reasons, not because they really have anything much to do with one another.

VI

And so the King James Bible and the 'Complete Works of Shakespeare' confront one another as counterparts and opposites, just as the old Globe Theatre confronted St Paul's Cathedral across the River Thames. In Shakespeare's day the church was a foundation of the state, and the theatre was very much on the outskirts of society, outside the city limits, part of the red light district where you would have been unlikely to find any of the KJV translators, except perhaps in disguise. For many people this face-off between pulpit and playhouse eventually consolidated into a clear opposition, in which the church gradually dwindled into insignificance, while the theatre became an incubator of secular modernity. In a secular age, the theatre can be seen as taking a leading role in areas formerly handled by the church, such as moral education, the building of community, understanding the human world, confronting its harshness, scouring it for hope. The works of Shakespeare continue to be read and performed and adapted, while membership of the church diminishes at least in the European west and the words of the Bible fall on increasingly deaf ears.

But is it quite so simple? The reconstructed Globe and the 'new' St Paul's mirror one another across a river now easily crossed by the Millennium Bridge. Their reflections on the oily surface of the Thames reach out to one another, as if seeking some form of reunion. And certainly, in 2011, the anniversary year of the KJV, Shakespeare's Globe did more than its fair share to promote such contact. The theatre undertook a recitation of the whole King James Bible, 'making Jacobean words become flesh', and hosted a number of public lectures on biblical and ecclesiastical themes. The Sam Wanamaker Fellowship lecture was devoted to Shakespeare and the King James Bible. Throughout 2011, the Globe encouraged people to seek out parallels and similarities between the two books, to pursue areas of contingency and convergence, rather than consigning the church and the Bible to history and regarding the theatre as a modern supercessor of the ecclesiastical role. Taking advantage of the partly accidental collision of Shakespeare and the KJV, the Globe facilitated a reversal of that dichotomy that appeared at the Reformation between church and theatre, and fostered a recognition of them again as co-equals, partners in a common enterprise; sharing a mutual dedication to the common good; striving, like Kipling's Shakespeare, for 'the betterment of the present age – and the age to come'.

VII

The short play that follows develops and extends the legend of Shakespeare and Psalm 46 that was exploited in fiction by Rudyard Kipling and Anthony Burgess. The play restates the basic idea that Shakespeare's hand somehow found its way into the KJV, then extrapolates this incident to devise a comic fantasy in which Shakespeare has to account for himself at the Gates of Heaven. In his interview with St Peter, Shakespeare carries the two books with him. The play concludes by suggesting some of the deeper parallels that can, in the light of this fortuitous collision of 2011, be discovered between Shakespeare's work and the English Bible. The play was performed at Shakespeare's Globe by Globe actors James Wallace, Kevin Quarmby, Rachel Winters, and Frances Marshall in June 2011; and again at the Shakespeare Birthplace Trust, Stratford, in July 2011, by RSC Associate Penny Downie, John Heffernan, and Sam Lesser.

CHAPTER 4

'Wholly Writ'
A Play in Two Acts

Act 1
New Place, Stratford. Summer 1611

Cast
Anne Shakespeare
Ben Jonson
William Shakespeare
Judith Shakespeare

Act 2
The Gates of Heaven. 1623

Cast
St Peter
William Shakespeare
Kiera and Katya (Recording Angels)
*With thanks to Rudyard Kipling, Anthony
Burgess, and Jorge Luis Borges*

ACT I

ANNE: (*shouts from off*) William! William!

> *Enter William, crosses stage, Exit.*
> *Enter Anne and Judith with Ben.*

ANNE: (*shouts*) William! Mr Jonson's here to see you! Judith go find him.

> *Exit Judith.*

So nice to see you again. How long's it been?

BEN: Like a winter, Mistress Anne.
ANNE: You men and your poetry. Killed anybody lately, have we, Mr J?
BEN: None of name, dear lady, none of name.

Enter William.

ANNE: Well that's nice. We don't hold with the brawling here in Stratford. (*to WILLIAM*) Oh, you're there.

WILLIAM: Do you know how he got off?

BEN: Pleaded benefit of clergy.

WILLIAM: Had to recite one verse of Scripture.

ANNE: Never! What if he'd recited two?

BEN: They'd have known I was over-qualified for the church.

ANNE: And three?

WILLIAM: They'd have made him a bishop. Peace now, woman, leave us. Where's your idle daughter?

ANNE: Looking for a husband.

WILLIAM: Send her to the tavern. Thence she may bring home both drink and man.

Exit Anne.

I'm hoping she'll marry Quiney the vintner.

BEN: You'd trade your daughter for a lifetime's supply of diluted sack? You are like to have *portly* grandchildren.

WILLIAM: Very funny.

William and Ben sit.

BEN: It's good to see you, Will.

WILLIAM: What brings you to the country?

BEN: Oh, you know: green pastures. Still waters.

Enter Anne with food and drink, and Exit.

Ah. Stay me with flagons, and comfort me with apples.

WILLIAM: What makes you so scriptural all of a sudden?

BEN: What d'ye mean? Can't a man employ the holy word in the course of ordinary conversation? Is it to be nothing but blasphemy and cursing?

WILLIAM: What's the news at court?

BEN: His Majesty ...

Enter Judith.

JUDITH: Young lady at the door to see you, Dad.

WILLIAM: What's she look like?

JUDITH: Dark.

WILLIAM: Tell her I'm not at home.

Exit Judith.

You were saying?

BEN: You know His Majesty hath commanded a new translation of the Bible? Which the church shall be bound to, out of all the translations that men use?

WILLIAM: Huh. Fifty priests wrangling over the correct Hebrew word for foreskin. They'll never improve on what we have.

BEN: Unless they drafted in . . . a real writer?

WILLIAM: Not . . .

BEN: The same. (*takes out papers*) The Word of the Lord has come unto Benjamin.

Enter Judith.

JUDITH: Young man at the door to see you, Dad.

WILLIAM: What's he look like?

JUDITH: A woman's face.

WILLIAM: By Nature's own hand painted?

JUDITH: I didn't look that closely.

WILLIAM: Tell him I'm dead.

Exit Judith.

They've asked *you* to help translate the Bible?

BEN: Why not? I know more Greek and Latin than the priests. I have more Hebrew than your average Rabbi. And I possess the gift of poetry.

WILLIAM: But you're a theatre poet. What happened to 'The Overthrowing of Stage Plays'? What about the 'School of Abuse'? Since when was there peace between platform and pulpit?

BEN: Yesterday's quarrels, Will. His Majesty smiles on all of us alike: priest and poet, papist and puritan. 'Violence shall no more be heard in thy land, wasting nor destruction within thy borders; but thou shalt call thy walls Salvation, and thy gates Praise.'

WILLIAM: Isaiah. Wait a minute. That's not right. I remember: 'Salvation thy wall, and praise thy gates.'

BEN: Yes: you remember the Geneva Bible. The meaning was just the same, but with all the poetry taken out. I, Ben, have replaced it. 'The sun shall be no more thy light by day; neither for brightness shall the moon give light unto thee: but the LORD shall be unto thee an everlasting light, and thy God thy glory.'

WILLIAM: It used to be: 'Thou shalt have no more sun.' Your version *is* better. Don't tell me that's your work?

BEN: 'Thy sun shall no more go down; neither shall thy moon withdraw itself: for the LORD shall be thine everlasting light, and the days of thy mourning shall be ended.'

WILLIAM: That's 'mourning' instead of 'sorrow'. Good God. It's better. I don't believe it.

Enter Judith.

JUDITH: Rival poet at the door to see you, Dad.

WILLIAM: There *is* no rival poet! I just made him up!

JUDITH: What d'ye want me to tell him then?

WILLIAM: Tell him to go and get a real job.

Exit Judith.

BEN: It's true, Will. You have no rival. In your own field, of plagiarising old stories and making them even more unbelievable, there is none can touch you.

WILLIAM: So you were chosen for this divinely appointed task on merit, were you?

BEN: Now, now, no rancour. You know I admire your work, this side idolatry.

WILLIAM: But nobody else does. They never called on me.

BEN: Come now: you've never laid any claim to divine learning. Small Latin. Less Greek. Remember? You've never shown yourself that way inclined. Why do you care?

WILLIAM: I don't. Bastard bishops.

BEN: No, really, why *do* you care? Do you lack advancement? Fame? Money? The respect of your peers?

WILLIAM: None of these. But what I have written, I have written for the betterment of the present age. Aye, and that of the next. But if this Bible is to carry a greater share of that – hope – to the future; why then, I need never have set pen to page.

BEN: This Bible will be a great work, no doubt. It will transmit the holy word with a new rhythm, a new sonority, a new beauty. But what we do is merely to burnish the lamp. That light that has shone so brightly these fifteen hundred years will go on shining, bright as ever. All we are doing is to take sound doctrine, and true story, and set them to a new music. Just as you have done, in your work for the stage.

WILLIAM: I'm like my Autolycus then, in that? 'A snapper-up of unconsidered trifles'?

BEN: Look. I pull no punches in lashing your work with the crop of my wit. We dance to different tunes, you and I. My work adheres to probability. I set no landward principalities on sea-beaches. I devise my own plots. I build them on my own foundations. I adorn them justly, as befits time, place, and action.

WILLIAM: Spoken like a bricklayer's apprentice.

BEN: To the son of a butcher. You rip the skin off a dead carcass and use it
to clothe an emperor. You filch, botch, and clap your plays together
out of ballads, broadsheets, old wives' tales, chapbooks. You're written
forty plays, and all but six of them have plots as common as
Moorditch. You steal everything for your writing. I've know more
discerning magpies.

WILLIAM: Go on, say what you really think.

BEN: And yet you have the right alchemist's touch: whatever you handle,
you turn to gold. You redeem your vices with your virtues. There is
ever more in you to be praised, than to be pardoned. I confess, to all
those who have ears to hear, that your writing is such, as neither man,
nor Muse, can praise too much. You know some of this is really good.
I'll have to note it down and save it for your obituary.

WILLIAM: You won't have to wait long.

BEN: Why man, what's wrong? Are you ill?

WILLIAM: No, Ben, no. Not ill. Just tired. Finished. Emptied out.

BEN: Now look. I'll have none of this. Get hold of yourself. Why, you
must know that your reputation is unrivalled. You are the soul of our
age. The applause, delight, and wonder of the stage. Your work is –
not for an age, but for all time. If I'd known you'd be discouraged by
this Bible business, I'd never have brought it up.

WILLIAM: Not discouraged. Only fearful. That in the days to come, the
voice of the priest may drown out the song of the poet.

BEN: Until priests learn to speak with the tongue of the poet, no one will
heed them. The words may lodge in the ear, but will never penetrate
the heart.

WILLIAM: But you, a poet, are here lending your music to the language of
the priests. Why not let your verses speak for you, and have done?

BEN: It's the Word of God, Will, not the language of men. God has given
me the gift of words, and I am paying Him back, that's all. Mere
charity. You may speak with the tongues of men, and of angels. But if
you have not charity, you are nothing. And now I must go and relieve
myself, or I will be as him that pisseth against the wall.

WILLIAM: Third on the left.

Exit Ben, leaving his papers on the table.

I'll give him charity. What else has he got here? The Psalms. Let's see. I'll
show them. Psalm forty-six: my age this birthday. One, two three . . . forty-
six words from the top. 'Tremble'. Perfect! Let's just cross that out and
make it 'shake'. Now. Forty-six words from the end. 'Sword'. Change it to
'spear'. It's done. Among the psalms of David, a psalm of – Shakespeare. By
the time they notice, it'll be too late.

Enter Ben.

BEN: I must be off now, Will. There's a meeting of the committee at Westminster tomorrow. They'll be wanting my Isaiah.

WILLIAM: God go with you, Ben. And I'm truly glad you have a part in the great work.

BEN: Not that anyone will know.

WILLIAM: God will know. Let's hope he's listening.

BEN: No hard feelings now?

WILLIAM: Of course not. Let's meet up in town. I have to be there next week.

BEN: At the Mermaid?

WILLIAM: At the Mermaid. Until then.

Exit Ben.

William stares after him. Then Blackout.

ACT 2

St Peter sits at the table, centre. Chair to his left. Large folio volume open before him. He reads.
Enter William, ushered in by Katya. He carries two folio volumes, one under each arm (First Folio and KJV).

ST PETER: Next!

KATYA: So nice to talk to you. Look me up on the way out – don't forget – Katya. If you do come back this way, that is.

WILLIAM: If I come back ... that way? ... Oh Lord. St Peter?

ST PETER: Who else? Name?

WILLIAM: William Shakespeare.

ST PETER: Not another one! Your *real* name?

WILLIAM: No, I really am William Shakespeare. See ... my book. See ... my picture.

ST PETER: Doesn't look a bit like you. Stage plays ... hmm. Is it 1623 already? Time flies. Hang on ... didn't you die seven years ago?

WILLIAM: Sorry. I had to wait for the book to come out.

ST PETER: Where've you been?

WILLIAM: Oh, backstage. Putting in the occasional appearance ...

ST PETER: As a ghost?

WILLIAM: I knew the lines.

ST PETER: Sounds like typecasting to me. What's the other one?

WILLIAM: This, your ... grace, is the King James Bible. To which I was a contributor. In a small way.

ST PETER: Were you just? Well you can put them down. This is the only book we're going to need for this interview. The Book of Life.

WILLIAM: My life?

ST PETER: Yes. William Shakespeare, this *is* your life.

WILLIAM: Oh dear.

ST PETER: Sit down. Now let's see. Baptized Stratford 1564. That's good. Butchering, school, gloves ... ah. What's this? 1582: fornicated with one Anne Hathaway in a field near Shottery. True?

WILLIAM: Indeed, your grace. We were betrothed.

ST PETER: We must tighten up those rules on pre-contract. But you stayed with the wench?

WILLIAM: Till death did us part.

ST PETER: Well then. You poached deer in the park of Sir Thomas Lucy.

WILLIAM: He called it his park.

ST PETER: That's just geography. Wherever it was, you coveted your neighbour's goods. What's this? There's a gap in this record. Something missing ... some ...

WILLIAM: ... Lost Years?

ST PETER: Exactly. What is all this? 'A schoolmaster in the country'? 'A musician in the household of Alexander Hoghton'? 'Holding horses at the playhouse door'? (*shouts*) Kiera!

Enter Kiera.

ST PETER: This file's incomplete! Look at this! Nothing but question marks!

KIERA: Let's have a look. 'Shakespeare, William'. Oh yes. All we could get were vague reports. No corroboration. Nothing conclusive. Sort of ... lost years, really.

ST PETER: Highly irregular. Stop here in case there are any more of them. (*to WILLIAM*) Do *you* know what you were doing all that time?

WILLIAM: (*pauses to look at the audience*) I haven't a clue.

ST PETER: Lucky for you, neither does anybody else. Now let's see ... oh, here we are. 1592. London's theatre-land. You consorted with prostitutes.

WILLIAM: Everybody did!

KIERA: (*to WILLIAM*) Doesn't really make it any better.

WILLIAM: I was drunk.

KIERA: (*to WILLIAM*) Actually makes it that little bit worse.

WILLIAM: I was a simple country boy, and they were practised London whores.

KIERA: Blame the woman, why don't you.

ST PETER: Will you get out!

Exit Kiera.

ST PETER: Now. You committed adulterous fornication with a Dark Lady.

WILLIAM: I did. But she betrayed me and went off with my best friend.

ST PETER: And he was ... oh good God I can't look at this.

WILLIAM: But I was an innocent country lad, and he was a peer of the realm.

ST PETER: I was a simple fisherman, but I never attempted anything like *that*. (*shouts*) Katya!

Enter Katya.

Have you got the file on the Earl of Southampton?

KATYA: No need to consult it, sire. We pass it round the office every day for a laugh. Off by heart.

ST PETER: How stands his audit?

KATYA: Completely full I'm afraid.

ST PETER: (*to WILLIAM*) Sorry. It appears this guilt is not transferable.

Exit Katya.

WILLIAM: Worth a try.

ST PETER: You perjured yourself on oath in court.

WILLIAM: When?

ST PETER: 1612. *Mountjoy* v. *Bellott*. Your landlord and his apprentice. Some dispute about a settlement?

WILLIAM: Oh that.

ST PETER: You said you couldn't remember the amount of the dowry.

WILLIAM: It wasn't so much that, your grace, as that I never understood a word Mountjoy was saying anyway. (*French accent*) 'Monsieur Chequespierre, weel you s'il vous plaît marche down da Palais de Justice an' defender moi against zis naughty garçon?' I just used to ag-rrree to, 'ow you say, everysing (*end of French accent*). It seemed easier.

ST PETER: You stole land from the poor people of Stratford.

WILLIAM: I think that's an exaggeration! They weren't *that* poor. Who told you that ... (*notices ST PETER'S expression*) But now you come to mention it ... indeed, I am most heartily sorry, repent of all my sins, and will pray for the welfare of the poor of Stratford.

ST PETER: That's better. Now we're getting somewhere. But at the final count, you've scored a total of five commandments broken.

WILLIAM: Which ones?

ST PETER: The commandments against adultery, theft, bearing false witness, coveting your neighbour's wife, and coveting his goods.

WILLIAM: Can't the last two count as one?

ST PETER: Not in the Roman Catholic Church. My house, my rules. But five out of ten? Divers weights are an abomination unto the Lord; and a false balance is not good. We really need another one as decider. Worshipped any false gods? Killed anybody? Graven images? No? There must be something else in here.

WILLIAM: Begging your grace's pardon, I have a suggestion.

ST PETER: Yes?

WILLIAM: Couldn't you perhaps take into account the fact that I was one
of the – well, translators – of the King James Bible?

ST PETER: That could make a difference.

WILLIAM: See here, Psalm forty-six. I was forty-six years old at the time.
Count forty-six words from the beginning. See? 'Shake'. Then count
forty-six words from the end. That's it: 'spear'. I put that in. 'Shake-
spear'. That's my work.

ST PETER: So your contribution to the King James translation of the Bible
was – to put your name into it?

WILLIAM: I understand it's a good translation. Master Tillotson told me
that the sense was thereby improved.

ST PETER: Do you know why someone would write his name into
someone else's book?

WILLIAM: Vicarious immortality?

ST PETER: No. Ontological insecurity. It's because he doesn't know who
he is. Look, William, this is not all about wrongdoing and
punishment, sin and repentance. It's also about self-knowledge. Have
you ever felt the need to *be* someone? To feel comfortable in your own
skin? To know yourself? Just – to be? Not – *not* to be?

During the next speech the two Angels enter and stand behind St Peter.

WILLIAM: That *is* the question. Truthfully, I've never really felt that I was
anyone. Inside I've always felt a kind of – hollowness. I wrote about so
many people because I wanted to know what it felt like to be a
character. I acted so many roles because I wanted to know what it felt
like to inhabit a personality. No one man was as many men as me. But
I never felt there was anyone inside me. As if I was a dream someone
had failed to dream. I was everyone, and no one. Do you understand
what I mean?

KIERA: We get it quite a bit.

KATYA: From artistic types.

ST PETER: I've heard them telling God about it.

WILLIAM: What does he say?

ST PETER: He's not all that sympathetic. 'So you found it hard trying to be
yourself while inhabiting innumerable other people? You feel as
though you are many, but no one? You poor love. Tell me about it.'
Still, he might be interested in your version. You never know.

WILLIAM: (*pause*) Does that mean I'm in?

ST PETER: In?

WILLIAM: You mentioned talking to God. Does that mean I can enter the
Celestial Court? Join the Choir Invisible?

ST PETER: Choir?

(the girls control their laughter)

WILLIAM: I don't have to go to … the other place?

ST PETER: Other place?

WILLIAM: *(it dawns on him)* There is no other place, is there?

ST PETER: Not as you imagine it.

WILLIAM: Oh Jesus. What was this all about, then?

ST PETER: Oh, procedure. Protocol. Red tape.

KATYA: And it was awfully funny.

KIERA: You should have seen your face!

WILLIAM: Kit Marlowe was right, then. 'Hell's a fable.'

ST PETER: Not exactly. It's more like an Italian church: 'closed for restoration'. Could always be opened up again.

WILLIAM: So everybody's in here, then? Even people who don't want to be there?

KATYA: They have their own area.

KIERA: 'Atheist's Corner'. You know: 'Many mansions'.

WILLIAM: And people of other faiths?

ST PETER: A bit embarrassed, but mainly relieved.

WILLIAM: What about those who sold their soul to the devil?

ST PETER: I think that's what you call a 'win-win situation'. He was never in a position to collect.

WILLIAM: No! But what happens to the truly wicked? Hardened sinners? Unrepentant malefactors? People who just won't see the error of their ways?

KIERA: We send them to the back of the queue.

WILLIAM: No.

St Peter and Angels nod.

So Purgatorial punishment is – queuing?

ST PETER: We find it works.

WILLIAM: I can't believe it.

KATYA: That's what we said.

KIERA: About your late plays.

ST PETER: What was that one called … *The Winter's Tale*?

St Peter and Angels laugh.

KATYA: 'The sea-coast of Bohemia.'

KIERA: 'Exit pursued by a bear.'

ST PETER: How did it go again? A jealous king, a virtuous wife suspected, a son dead from grief, a daughter left to die on a distant shore, a man torn to pieces by a bear. An improbable fiction!

KATYA: All brought together at the end.

KIERA: Reconciliation and forgiveness springing between them.

ST PETER: A lost daughter returned.

KATYA: A wife back from the dead.

KIERA: A statue that moves and speaks.

ST PETER: Ring any bells? 'Like an old tale still, which will have matter to rehearse, though credit be asleep, and not an ear open.'

WILLIAM: You know my work?

ST PETER: There will come a time, William, when everyone will know your work. No one ever said the Scriptures had the monopoly of wisdom. 'Whatsoever things were written aforetime were written for our learning, that we through patience and comfort of the scriptures might have hope.' Likewise everything written afterwards. The Lord's word also speaks through the mouths of men. (*to ANGELS*) Give me those lines from Deuteronomy again.

KATYA: 'My doctrine shall drop as the rain ...

KIERA: ... and my speech shall still as the dew ...

KATYA: ... as the shower upon the herbs ...

KIERA: ... and as the great rain upon the grass.'

ST PETER: Beautiful, isn't it? Hard to believe it could be improved on. And yet you did it. In your *Merchant*.

KATYA: 'The quality of mercy is not strained ...

KIERA: ... It droppeth as the gentle rain from heaven ...

KATYA: ... Upon the place beneath.'

ST PETER: Which one is easier to remember? Which one do you think will become part of everyday language? Which one will schoolchildren learn by heart in class? Ours, or yours? We're on the same team, you see. And that, William, is what it's all about.

WILLIAM: Mercy? Forgiveness? Reconciliation? I think I see.

ST PETER: Yes, mercy. It blesseth him that gives, you see; and him that takes.

WILLIAM: Twice blest.

ST PETER: As are you. With a good life, and a good death.

WILLIAM: I suppose so. Not at all amused, though, by your little audition.

ST PETER: But you got the part! No need to take it personally. Most people are more relieved than disposed to complain.

WILLIAM: Understood. I won't say a word when I talk to ... the Man. Well, I'd better be off, then.

ST PETER: You can take the Bible. But don't say too much about being a translator. Some of them are already in there.

WILLIAM: Can I take the other one too?

ST PETER: No. It's the Kingdom of Heaven, not a desert island.

KATYA: Fare thee well, Master Shakespeare.

KIERA: Enjoy the rest of your day.

WILLIAM: Bye.

Exit William.

St Peter picks up the First Folio. Opens it.

KIERA: Do you want the next one in, sire?
ST PETER: Hold the queue for a while, will you.
KATYA: How long?

St Peter checks the length of the book.

Let's say five years.

Exit the Recording Angels.
St Peter starts reading the First Folio.
Long pause, then Blackout.

PART III

CHAPTER 5

The Coriolanus *myth*

I

Coriolanus seems to me very much a play for today, if anything more contemporary than it ever has been since the early seventeenth century. This chapter, and its accompanying story, are about Coriolanus as a folk-hero for the third millennium, and as the source of a generic cultural formation I will call 'the Coriolanus myth'. The history of how this rapprochement came about is, however, nothing like a natural process of evolution, or a symptom of Shakespeare's permanent universality. It arises rather from a long series of collisions between Shakespeare's play and the various political ideologies that have appropriated it in very different ways. The specific collision between *Coriolanus* and our own time can best be described by linking the play, and its contemporary film version, to other cultural products that are entirely other than Shakespeare. In short, once again, in order to locate Shakespeare, we have to examine the apparently accidental entanglements of Shakespeare with 'not-Shakespeare'.

Coriolanus is recognised as one of Shakespeare's 'Roman' plays, but is generally considered more difficult and intractable than either of its fellows, *Antony and Cleopatra* and *Julius Caesar*. Extraordinarily, Ralph Fiennes's film version *Coriolanus* (2011) is that play's first cinematic adaptation.[1] The play may be a Roman play, but this is not a Roman film. The film chooses for its scene-setting epigraph the descriptive phrase employed by John Osborne when he adapted Shakespeare's play in 1973,[2] 'a place calling itself Rome', and is set in the war-devastated landscape of the Balkans (much of the shooting was done in Belgrade, Serbia).[3] The play is transplanted, in other words, much as a Shakespeare play can be transplanted into a foreign culture, language, and tradition, to grow and bear fruit from a process of hybridisation. 'The way to test a great work of art,' claims Slavoj Žižek, 'is to ask how it survives decontextualisation, transposition into a new context.'[4] The language of the play speaks continually of 'Rome', but the film operates by extracting various meanings from that master-concept – militarism, physical violence, family and class, loyalty and betrayal – and applying them in a different and easily recognisable geopolitical context.

I will be arguing in the following pages that although *Coriolanus* the film struggles with some of the play's essential attributes and preoccupations, since the soil the adaptor has chosen for replanting is in some ways unsuitable for that particular variety, it nonetheless manages to reproduce some of the play's most transferable meanings. The play dwells obsessively on certain arenas of experience that are not difficult to translate out of their original Roman dialect and idiom. It focuses powerfully on a kind of intense homoerotic bonding between men that is achieved through violent physical combat; on a synchronisation of family honour with military success; and on an uneasy rapprochement between military conquest and political popularity. All of these fit naturally into Shakespeare's context of the early Roman republic, and are easy to dramatise on stage. Fiennes's attempt to relocate these themes into the former Yugoslavia, in the medium of realistic 'documentary' and news-mediated film, comes up against certain forces of resistance embedded in the play itself, but in my view succeeds in reproducing a *Coriolanus* for today.

I then take this argument further by suggesting that in order to deepen our sense of what Shakespeare's *Coriolanus* has to offer us, we need to take the hero out of the play altogether, and to dramatise his character and actions in a context that sits more agreeably with Shakespeare's Rome. In other words, I am searching contemporary culture not just for signs of Shakespeare's *Coriolanus*, but also for examples of the Coriolanus figure, reproduced as a kind of contemporary folk-hero and cultural mythos. I find this figure active in a number of different genres, notably in narratives that deal with post-9/11 warfare, and in the popular conventions of the spy thriller. I will argue this case by showing that two other current films, Kathryn Bigelow's *The Hurt Locker* and Sam Mendes's James Bond thriller *Skyfall* (both of which are connected with Fiennes's *Coriolanus*) actually produce the Coriolanus-figure as a typical contemporary culture-hero. These genres allow Shakespeare's character and themes to flourish in startling and unexpected ways. In these film dramas, Shakespeare's Coriolanus finds himself in new forms: in the breathtaking riskiness of bomb disposal, or in the brutal physical violence of unarmed combat. Shakespeare's Rome discovers new adoptive *loci* in the booby-trapped streets of Baghdad, or in the twisted allegiances of modern espionage.

II

We begin with the play. Shakespeare's play begins with a popular insurrection against the power and authority of the Roman patricians and their Senate, prompted by food shortages. The people are desperate, starving, prepared to die for their cause. They are armed '*with staves, clubs, and other weapons*'; they are resolved 'rather to die than to famish'; and the focus of their class resistance is one particular member of the patrician order, Caius Martius, described as 'chief enemy to the people'. Shakespeare depicts the Roman populace as an organised body, capable of real violence, armed and dangerous, ready to kill or be killed, and irrationally focused on one hated individual, rather than on the economic and political structures they are challenging. They are a mob.

At the same time, Shakespeare gives the plebeians a reasonable voice and a defensible viewpoint, in the speech of the First Citizen:

What authority surfeits on would relieve us. If they would yield us but the superfluity while it were wholesome, we might guess they relieved us humanely. But they think we are too dear. The leanness that afflicts us, the object of our misery, is as an inventory to particularise their abundance; our sufferance is a gain to them. (1.1.14–20)[5]

Like some of the great humanitarian speeches in *King Lear*, the First Citizen's protest accurately diagnoses the root of the social problem, in inequality and the disproportionate division of resources between rich and poor in Republican Rome. The patricians could easily feed the people with the 'superfluity' of their excessive wealth. But the poverty of the people is what defines the privileged position of the rich: without that benchmark of deprivation they would have no sense of their own contrasting 'abundance'. They need to keep the people poor so they can feel all the richer.

 Coriolanus himself is thus first introduced as the object of popular disaffection.

> 2 CITIZEN:
> Would you proceed especially against Caius Martius?
> ALL:
> Against him first. He's a very dog to the commonalty.
>
>   1.1.24–6

This collective hatred is then mollified by an appeal to Martius's public service, his patriotic contribution to the defence of Rome against her enemies. The initial suggestion here is that military honours achieved in warfare should compensate for, transcend, and neutralise an otherwise unacceptable class-contempt for the people.

> 2 CITIZEN:
> Consider you what services he has done for his country?
>
>   1.1.27

The First Citizen responds however by pointing out that military service and defence of the Republic is precisely the patrician's job, which should not therefore be remunerated twice over, in both wealth and adulation.

> 1 CITIZEN:
> . . . he pays himself with being proud.
>
>   1.1.30

The same speaker goes on to make the connections between military service, public duty, personal pride, and family honour that could be described as the very texture of the play's ethical environment.

> 1 CITIZEN:
> I say unto you, what he hath done famously, he did it to that end.
> Though soft-conscienced men can be content to say it was for his
> country, he did it to please his mother and to be partly proud – which
> he is, even to the altitude of his virtue.
>
>   1.33–7

 Martius may have distinguished himself by defending the city; but such distinction scarcely deserves admiration if its motivation was, in fact, not civic duty and public loyalty, but individual arrogance and family pride. In other words, Martius's service to the Republic is exactly what sets him against the Republic. His allegiance is to himself, his loyalty to his family; pride and honour place him at an 'altitude' far above his fellow citizens. It is not merely that Martius courts unpopularity; it is rather that the very 'nature' of his public identity creates a contradictory relationship with his society. He serves Rome, but looks down on its common population; he fights her battles, but hates her people. He loves Rome, but hates Romans.

The voice of the Senate is then articulated in the placatory speeches of Menenius, who tries, through rhetoric and persuasion, to reconcile the manifest contradictions fissuring the Roman state. The patricians, he insists, observe a 'charitable care' of the people. And yet, he admits, the state will crush any popular insurrection that threatens its power. The Senate, he pleads, is doing what it can to alleviate popular distress. And yet, he acknowledges, the Senate absolves itself of any responsibility for the crisis, and recommends an appeal to the gods:

MENENIUS:
I tell you, friends, most charitable care
Have the patricians of you. For your wants,
Your suffering in this dearth, you may as well
Strike at the heaven with your staves, as lift them
Against the Roman state, whose course will on
The way it takes, cracking ten thousand curbs,
Of more strong link asunder than can ever
Appear in your impediment. For the dearth,
The gods, not the patricians, make it, and
Your knees to them, not arms, must help.

1.1.60–9

Menenius's defence of the status quo is however confronted by the First Citizen's furious and dissident protest, which exposes the true hypocrisy of the patrician's moderate and liberal ideology. The rich and powerful claim concern for the people, yet deny them access to the food they themselves are hoarding; increasingly they seek to extend patrician power, while restricting popular liberties.

I CITIZEN:
Care for us! True, indeed! They ne'er cared for us yet. Suffer us to famish, and their store-houses crammed with grain . . . repeal daily any

wholesome act established against the rich, and provide more piercing
statutes daily to chain up and restrain the poor.

I.I.74–9

Menenius's 'fable of the belly' gives metaphorical shape to his
clearly contradictory defence of Roman society as a perfectly harmoni-
ous totality in which each member of the commonwealth has a
different but complementary role to play. Meeting an obdurate radical
resistance to his avuncular parable, his liberal apologetics collapse
immediately into the beleaguered accent of a threatened conservatism:

MENENIUS:
Rome and her rats are at the point of battle;
The one side must have bale.

I.I.157–8

The people are after all nothing more than 'rats' to Rome, vermin
who threaten the resources and health of the body politic. They are
like rats in their intention to raid the city's granaries for food; and
like the rats of sixteenth-century London, they potentially carry
infection and plague into the otherwise healthy heart of the Republic. In the mind of the patrician this insurrection is not an equal
contest, like a noble warrior facing an honourable opponent, but
more like a farmer confronting the rats who would destroy his crops
and devour his sustenance. The people of Rome are Rome's own
internal enemies: subhuman, bestial, they are the very embodiment
of the alien.

And this is exactly the right moment for us to meet with Caius
Martius.

MARTIUS:
What's the matter, you dissentious rogues,
That, rubbing the poor itch of your opinion,
Make yourselves scabs?

I.I.159–61

In stark and direct contrast to Menenius's defensive and propitiatory
rhetoric, Martius immediately abuses the people as mutinous, ignorant, and (at least metaphorically) diseased.

Martius's attack on the people is predicated on a fundamental
distinction between him and them: he is a warrior; they are not. War
is the natural nursery of virtue, and those who will not fight can lay

no claim to honour. As such they cannot be trusted with civic responsibility. In war they prove cowards; in peace, comforted by the absence of military threat, they become complacent and sufficiently arrogant to convince themselves they could shoulder political responsibility. As such they are untrustworthy, and cannot be relied upon by the state's rulers. Rome needs predators, lions and foxes, and the people are merely prey, geese and hares. The heat of their anger melts the solid foundation on which it rests, as a burning coal reduces ice to liquidity.

MARTIUS:
What would you have, you curs,
That like nor peace nor war? The one affrights you,
The other makes you proud. He that trusts to you,
Where he should find you lions finds you hares;
Where foxes, geese you are – no surer, no,
Than is the coal of fire upon the ice,
Or hailstone in the sun.

                                                                    I.I.163–9

Both sides in this dispute trade the same insult, each accusing the other of 'pride'. To the people, Martius displays the patrician arrogance of a natural ruling class. To Martius, the people are able to indulge in a pride of aspiration generated by the lack of military threat. If they were obliged to defend their country, then they would realise the true price of freedom. As it is they are spoiled, cosseted, enjoying freedom without the responsibility of preserving it. Martius invokes the aristocratic principle, insisting on the innate superiority of the military patrician class over the popular majority. The natural political order is one in which the mob obediently accepts the rule of the minority. Left to themselves, they would create only anarchy, feeding not on the state's superfluous stocks of food, but on one another.

MARTIUS:
What's the matter,
That in these several places of the city
You cry against the noble senate, who,
Under the gods, keep you in awe, which else
Would feed on one another?

                                                                    I.I.179–83

Martius's preferred solution to this stand-off would be force. As the natural ruler, the Roman warrior should defend his country against all enemies, foreign and domestic. If the people rise against the state, the state should treat them in exactly the same way as it treats its foreign enemies, casting aside all pity and compassion, and subjecting the mob to the uninhibited violence of state power:

> MARTIUS:
> Would the nobility lay aside their ruth
> And let me use my sword, I'll make a quarry
> With thousands of these quarter'd slaves as high
> As I could pitch my lance.

I.I.192–5

The common people naturally retreat from this direct threat, showing no instinct for physical combat: they slink away, disappear, evaporate. In Martius's words they are 'dissolved', just as the ice in his metaphor turns to liquid at the touch of fire. But then immediately what seems to Martius to be a decisive victory, with the 'cowardly' enemy in flight and the victor left in command of the field, is fatally compromised by news of a political concession. Martius hears that the Senate has granted the people a tribunate. Elected representatives of the people are invited to membership of the Senate. The grievances of the people have been heard; the protests of the people addressed; the demands of the people met by political incorporation. The crisis has been resolved by democracy, not by military force. Naturally Martius sees this development as an incipient destruction of the commonwealth. He would rather see the city destroyed than its dissident people gratified. And he foresees, correctly in the event, that this encroachment of popular power upon patrician privilege is the thin end of a dangerous wedge. The granting of a measure of popular power will increase the people's appetite for more, and in time, rather than palliating the mob, will foster further insurrection.

> MARTIUS:
>   'Sdeath,
> The rabble should have first unroofed the city
> Ere so prevailed with me! It will in time
> Win upon power and throw forth greater themes
> For insurrection's arguing.

I.I.212–16

Almost as soon as Martius's pyrrhic victory over the people has been eclipsed by the news of the Senate's democratic concessions, further news arrives that offers him the opportunity of another victory over an inveterate enemy, the Volscians, who are in arms and threatening Rome. Martius sees this emergency as a much more promising way of solving the state's political problems:

> MESSENGER:
> The news is, sir, the Volsces are in arms.
> MARTIUS:
> I am glad on 't: then we shall ha' means to vent
> Our musty superfluity.
>
> I.I.219–21

The same word was used earlier by the Citizens in a very different sense. To them the obvious 'superfluity' of the Republic is the excess of wealth and power held by the patricians. To Martius there is a 'superfluity' of unnecessary and wasteful energy, the heated discontent of the plebeians, the hot air of Senate debates, the bad smell of political compromise. All this produces a kind of gas that needs to be 'vented' if the state is to recover its health. War is the rigorous physical discipline that will force an evacuation of noxious and toxic elements.

In his discussion with Rome's senior politicians, we find Martius restored to his true element. To talk of war, of military prowess, of courage on the field, of undying honour in battle, these are the themes that come naturally to him. And again we immediately realise that this soldier of Rome has a peculiarly perverse view of allegiances in combat. For while he despises his own Roman people, he has nothing but admiration for the leader of the enemy forces, Tullus Aufidius.

> MARTIUS:
>   They have a leader,
> Tullus Aufidius, that will put you to 't.
> I sin in envying his nobility,
> And were I any thing but what I am,
> I would wish me only he.
>
> I.I.223–7

'I sin in envying his nobility'. This envy is 'sinful' because it sets Martius in opposition to his own political allegiance. The kinship of warriors on the battlefield is stronger than the political ties that bind members of the same commonwealth, and this cuts across the proper borders of loyalty and enmity. If Martius had to choose another identity, it would not be a Roman one. He would not wish to be another Roman patrician, still less a mere Roman citizen. He would wish only to be Rome's foremost enemy.

This sense of kinship is one that has been fostered on the battle-field, by direct physical engagement in combat, body to body, hand to hand.

> COMINIUS:
> > You have fought together!
> MARTIUS:
> Were half to half the world by th'ears and he
> Upon my party, I'd revolt to make
> Only my wars with him. He is a lion
> That I am proud to hunt.

> 1.1.227–31

In one sense, the hunter respects his prey, but yet has no hesitation in killing him when the opportunity presents itself. The hunter would with alacrity kill the lion he admires, and Martius would give no quarter to Aufidius on the battlefield: 'thou / Shalt see me once more strike at Tullus' face' (1.1.235–6). In another sense, Martius acknowledges that his sense of brotherhood with his enemy is a stronger bond than anything that ties him to his own country. The feeling is mutual, as we learn presently from Aufidius himself, who shares this sense of blood-brotherhood in mortal hatred:

> If we and Caius Martius chance to meet,
> 'Tis sworn between us we shall ever strike
> Till one can do no more.

> 1.2.34–6

Shakespeare's dramatic rendering of the engagement between the Romans and the attacking Volscians is cut down from Plutarch's very long and detailed narrative, but still occupies considerable space in the play. It shows us Martius in his natural element, involved in violent physical combat and effectively leading soldiers into battle. Like a true military commander, he puts himself at risk by fighting in the forefront of the battle. He hates to see cowardice, and would prefer to fight with his soldiers than see them retreat. He is the kind of officer who would shoot his own men in preference to permitting them to run away:

> You souls of geese
> That bear the shapes of men, how have you run
> From slaves that apes would beat! Pluto and hell!
> All hurt behind, backs red, and faces pale
> With flight and agued fear. Mend and charge home,
> Or by the fires of heaven, I'll leave the foe
> And make my wars on you.
>
> 1.4.35–41

There is no trace of military strategy in Martius's next foolhardy move. Finding the gates of Corioli open, he takes the opportunity of entering the defended city, expecting his men to follow. They refuse, displaying less courage but more sense than their commander:

> 1 SOLDIER:
> Fool-hardiness! not I.
> 2 SOLDIER:
>   Nor I.
>
>   *Martius is shut in.*   1.4.47–8

The Romans naturally assume that they have seen the last of their hero. Trapped alone in the beleaguered enemy city, he cannot possibly survive. The soldiers report the event as an instance of supremely heroic bravado:

> 1 SOLDIER:
> Following the fliers at the very heels,
> With them he enters, who, upon the sudden,
> Clapped to their gates. He is himself alone
> To answer all the city.
>
> 1.4.53–6

'He is himself alone'. Nobody ever won a war in this way. Martius's entry into Corioli is utterly contrary to any notion of military tactics. It represents a failure of leadership, since he has no tactical support; a failure of strategy, since he allows himself to be cut off and isolated; and a textbook example of the pursuit of vainglory by a man who has disaggregated himself from the very body politic he is purporting to defend. Martius takes upon himself the identity of Rome, and is its sole representative; he internalises the state within himself. But by placing himself in danger he also runs the risk of bringing Rome to ruin.

And yet there is another perspective on this incident, and on the way Shakespeare dramatises it. Martius has placed himself in the heroic position of the last man standing, the ultimate bulwark of defence against the enemy. It is precisely the position and the status he chooses: at that moment, all that is left of Rome is he himself, *contra mundum*. At the same time this pregnant descriptor implies the broader, more existentialist explanation that Martius is truly himself, perhaps only himself, when he is alone and surrounded by enemies. The heroic tradition favours such acts of reckless bravado, and always validates the hero who stands alone, especially the hero who is prepared to take on his enemy one to one, *mano a mano*, in single combat.

Assuming Martius is already dead, the Romans waste no time in constructing his obituary:

> LARTIUS:
>   Thou art left, Martius.
> A carbuncle entire, as big as thou art,
> Were not so rich a jewel. Thou wast a soldier
> Even to Cato's wish, not fierce and terrible
> Only in strokes, but, with thy grim looks and
> The thunder-like percussion of thy sounds
> Thou mad'st thine enemies shake, as if the world
> Were feverous and did tremble.
>
>   1.4.58–65

But like someone appearing to interrupt his own funeral, a bleeding Martius rushes on to the stage to reveal that reports of his death are greatly exaggerated.

> *Enter Martius, bleeding, assaulted by the enemy.*
>
>   1.4.64

Martius has survived his foolhardy attack, and is already seeking another fight, since he has not come face to face with his true enemy, Tullus Aufidius.

LARTIUS:
                    Worthy sir, thou bleed'st.
Thy exercise hath been too violent
For second course of fight.
MARTIUS:
                         Sir, praise me not;
My work hath yet not warmed me. Fare you well.
The blood I drop is rather physical
Than dangerous to me. To Aufidius thus I will
Appear and fight.

                                                    1.5.14–21

And so Martius rushes off to join the other Roman army commanded by Cominius, regretting only that he may have come too late. He greets Cominius with another speech confounding military with sexual emotions, drawing a parallel between the eager bridegroom on his wedding night, and the veteran soldier greeting his comrade-in-arms.

MARTIUS:
                         O, let me clip ye
In arms as sound as when I wooed, in heart
As merry as when our nuptial day was done
And tapers burned to bedward! [*They embrace*]

                                                    1.6.29–32

Fired by this perverse amalgamation of sex and violence, Martius once again reveals his capacity for leadership. Displaying to the troops the vivid traceries on his body of the dangers he himself has invited, inciting their sense of honour, invoking their common patriotism, he stirs their courage and fortitude to battle pitch.

MARTIUS:
                         Those are they
That most are willing. If any such be here,
(As it were sin to doubt) that love this painting
Wherein you see me smeared, if any fear
Lesser his person than an ill report,
If any think brave death outweighs bad life
And that his country's dearer than himself,
Let him alone, or so many so minded,
Wave thus to express his disposition,
And follow Martius.

                                                    1.6.66–75

The appeal works. The Roman soldiers become a unified fighting force, sharing a common enthusiasm, at one in their loyalty to their leader:

They all shout and wave their swords, take him up in their arms, and cast up their caps.

1.6.76

Martius is in his element:

> O, me alone! make you a sword of me?
> If these shows be not outward, which of you
> But is four Volsces? None of you but is
> Able to bear against the great Aufidius
> A shield as hard as his.

1.6.76–80

'O, me alone!' Another double entendre. 'Only me', no one else but me, exclusively me as the chosen leader. But also that telling emphasis on the essential solitude of the warrior, alone on the battlefield with his own rage and his own fear. Holding him above their heads, the Roman troops seem to turn him into the very embodiment of their fighting spirit: they brandish him aloft as if he were a sword, and point him towards the heart of the enemy. What we see on stage is a total synthesis of leader and men, a seamless unity of collective violence. But the sword is not of the same nature as its handler. For himself, Martius has reached the perfect resolution of his military aspiration, becoming a pure weapon, a thing of irreducible and irrefutable deadliness and anger.

And this is exactly how he enters the next stage of the combat, seeking not a generalised enemy of Rome, but his own implacable enemy, Aufidius.

> MARTIUS:
> I'll fight with none but thee; for I do hate thee
> Worse than a promise-breaker.
> AUFIDIUS:
>   We hate alike:
> Not Afric owns a serpent I abhor
> More than thy fame and envy.

1.8.1–5

Martius boasts to Aufidius about his recent foray into the city as a spectacular achievement:

MARTIUS:
>   Within these three hours, Tullus,
> Alone I fought in your Corioles' walls
> And made what work I pleased.

                                                1.8.8–10

'Alone'. The act of valour he wishes to share with Aufidius is not an instance of effective leadership, for example a successful assault in which other members of the Roman army could reasonably share in the honourable spoils of victory. No: it is rather that reckless act of courage that rendered him an isolated and irreducible fighting principle. And this is the position he hopes his enemy will fully understand.

The scene now shifts to the Volscian camp, and to the state of mind of that very same enemy, which proves, not surprisingly, to be similar to that of Martius himself. Aufidius would rather be a Roman than endure life as a defeated Volscian. Clearly the wish to be the enemy when circumstances dictate is very strong for both parties. Each would rather be the other than accept the common lot of his own society.

AUFIDIUS:
> Condition!
> I would I were a Roman; for I cannot,
> Being a Volsce, be that I am.

                                                1.10.4–6

Aufidius goes on to fantasise about physical combat with Martius in much the same way as the other fantasises about him.

>   By th'elements,
> If e'er again I meet him beard to beard,
> He's mine, or I am his.

                                                1.10.10–12

The combat Aufidius dreams of is again physically up close and personal, face to face, 'beard to beard', intimate and quasi-sexual. The language seems more appropriate to an erotic relationship than to a military one, as in the Song of Songs, where 'my beloved is mine, and I am his'. But Aufidius differs from Martius in one respect: he cares more about winning than about honour. He is prepared to cheat. He would prefer to beat Martius in a straight combat. But rather than continue to endure successive defeats at the hands of the enemy he hates, Aufidius will consider subterfuge and chicanery:

Mine emulation
Hath not that honour in't it had, for where
I thought to crush him in an equal force,
True sword to sword, I'll poach at him some way.
Or wrath or craft may get him.

1.10.12–16

Coriolanus's desire for Aufidius is perverse but pure. Aufidius feels the same intense attachment, but it is contaminated by the will to win by any means. The latter is as pragmatic as the former is absolute. And their collision generates a modern tragedy.

III

Although Shakespeare's tragedy is deeply embedded in the Renaissance conception of Rome, derived mainly from North's translation of Plutarch's *Lives of the Noble Grecians and Romans*, the play has long lent itself to contemporary appropriations. The clash of political philosophies within the play – despotic and democratic, authoritarian and libertarian, aristocratic and republican – has strongly attracted adaptors from both extremes of the political spectrum. In the 1930s, German, French, and Italian fascists mined the play for its anti-democratic tendencies, its apparent contempt for liberal democracy, its celebration of the martial heroism of a fearless leader. A German school text of the 1930s drew an admiring parallel between Coriolanus and Hitler. But the play was equally attractive to communists such as Bertolt Brecht, who adapted the play as a model for popular revolt against military dictatorship and political corruption.

Ralph Fiennes's film version of *Coriolanus* also modernises the political background so as to detach the drama from any but the most vestigial relationship with a historical Rome.[6] This really is a place that only 'calls itself' Rome, or is rather only being called Rome in deference to its source. The film's social world is a modern eastern European state, with a strong and heavy-handed military elite, a weak but unscrupulous political class, and a refractory, discontented civilian population desperate enough to resort to violence. The opening shots display a shabby urban landscape of graffiti-daubed concrete and post-communist economy housing. The common people are organised and conspiratorial rather than carried along in the spontaneous mob uprising we see in Shakespeare. The grievances and injustices the people profess in the film appear to be genuine, and the viewer is probably expected to respond sympathetically to their histrionic displays of indignation and resentment, which often evoke press photographs of rehearsed popular protest.[7] This prejudice in the people's favour is certainly confirmed when an organised demonstration against the state's hoarding of grain is met with the crude and impersonal violence of a line of riot police.

Caius Martius is depicted in the film as a military commander who seems nominally in charge of the police: he alights from an armoured car, crosses the line of riot police, and addresses the protestors. This is quite different from Shakespeare's portrayal of Martius as a warrior patrician whose role is that of taking on external enemies, not policing internal domestic politics. Shakespeare's Martius makes it plain that only the Senate can decide how to deal with the people: he would use violence against them if he could, but is not in a position to do so. In the film it is Martius who gives the command for the riot police to charge and ruthlessly attack the protestors. He represents the violence of the state.

Thus immediately the warrior caste of the film's 'Rome' is unlike the patrician military order of Shakespeare's Roman republic. In the play, Martius despises the common people for a range of reasons: because they are ignorant and aspire to a knowledge of public affairs; because they assert rights to which they should not be entitled; and principally because they have no taste for war, being bold in the protected environment of peacetime but cowardly in the face of attack. The abbreviated text given at this point to the film's Martius restricts his contempt to a visceral militaristic hatred of the cowardly populace, who make no contribution to the state's defence, yet expect the state to confer on them privilege and protection.

The Balkan setting is not only generally suggestive of regional civil wars, but specifically echoes particular identifications of parties with causes. Slavoj Žižek for instance sees the Romans as Serbs, and the Volscians as Albanians from Kosovo. In changing sides, Coriolanus abandons a bankrupt quasi-fascist state to become a freedom fighter for national liberation. The suggestion seems in some ways apposite: the men Martius fights with are all clean-shaven Caucasians, while the bearded or moustachioed Volscians look much more like an oppositional guerrilla minority. On the other hand the political leader of Rome, Shakespeare's Cominius, is a black African, and the professional politicians are pan-British, English, Scots, and Irish. The common people are presented as the kind of rainbow coalition of ethnicities that is generated by equal opportunities casting in the theatre. In which case, in the film, Martius seems to be espousing a supremacist ideology with no nationalist context to support it. There is no opportunity afforded to him for ethnic belonging. Nationalist leaders don't need to hate their own people: they have plenty of opportunities to hate everyone else. Hence the film's Coriolanus is even more isolated than he is in Shakespeare's play, even more of a 'lonely dragon', already from the beginning behaving 'as if a man were author of himself, and knew no other kin'.

Fiennes's Coriolanus, as critics have pointed out, specialises in disgust. His social feelings, whether towards family, political elite, or the common people, range on a fairly narrow spectrum from antipathy to revulsion. He is indifferent to his wife, seems little interested in his son, and edgily anxious in the face of his mother's manifest domination of his personality. His strongest emotion, a kind of dreadful joy, awakens only in the prospect of battle, as does that of Shakespeare's hero. Conflict gives him a reason to live, and the purifying rage of battle violently endorses all his contempt for peace, social order, and the rituals of public office.

Small wonder, then, that his only strongly physical relationships are with the men he fights with, and with the men he seeks to kill. Warfare in the film is cleverly presented as the close engagement of guerrilla street conflict, with the Romans fighting their way, house to ruined house, through the battle-devastated streets of Corioli, encountering small-arms resistance, sniper fire, and the menace of improvised explosive devices (IEDs). There is nothing remote or long-range about this kind of fighting: here men shoot one another at close quarters. The scene in Shakespeare which shows Martius advancing into the enemy city of Corioli alone, leaving his comrades behind and becoming trapped within the gates, is reimagined as Fiennes's Martius fighting his way into a building and being obliged to close with the enemy hand to hand. Attacked from behind by a Volscian soldier with a knife, Martius grapples with him in a violent embrace, and stabs him to death. The blood that is spilt in this intense struggle between two male bodies liberally soaks and streaks Martius's shaved head, creating the signature image deployed in the film's poster.

His troops, having given up hope for his survival, greet his return with manifest delight. Beaming through the veil of blood, Martius embraces Titus Lartius with a frank physical intimacy reserved only for other men, and only for the battlefield. He explicitly draws a parallel between such quasi-sexual male bonding and the anticipatory desire of a bridegroom for his bride:

> MARTIUS:
> O, let me hold you
> in arms as sound as when I woo'd, in heart
> as merry as when our nuptial day was done . . .

Eager to fight a second battle, fearing only that he may have come 'too late', Martius inspires his troops to follow him. The phrase 'me alone?' is uttered in response to some momentary reluctance on the part of his soldiers to press another attack. The hesitation is soon over. The men and their leader fuse into a single fighting unit, and Martius is thrust forward as their collective weapon:

> Make you a sword of me?

But Aufidius is Martius's true bride of battle, and his desire is only for him. The Romans assault the building where the Volscians are holed up, forcing them to retreat. In the course of their withdrawal, the two forces meet and join in a reciprocal stand-off. Martius and Aufidius come face to face. The two armies train their weapons on one another.

At this point the film's attempt to sustain the parallel between the 'Roman' play and the twentieth-century context becomes stretched and difficult. For it is absolutely imperative, both for the play's fiction and the film's appropriation of it, that Martius and Aufidius are able to engage in physical conflict. On the other hand this is not how modern warfare is actually fought. The film solves the problem by invoking conventions around single combat that are as old as the *Iliad*, as new as the latest Hollywood western. Aufidius emerges from a stairwell with weapon lowered, and Martius has him in his sights. But he refrains from killing him, thus enabling the Volscians to regain an advantage. Martius is not interested in a general shoot-out, only in a duel between himself and his mighty opposite:

> I will fight with none but thee.

Such an invocation of the heroic convention of single combat to the death chimes perfectly with the Roman background of the play, though it sits uneasily within the film's largely realistic evocation of modern battle. This is Roman warfare as Shakespeare imagined and realised it: an epic struggle of hero against hero, a hand-to-hand physical combat entailing the intimate embracing of two male bodies. Like warriors in Homer, or in Old English heroic verse, the two soldiers exchange expressions of mutual hatred, and lay aside their rifles, fighting only with knives. The duel is the kind of struggle conventional in action films, the two men closely grappling and trading violent blows. At one point they crash through a glass window and fall to the ground. But with Shakespeare's portrayal of the homosexual culture of war in the background, the vision of two men locked in so violent an embrace could as easily suggest sexual congress as military engagement. Martius lies on top of Aufidius, arms intertwined, nose pressed against nose, both uttering quasi-sexual groans of pleasure or pain. Only an explosion tears them apart, and they are borne away by their respective troops.

This, then, is the emotional heart of Martius's being, and of the film's society. Nothing else in this transplanted 'Rome' affords Martius anything like the pure and absolute rapture of fighting with the man he hates so vehemently that the passion resembles love. For Martius, now Coriolanus, the embraces of family, the friendship of other patricians, the humiliating demands of political office, all pale into insignificance beside this one true and absolute devotion to war, to other men of war, and to the violent delights of physical consummation with the enemy of his heart. Commentary on the film frequently uses the term 'fighting machine' to describe Coriolanus's impersonal dedication to his craft.[8] But no machine derives such pleasure from conflict. Coriolanus represents a certain existential purity of existence in which the physical being, the controlled body, is wholly conscious and fully alive only in danger, risk, exposure, pain. The hard muscular physique that collides so violently with other bodies; the vivid tracery of wounds on the battle-scarified skin;

the stained face that wears the enemy's blood as a mask, defying all personal risk in the obsessive pursuit of victory: these are the defining lineaments of the modern man of war.

Small wonder, then, that Coriolanus cannot meet the obligations and requirements of his society. On the battlefield he knows an absolute extremity of desire, shared only with his chosen peers, impossible to convey to civilians. His real, but only, claim to high political office is his military success. But the nature of that success cannot be translated into social or political terms. Hence Coriolanus is so radically disengaged from any human society but that of the battlefield that it is impossible to envisage him fully reconciled to any political process, let alone the fraught, conflicted, and demeaning ritual required by the Roman republic. The lengthy unravelling of this problem, as played out in Shakespeare, can have only one end, and that is Coriolanus's withdrawal from the compromises of public life. But where is he to go? The tribunes persuade the common people to demand his banishment from Rome. Such a conception can have no meaning for Coriolanus, who does not recognise his society as an objective reality, but rather solipsistically internalises the heroic and military values of Rome within himself. The actions of all those around him, even his mother who shares his value system, serve only to cheapen and contaminate those values. Coriolanus can preserve them in no other way but by alienating himself from his own corrupt society, bearing its core values away with him. 'I banish you,' he says to Rome, with an absurd but strangely impressive hubris: 'I banish you.'

The next step seems equally inevitable, though utterly self-contradictory. If Coriolanus's only positive relationship is with Aufidius, with whom he shares a deeper kinship than with any member of his own community, then it follows naturally that he should seek out the enemy and join himself to their cause. To preserve Rome, he must unite with Rome's enemies. To save Rome, he must attack and defeat it.

CORIOLANUS:
O world, thy slippery turns! Friends now fast sworn,
Whose double bosoms seem to wear one heart,
Whose hours, whose bed, whose meal, and exercise
Are still together, who twin, as 'twere, in love

Unseparable, shall within this hour,
On a dissension of a doit, break out
To bitterest enmity. So fellest foes,
Whose passions and whose plots have broke their sleep
To take the one the other, by some chance,
Some trick not worth an egg, shall grow dear friends
And interjoin their issues. So with me:
My birth-place hate I, and my love's upon
This enemy town. I'll enter. If he slay me,
He does fair justice; if he give me way,
I'll do his country service.

Based on *Coriolanus* 4.4.12–26

Exiled and alone, the world reveals nothing to him but the 'slippery turns', the fluid alternations of loyalty and enmity, hatred and love. Friends become bitter foes; enemies who can barely sleep for dreaming of revenge grow amicable and intermarry their sons and daughters. Coriolanus's world is inverted: hating his own state, the natural law of conflict forces him to love its opposite: 'my love's upon / This enemy town'. Rome has betrayed itself. The true Roman can only be a traitor.

In the film, Fiennes prepares for this transition by enduring a prolonged period on the road, sleeping rough and shunning human society. During this ordeal he acquires the beard, long hair, and scruffy appearance of a backpacking itinerant. By the time he reaches Antium, represented by the coastal town of Kotor, Montenegro, he has grown to resemble more closely his Volscian enemies than the clean-cut Romans. He finds the Volscian headquarters, and offers himself to Aufidius, who welcomes him with a restatement of the intense quasi-sexual passion they have shared on the battlefield.

AUFIDIUS:
O Martius, Martius!
Each word thou hast spoke hath weeded from my heart
A root of ancient envy. If Jupiter
Should from yond cloud speak divine things,
And say ''Tis true', I'd not believe them more
Than thee, all noble Martius. Let me twine
Mine arms about that body, where against
My grained ash an hundred times hath broke
And scarred the moon with splinters.

[Embraces CORIOLANUS] Here I clip
The anvil of my sword, and do contest
As hotly and as nobly with thy love
As ever in ambitious strength I did
Contend against thy valour. Know thou first,
I loved the maid I married; never man
Sighed truer breath. But that I see thee here,
Thou noble thing! more dances my rapt heart
Than when I first my wedded mistress saw
Bestride my threshold.

4.5.103–21

Hitherto Aufidius has regarded the body of Coriolanus as an obdurately resistant object, to be broken and penetrated with the weapons of war. Now he can 'twine [his] arms' about that same body, relishing its scarred hardness, with a 'love' both 'hot' and 'noble'. Earlier Coriolanus had embraced Titus with the excited thrill of a bridegroom, and Aufidius also resorts to the language of *prima nox* to express his feeling for Coriolanus. Like a bridegroom on his wedding night, relishing the imminence of passion, Aufidius's heart dances in rapture at being able to call Coriolanus his 'noble thing'.

We see in Aufidius's language how closely bonded vindictive obsession is to sexual fantasy. His recurrent dreams of fighting with Coriolanus constantly return to imagined 'encounters' of a transparently erotic kind, in which the two men are 'down together', removing one another's helmets, each 'fisting' at the other's throat. The imaginary enacting of these perverse fantasies leaves Aufidius hollow with post-coital emptiness:

thou hast beat me out
Twelve several times and I have nightly since
Dreamt of encounters 'twixt thyself and me –
We have been down together in my sleep,
Unbuckling helms, fisting each other's throat –
And waked half dead with nothing.

4.5.123–8

In the film Aufidius responds to Coriolanus's surrender of himself with a baffled mixture of mistrust and desire, grappling him closely, but with a knife at his throat. Suspicion put aside, the two men embrace with the unabashed intensity of lovers, the passionate camaraderie of comrades-in-arms.

Responding to the film's bonding and isolation of the two principal characters, Peter Holland proposes that it is presented, and certainly marketed, as a kind of 'buddy movie of an unusual kind'.[9] If so, it is more than an unusual example of the convention. In popular film 'buddies' usually experience a deeply conflicted relationship, but what binds them together is stronger than what drives them apart. Through conflict the two men in a buddy movie discover and negotiate the shared experience they have in common, that which makes them kin. In the film version of *Coriolanus*, everything the two heroes share is fatally destructive to one or both of them. Drawing on the play's language of animal loyalty – 'Who does the wolf love?' – Holland describes Coriolanus and Aufidius as 'friendly beasts'. But such a strained friendship between creatures who are natural enemies is unlikely to survive the enmity that is constitutive of their nature. The essence of their passionate entanglement is a mutual pleasure in annihilation. For a brief period following Coriolanus's desertion, their reciprocal desires are balanced and counterpoised in a fragile equilibrium. But very soon that delicate equipoise begins to break down, and the inevitable tragic denouement lurches into motion. Coriolanus becomes more popular among the Volscians than Aufidius. Some of the enemies of Rome start to style themselves after the model of the quintessentially Roman hero, shaving their heads to emulate his signature skinhead baldness, while Coriolanus dresses down to their informal partisan attire of sleeveless vest and combat fatigues. Aufidius vows to find some means of ridding himself of his now intolerable partner.

At last, leading the Volscian army in an assault on Rome, Coriolanus's conviction of the rightness of his action is tested to its limits, and beyond, by the intercession of his family. Let us first follow this denouement in Shakespeare's play.

> *Enter Virgilia, Volumnia [Young Martius, Valeria] with Attendants.*

My wife comes foremost; then the honoured mould
Wherein this trunk was framed, and in her hand
The grandchild to her blood.

                                                          5.3.22–5

The women wear the garb of mourning to signal that Coriolanus is dead to them, and to Rome. Initially he struggles to resist the promptings of natural affection in order to safeguard his resolve:

> But, out, affection!
> All bond and privilege of nature break!
> Let it be virtuous to be obstinate.
>
> 5.3.24–6

He will continue his course of treachery and betrayal, however strongly his loved ones invoke in him the rejected desire to belong:

> Let the Volsces
> Plough Rome and harrow Italy, I'll never
> Be such a gosling to obey instinct, but stand,
> As if a man were author of himself
> And knew no other kin.
>
> 5.3.33–7

Coriolanus predicates his existence as a supreme isolation, a perfect loneliness in which he knows no equal, no peer, no partner, no kin. Like God he is self-begotten, self-renewing, self-directing. Resisting all appeals, from ally, wife, and son, he is finally moved to capitulate by his mother's persuasions:

> VOLUMNIA:
> how can we,
> Alas, how can we for our country pray,
> Whereto we are bound, together with thy victory,
> Whereto we are bound? Alack, or we must lose
> The country, our dear nurse, or else thy person,
> Our comfort in the country ... For either thou
> Must, as a foreign recreant be led
> With manacles thorough our streets, or else
> Triumphantly tread on thy country's ruin
> And bear the palm for having bravely shed
> Thy wife and children's blood.
>
> 5.3.107–18

Volumnia expresses the intractable nature of the crisis she faces: if the battle goes ahead, she will be obliged either to mourn her son's death, or behold his victory over her own country. This is not maternal remonstrance, or an appeal to family loyalty, but an appeal from one warrior to another. The mother succeeds, where the wife and son fail, because she shares her son's values, she is indeed more counterpart than companion. She is, in Philip French's words, 'the very woman who has turned him into an uncompromising warrior'. 'Thou art my warrior,' she says to him later: 'I holped to frame thee.' Or as Greenblatt puts it, 'Volumnia makes clear her aristocratic hauteur, her zealous patriotism, her ferocious cult of martial honor, and her limitless investment in the son she has shaped to act out her fantasies.'[10]

Coriolanus, fully aware of the fatal destiny entailed in any recantation, expresses his emotions through an eloquent silence, but cannot forbear disclosing the personal betrayal his civic treachery has occasioned:

([He] holds her by the hand, silent)

CORIOLANUS:
O mother, mother!
What have you done? Behold, the heavens do ope,
The gods look down, and this unnatural scene
They laugh at. O, my mother, mother! O!
You have won a happy victory to Rome;
But, for your son, believe it, O, believe it,
Most dangerously you have with him prevail'd,
If not most mortal to him.

5.3.183–90

In the film, as in the play, this moment is played out with an audience of Volscian officers and soldiers. The mother, wife, and son are led past tanks and heavily armed soldiers to the ruined building that is the Volscian base. Coriolanus receives the delegation from Rome seated in a barber's chair, a bizarre parody of a chair of office. We have seen the same chair earlier in the film, in a scene where one Volscian soldier shaves a comrade's head, in a heavily charged masculine environment, rank with sweat and lurid with tattoos. So Coriolanus presents himself, to the diplomatic embassy that is his own family, as wholly embedded in the Volscian military community, and correspondingly indifferent to the imminent sufferings of Rome. And he succeeds in resisting all entreaties, though their effects are no doubt cumulative, until the very final moment where his resolve breaks and his eyes cloud with emotion. And this is the point where Volumnia asserts that as far as she can see, Coriolanus really has turned, and become an enemy of the state. If he truly has betrayed both Rome, and her matriarchal pact with him, then the man before her cannot be her son. If he has so disinvested himself of all Roman piety, then he must indeed belong to the enemy he has joined.

> This fellow had a Volscian to his mother;
> His wife is in Corioli and his child
> Like him by chance.

Coriolanus breaks down, buries his face in his mother's clothing, weeping like a child, and acknowledges the multi-layered perversity of this 'unnatural scene'. He concedes that she has won, but conveys an awful clarity of vision about the repercussions her victory will have on him. He renounces his treachery, and faces his inevitable end with stoic fatalism:

> Let it come.

Coriolanus meets his death on a featureless, empty road, hacked by the Volscian troops with knives and bayonets while Aufidius stands back and watches. It is the latter, however, who delivers the *coup de grâce*, with the blade he was already honing at the opening of the film. He takes Coriolanus again in his arms and delivers a knife-thrust to the body, while cradling the blood-boltered head in his hands with a perverse tenderness. As Coriolanus falls, in a strange and eery sunlit silence, Aufidius literally kisses him into death. Clearly moved, Aufidius takes his last embrace of the enemy he loves.

IV

I will now proceed to examine the contingencies between this film version of Shakespeare's play and two other contemporary films, one a war film, the other a spy thriller. All three display what might be considered marginal connections with one another. *Coriolanus* and *The Hurt Locker* shared a cinematographer, Barry Ackroyd, and a sound mixer, Ray Beckett; while the principal screenwriter for *Skyfall*, John Logan, did the screen adaption of *Coriolanus*. Ralph Fiennes, director and star of *Coriolanus*, has minor role in *The Hurt*

Locker and a major role in *Skyfall*. But as I propose to demonstrate, the three films belong together, in that they share a common investment in what I have called the 'Coriolanus myth', a peculiarly contemporary realisation of the classic man of war.

The hero of *The Hurt Locker*[11] is an American bomb disposal expert working in Iraq. The theatre of war is not that of the battlefield, but rather that of a military occupation threatened by the covert tactics of car bombs and concealed snipers. The American troops spend their time nervously patrolling the silently menacing streets of Baghdad, anxiously seeking an invisible enemy. The insurgents in this environment do not appear in any frontal assault, but rather hide themselves to detonate IEDs, pick off unwary American soldiers with sniper fire, and try to capture hostages if they can. The tactics of the enemy are, in other words, those of an insurgent guerrilla army such as the displaced Taliban, or an organised terrorist group like Al-Qaeda.

The American soldiers are thus placed, by their government, in a defensive position, unable to engage with an enemy they cannot see. Their presence in Iraq is as much political as military, restricted to a civilian 'peacekeeping' role. Confined to a passive military stance, they are denied the adrenalin rush of battle. Their daily experience is thus a constant endurance of risk without excitement, exposure without action, danger without any corresponding thrill of combat, suspense with no fulfilment or resolution. They live and work in the midst of a civilian population that is partly friendly, partly hostile, and often found silently observing events in an apparent indifference that could conceal mere antipathy to the occupying troops or collusion with their enemies. Who can tell? In one scene a man is observed filming the Americans at their dangerous work from the minaret of a mosque. He could be an interested bystander or the terrorist who has planted the bomb. The cinematic spectator watches Iraqi people watching the American soldiers, but has no more idea who to trust than they do:

The engagements between Delta Company and its shadowy adversaries contain an element of theater. The bomb-makers mingle with Iraqi bystanders to observe and assess their work, standing on balconies and at windows watching impassively as the Americans shout, sweat and gesticulate, actors in a show whose script they are fighting to control.[12]

The story of the film concerns the three men who constitute 'Delta Company'. Sergeant Sanborn is a professional soldier who has come to hate his assignment, and who trusts that a painstaking adherence to discipline and procedure will enable him to survive and return home. Specialist Eldridge is very young, and pathologically terrified. The film begins with their principal bomb disposal expert being killed by an IED he has failed to defuse, when the robot device designed to explode the bomb on contact undergoes mechanical failure and the bomb is triggered with a mobile phone by a man innocently standing in the front of his butcher's shop. His replacement is Staff Sergeant James, who is the 'Coriolanus' figure of the film. James is a soldier who has found a way of infusing the tightly restricted protocol of their passive military role with the kind of intoxication, excitement, and transcendence available to soldiers in combat. His approach to bomb disposal appears to be incredibly cool, systematic, and untroubled by circumambient danger. He has no use for the remote control of a robotic safety device. While he works, his comrades become increasingly anxious, urge him to hurry, and eventually order him to withdraw. He ignores their concerns, and finding that they trouble his concentration, switches off his intercom.

In this action of disengagement, James displays a characteristic refusal to adhere to military discipline. He literally switches off from any concern with the safety of the company as a collective unit. He has no time for protocol. His rapt concentration and technical brilliance make him seem more like an artist than an engineer. He requires an absolute stillness of focus on the task in hand, the elimination of all distraction, a Zenlike transcendence of fear, of any concern for personal safety. With a total disregard for personal safety, he places himself directly in the 'Kill Zone', the area that would be devastated should the bomb explode.

This apparent artistic detachment and focus to some extent disguise the true psychological condition that brings James to such points of transcendence. In truth, like Coriolanus, his deepest happiness lies in reckless exposure to danger, in a terrifying level of risk. James will even remove the helmet from his protective suit when its confinement becomes an irritation: 'If I'm going to die, I'll die comfortable.' To him the bomb is not merely a machine that needs to be powered off; it is more like a living enemy he will close and grapple with in a perverse form of single combat. He removes his armour to show his face to the enemy, just as Coriolanus in the film version lays aside his rifle to fight with Aufidius. Both actions treat war as a kind of game or sport with a set of rules that are quite different from those to be found in the service manual. In this kind of fighting the individual male body is an implement, a finely honed tool that can be pitted against an opposing force with heroically reckless abandon and utter contempt for peril.

From the viewpoint of Sanborn, James's actions are reckless to the point of insanity. Sanborn's concern is with following procedure, safeguarding the lives of the men in his company. But James is only truly sentient in the existential crisis of absolute risk. Only in the extremity of danger does he feel fully alive. As Peter Bradshaw comments in the *Guardian*, the film shows that 'the danger of war is deeply exciting' (19.01.12); or as the *New York Times* reviewer puts it, while absorbed in his perilous work, James appears to be 'having the time of his life' (01.12.11). Sukhdev Sandhu in the *Telegraph* writes of James's 'addiction to danger' (21.01.12), while Anthony Quinn in the *Independent* says: 'This bomb specialist gets his kicks from being as close to obliteration as humanly possible' (22.01.12). His two comrades are able to perceive something of this heroic warrior code, finding James's risk-taking thrilling, even admirable. At the same time they recognise the extent to which his suicidal bravery puts them at risk of their lives. They even at one point seem tempted to kill him and 'make it look like an accident'.

James shares another characteristic with Coriolanus: an almost complete disengagement from any kind of society other than that of the particular 'battlefield' he fights in. Though he has a family back home in the States, he has no contact with them. He telephones his wife, but can say nothing to her, and rings off. This alienation extends to the very army he fights in: his recklessness and disregard for protocol separate him from the majority of his own comrades, who want to survive the war and go home. His only positive relationships are with his comrades-in-arms. He displays a tender care for the young soldier Eldridge, and a strong though perverse attachment to Sanborn. Culturally these two are polarised, since Sanborn is an African-American and James, to use Sanborn's phrase, 'a red-neck piece of trailer-trash'. Their continual disagreement over tactics is punctuated by moments of intimacy of a quasi-erotic kind. In one scene James and Sanborn engage in a mock-wrestling match that generates, like the knife fight between Coriolanus and Aufidius in the film version, both homoerotic emotion and real violence. In a prolonged vigil in the desert in which Sanborn has to keep his rifle trained on a building containing insurgents, his face masked with sand, his eyes visibly smarting with the prolonged exposure, James gets a sachet of juice and holds it near Sanborn's mouth for him to sip it. The moment is one of delicate tenderness, more like a father feeding a baby than one soldier helping another. As in *Coriolanus*, there is throughout *The Hurt Locker* a symbiosis between erotic, homicidal, and masochistic desires.

The film's title derives from a metaphor initially used in extreme sports, then absorbed and commonly used by the military. A 'hurt locker' is a space of both confinement and agony, a microcosmic 'world of pain'. To be in the 'Kill Zone' of an IED is to be perilously close to the hurt locker. The grotesque protective suit worn by the bomb disposal technician in itself suggests a 'hurt locker', a confined space of extreme peril, inches and seconds away from agonising annihilation. The enforced passivity of the US soldiers renders their everyday experience a 'hurt locker'. And the total environment of this very modern style of warfare, with an army defensively restricted to a civilian role and confronted by an invisible enemy who recognises no rules of combat, could be described as the very macrocosm of the 'hurt locker', a universal world of pain.

The film's title was most likely derived from a poem of the same name written by former soldier Brian Turner.

> Nothing but hurt left here
> Nothing but bullets and pain . . .
> Nothing left here but the hurt.
>
> Believe it when you see it.
> Believe it when a twelve-year-old
> rolls a grenade into the room.
> Or when a sniper punches a hole
> deep into someone's skull.
> Believe it when four men
> step from a taxicab in Mosul

to shower the street in brass
and fire. Open the hurt locker
and see what there is of knives
and teeth. Open the hurt locker and learn
how rough men come hunting for souls.[13]

The achievement of the film is to show the cinema audience exactly
what is contained inside the hurt locker; and then to explain how
and why a man like James, or indeed like Coriolanus, should desire
so passionately to penetrate its ultimate mysteries.

v

Skyfall, the latest James Bond movie, overlaps significantly with the
Coriolanus film, a fact that is unsurprising given their common
'authorship' in the screenwriting of John Logan.[14] As the film is
not based on any of the Ian Fleming Bond stories, the writers were
free to appropriate the Bond formula in radically innovative ways,
taking James Bond into dubious moral territory where the simple
tough patriotism of Ian Fleming would have been very unlikely to
go. *Skyfall* also contains the main ingredients of the Coriolanus
myth: the hero whose loyalties are so badly misused, that he is
strongly tempted to undertake self-banishment; the villain who is a
kind of double to the hero, a brother destroyed by sibling jealousy, as
much counterpart as opposite; and a mother figure who is so much a
matriarchal warrior that she will readily sacrifice her own sons, rather
than see them dishonoured by failure.

The Secret Service in the film is a modern organisation with an
accessible public face; housed in SIS, the real MI6 building on the
banks of the Thames; vulnerable to terrorist attack, and accountable
to parliamentary scrutiny. Its leader, 'M', originally Ian Fleming's
veteran admiral, was recast as a woman earlier in the Bond movie
series. In the Bond books, the Head of the Service is called M, simply
because it is the initial letter of his name (Miles Messervy), as is the
case with the character who replaces M at the end of *Skyfall* (Mallory).
Conferred on a woman, the initial becomes explicitly a codename for
'Mother' (it is what Ian Fleming called his own mother).

M, played by the veteran actress Judi Dench, is as much a warrior
as any of her 'sons', the agents she runs, and as uncompromising and

ruthless, in decision and in action, as any of the men she commands. Directing operations from her HQ, she displays no compassion for her agents in the field. The film begins with Bond on an assignment in Turkey, pursuing a stolen computer containing the names of agents embedded in terrorist organisations, and being instructed directly by M via electronic transmission. He comes across a fellow agent who is wounded and in need of medical attention, and stops to give him first aid. M orders Bond to leave the casualty and proceed with the mission. This callousness towards her agents is then climactically compounded when M orders another agent to shoot at the man Bond is struggling with on top of a train, despite the obvious danger to Bond himself. The shot misses the target and hits Bond. In a long, silent tumble from a viaduct into a river far below, Bond falls from the train, wounded by friendly fire, shot by command of his own superior officer, sacrificed by his own surrogate mother.

Somehow Bond survives and escapes, but he makes no attempt to return and report for duty. We see him instead 'Absent Without Leave', taking a prolonged unofficial holiday, naturally in the company of a beautiful girl, in some tropical paradise. He has, at least temporarily, disengaged himself from patriotic loyalty and military discipline, rejected the claims of his service upon him, and made a separate peace. Both wounded and hurt by his commander's indifference, disillusioned by his country's disrespect for the life he has often risked for it, drinking heavily, he becomes more like a figure from John le Carré or Graham Greene than the unflinchingly loyal James Bond of Ian Fleming.[15] Like Coriolanus, he banishes his own country from himself, rather than allowing it to banish him.

Bond, however, recovers from his Coriolanus moment, and he returns to London. Clearly the worse for wear and for drink, he confronts M in her flat and reports himself for duty. What has brought him back out of his self-imposed exile is the resurgence, from the past, of a character who proves to be another Coriolanus figure, this time one who has turned with no hope of reclamation, and who becomes the arch-villain confronting and threatening Bond, the Secret Service, and England. This is Raoul Silva (played by Javier Bardem), a former MI6 agent who worked under M and who has undergone a parallel experience to Bond, being abandoned and left for dead by his own service. Silva, however, is the son who can never forgive his mother (he refers to M repeatedly as 'Mother' and 'Mommie'). His response to this betrayal, unlike Bond's, is neither temporary nor forgiving, and he commits to killing M, destroying the Secret Service, and inflicting as much damage as he can on the country. His initial, very modern, methods involve cyber-terrorism, a sabotaging of the MI6 computer systems, and the planting of explosives to cause a huge blast in the SIS building.

In a sense Bond and Silva share the Coriolanus myth between them. Both are basically public servants who are sacrificed by their service, victims of their own loyalty, and of the ruthless discipline of a military organisation. Like Coriolanus, Bond turns his back on his country and his service, and also like Coriolanus, he relents and surrenders himself when his 'mother's' life is threatened by his own actions. Bond is then however restored to his constitutive position in the Bond formula, as national hero and saviour. Silva is equally like Coriolanus in his vow of vengeance against his (adoptive) country, for what it has done to him. In him however there is no relenting, and no forgiveness.

The two principal male characters, like Coriolanus and Aufidius, thus share a kinship, a commonality of loyalty and betrayal. Both display reciprocally parallel and contrasting responses to their experience. There is between them a wary mutual respect, since both realise how closely matched they are in terms of warlike intelligence and destructive capacity. There is even an attempt, on the part of Silva, to introduce homosexual desire into their relationship: with Bond tied to a chair, Silva fondles him in an explicitly homoerotic way. But Bond is still sufficiently Ian Fleming's creation to want no truck with homosexuality, and the advances are unreciprocated.

What binds Bond and Silva together is that they share the same 'mother', M, and that Bond's instinct to protect her is as strong as Silva's desire to see her dead. The entwined infantile instincts of possession and destruction towards the mother are dispersed between them. It is M they fight over, rather than service or country or principle. Bond rescues M from interrogation by a parliamentary committee, spirits her away in the iconic Aston Martin DBVI driven in *Goldfinger*, and takes her to Skyfall, his family estate and childhood home in Scotland, where they arm themselves and wait for Silva to find them. M participates in the fighting along with the men, and is fatally wounded in the action. When Silva eventually corners them, in a moorland chapel, he displays genuine compassion for M's injury, as if he really does see her as his mother. 'You're hurt. What have they done to you?' He forces M to take his gun, and begs her to kill them both with the same bullet. His destructive impulse towards the mother is twinned with the desire for self-destruction, a dark Freudian knot. Bond kills Silva, thus saving M from Silva's proposed suicide pact. But M dies of her wounds in any case.

VI

Each of the three films I have been discussing deals with war in one shape or another, and in each case the war is framed within a wider social and political context. In *Coriolanus*, the conflict between Rome and the Volscians plays out in the midst of a political crisis, the struggle for power of factions within the republic. *The Hurt Locker* has been praised for focusing on the everyday experience of soldiers, rather than pontificating, as so many other Hollywood movies have done, over the rights and wrongs of US foreign policy; yet the action of the film could not be understood without some grasp of America's post-9/11 presence in the Middle East. The politics of *Skyfall* naturally resemble those of the Ian Fleming novels, which vaguely invoke the Cold War but in practice construct shadowy global organisations like SPECTRE that strike at England with terrorism and sabotage, and which are run by demonic and grotesque arch-villains. Silva in *Skyfall* may employ tactics such as computer hacking, but in every other respect he is a true heir to master criminals like Ernst Stavro Blofeld or Dr No.

But the three films are less interested in war as a matter of armies and campaigns, or in the wider political context that informs the shape of each military confrontation, and much more interested in that fundamental trope of war fiction, the physical struggle of one man against another. In *Coriolanus*, as we have seen, the essence of war is represented through the single combat of Coriolanus and Aufidius. In *The Hurt Locker* James can engage with his enemies only through direct physical engagement with explosive devices, but his intimate struggles with these intricate machines constitute an alternative form of single combat. Ian Fleming's books focus obsessively on physical combat and bodily ordeal, which are Bond's only means of engaging with the crises he undertakes to resolve. *Skyfall* remains true to this formula, privileging direct physical struggle as ultimately the only way of fighting off a dangerous enemy. Although Silva is a renegade terrorist, and Bond and M represent the British state, the film's final show-down sees Silva commanding a helicopter gunship and a heavily armed platoon of men, while Bond fights back with the improvised tactics of the guerrilla or partisan, setting booby traps and detonating home-made bombs. He finally kills Silva not with a gun, but with an old-fashioned weapon, a knife. In all three films, war is a matter of human agency, and its outcome is dependent on the courage and hardihood of an individual combatant. Whether it is Coriolanus rushing alone into an occupied enemy position, or Segeant James courting extreme danger by renouncing military protocol, or Bond ignoring official orders and throwing himself instinctively into danger, the figure and its meaning are always the same: the code the hero lives by is not social order, moral principle or military discipline, but fearless, reckless abandonment of the body to absolute risk.

VII

Throughout this analysis I have been concerned with fiction, rather than history, as a source for more fiction. Our encounters with a play like *Coriolanus* invariably blend reality and fantasy, history and its continual fictionalisation. Both have become inseparable, of course, since there is no return to the past that can purport to be unaffected by the concerns of the present. Once these principles are accepted, the critic is obliged to reflect on the nature of his or her own interpretative discourse, since the solid historical base that provides the intellectual platform for most contemporary criticism is no longer there. If fiction breeds fiction, and there is no further recourse to a stabilising history, then criticism is forced back upon its original constitutive methodologies of linguistic analysis and formal exegesis.

Or there is another way: the way of the imagination. Criticism can meet creative work on its own ground, by adopting creative methods of interpretation through imitation, parallelism, analogy, adaptation. My study of *Coriolanus* could not be complete without adding to the critical analysis a creative response to Shakespeare's work, which takes the form of a spy thriller narrative adapting the plot of Shakespeare's play to the espionage genre. Within this narrative I have found the perfect complement to Shakespeare's Roman drama, a medium in which all the themes and preoccupations of the play can be accurately and creatively relocated. Like the Coriolanus of Ralph Fiennes's film, or the heroes of *The Hurt Locker* and *Skyfall*, my hero – named Guy Mars, after the Latin Caius Martius – encounters all the experiences that make Shakespeare's hero so memorable and distinctive. He does so within a largely fantasy world that bears little direct relation to reality, and is yet very much of our time.

CHAPTER 6

'The Lonely Dragon'

I

Most people preferred to walk round the edges of the so-called 'Peace Camp' that littered the neat turf and winding paths of St James's Park, but Guy Mars insisted on walking stolidly through. He had paced the same route, from the tube station to his office in Carlton House Terrace, for as long as he could remember, and he saw no reason to alter it now. As he picked his way gingerly amongst the shapeless tangles of plastic sheeting, guiding his handmade Italian shoes carefully around piles of unidentifiable decomposing matter, a few of the demonstrators noticed him, and began to hiss and jeer.

'Capitalist.'

'Tax-dodger.'

'Traitor.'

At this last flung accusation, Mars fetched up short against its utterer, a thin young man with round Trotsky glasses and a pony-tail, who thrust towards him a placard demanding 'Bread for the People'. Food shortages had become endemic and recurrent since England's withdrawal from the European Union. Emboldened anoraks gathered round. Mars stood his ground quietly, an incongruous figure in his camel-coloured cashmere coat and polished Asprey leather briefcase, and stared down his accuser with cold, dangerous eyes. The youth slunk backwards, and the crowd melted away to let Mars through. As he ascended the elegant white steps leading up to Carlton House Terrace, the demonstrators began to mutter amongst themselves.

'Who is he?' asked Trotsky, his courage returning.

'Guy Mars,' replied an older man with a military jacket and a nest of plaited, tramplike hair. 'War hero. A long time ago. Now he's in Intelligence. Homeland security. Bastard.'

'A true enemy of the people. He hates everything we stand for. He'd set the troops on us if he could.'

'Flaunts his wealth with flash cars and expense-account meals. We could live for a week on what he sends back to the kitchen.'

'We could fund a hospital with his bar bills.'

'He was a hero though, right? He did defend us.'

'Yes, but what for? Not for your benefit. Or mine. Out of his own pride, that's all. And to please his "Mother".'

'Who?'

'Not his real mother, tosser. You know,' said Tramp-head, pointing towards one of the tall Regency windows that looked out over the park. 'Her.'

II

The object of his gesture stood in the window-bay of a high-ceilinged room in one of the elegant mansions of Carlton House Terrace, surveying the amorphous mass of shanty town that disfigured the park. Tall and immaculately dressed, Dame Volumnia Marsden had been the first woman director of the Security Service. It was she who had personally engineered the controversial merger of MI5 with MI6. As the balance of threat between home-grown terrorism and foreign attack shifted in favour of the former, the international security apparatus of the SIS had ceased to be fit for purpose. All round the globe, British agents were idling in the bars and bordellos of Tangier or Bangkok, while at home a steady stream of fanatical jihadists was flowing from mosques and schools in Luton and Rochdale. Under cover of a government cost reduction programme, the two services had been quietly reunited, rendered more transparent, and held to strict accountability by a parliamentary committee. Cold War warriors like Guy Mars were brought home, shackled to desks, and busied with committees and audits, quality controls, and health and safety legislation. Though still called the Secret Service, everybody now knew all there was to know about it, so it was an easy target for the militant anti-capitalists of the

'Occupy London' movement, who had pitched their ramshackle tent city beneath its windows, and chanted their daily litany against the arbitrary power of capitalist lackeys and imperialist running dogs. In rueful recognition of her gender and her domestic reforms, Dame Volumnia had acquired the nickname, conferred on her in a mixture of affection and resentment, of 'Mother'. Though there was nothing maternal about her, she accepted the soubriquet, since it defined her matriarchal power over the men who served under her.

Beside Mother, at the window stood her second-in-command, Sir John Mennis, known in the service by his codename 'C' (for 'Control'). Mennis was a distinguished elderly man, his face just a little too red beneath the coiffed grey hair, his pampered flesh just a little too protuberant beneath the beautifully tailored Savile Row suit. Together they watched Guy Mars pass through the knot of protestors and walk resolutely up the steps towards them.

'No love lost there,' remarked C.

'What can he expect?' she replied, a touch of asperity in her usually musical voice. 'What does he do to make them like him?'

'I think it's respect he looks for, rather than affection,' said C.

'Things have changed. We're the face of government now. He was my best agent, and it's hard to see him committing slow suicide. Have you finished that Press Statement yet?'

Without replying, C offered her a sheet of paper. She pulled on her glasses, held by a string around her neck, and began to read.

III

On the other side of the Peace Camp two men sat side by side on a park bench at the edge of the ornamental lake, drinking take-away coffees. Both wore the anonymous raincoat and trilby hat favoured by minor government officials of the Foreign Office or Ministry of Defence. They too had observed Guy Mars pass through the encamped mob of discontented citizens, and had watched him unhurriedly ascend the steps to the terrace above.

'There goes yesterday's man,' observed the younger of the two, whose name was Bootles.

'He'd be proud of the title,' said the other, older man. 'He doesn't have much time for today.'

'Isn't he due for retirement?'

'Overdue. But they keep him around for some reason. For some emergency that might require his particular skillset.'

'He's a stumbling block to our public relations. The more we try to placate the people, the more he provokes them.'

'Perhaps we should be looking for some way of easing his path to retirement.'

'You have some ideas, Sicksmith?'

'They're setting up a review of the Department. He'll have to appear before a committee. Account for himself. Do some explaining.'

'He won't like *that*.'

'No. And if the committee puts enough pressure on him, he'll most likely walk.'

'Who's chairing it?'

The elder man tilted his coffee-cup, and poured the last dregs on to the grass beside him, as if it were a libation.

'I am.'

IV

Guy Mars slumped down at the desk in his office in Carlton House Terrace with the resignation of a man so enslaved to routine that even hope – of anything interesting, exciting, worth doing – had become a sentiment hardly worth nourishing. A cup of strong black coffee awaited him, but it was already cold. He badly wanted a cigarette, but would have to return to the ground floor and smoke on the pavement outside. The Secret Service had become a non-smoking environment. Wearily he pulled towards himself an in-tray piled high with correspondence: memos, circulars, requests for information. Everything was labelled TOP SECRET, as was the convention in his department, but nothing was of any importance. He opened a large buff Manila envelope and took out a memo. An instruction from the Chief Executive's Office: all staff to undertake refresher training in Equal Opportunities and Disability Awareness. Mars sighed, pushed the paper aside, and opened the next one. A new quality assurance methodology to be implemented: mandatory induction for all staff with operational responsibilities. Mars tossed the paper into his no-intention-of-ever-reading pile, leaned back in his chair, and looked at the leaves of the topmost branches in St James's

Park. They were edged with yellow. Autumn was entering his soul.
Perhaps after all it was time to quit.

v

The Peace Camp protestors had formed a ragged semi-circle around
the foot of the steps to Carlton House Terrace, and embarked on
their daily litany of protest against government, the police, the
army, tax avoidance. Suddenly an angry roar broke from the crowd,
as Sir John Mennis appeared at the top of the steps, flanked by a
heavily armed bodyguard. Sir John held out his hands, palms
downwards, in a placatory gesture, and tried to speak above the
noise.

'Who's he?' asked one protestor.

'Sir John Mennis,' answered another. 'He's one of the best of them.
He's always loved the people.'

'An honest man! If only the rest were like him,' put in a third man.

The mob fell silent as Sir John began to address them.

'My fellow countrymen. What's the trouble here? Where are you
off to, with your placards and banners? Tell me what you want. Tell
me what's wrong.'

'You know what's wrong,' shouted Tramp-head, who pushed himself forward as spokesman for the mob. 'We petitioned Parliament a
fortnight ago. If we don't get what we want, we'll find some way of
taking it.'

Sir John replied with the same propitiatory gesture. 'Good friends,
honest neighbours. Do you want to ruin yourselves?'

'We're already ruined,' came the furious reply from a hundred throats.

'No, no,' replied Sir John. 'Government has your best interests at
heart. The state cares for you like a father. You curse us as if we were
enemies. But if you try to lift your hands against us, you may as well
strike at heaven. Parliament has the power to crush you, and ten
thousand more who come behind you. It's not our fault there's a
shortage of bread.'

'You've put most of it in your belly, you fat bastard!'

'It's true I'm not as lean as I used to be. But what I put into my
stomach enables me to work for you. You think government is just a
huge belly: devouring your taxes, swallowing your income, hoarding

your food. But everything that goes into that stomach comes out again . . .'

'Yeah, in shit!'

'No, no, in energy. Heat and light for your schools and hospitals. Roads, railways, airports. The body can't manage without the belly. It drives everything: the limbs, the organs, the brain. That's the nature of society. Some do the hard labour, some manage the systems, some do the thinking. We all have our place. But nothing works, if we don't work together. I'm sorry you're short of food. Really I am. But don't blame the government. Blame the weather. Blame climate change. But blaming one another won't put food on the table. Which reminds me, my lunch is waiting for me.'

'Champagne and caviar, is it?'

'No, no, just bread and cheese. Maybe a small glass of wine.'

A few of the protestors tittered. Sir John was well known as the joker in an otherwise heavy pack.

'Come on, friends,' he went on. 'It's getting cold. You know we're doing what we can, in very difficult circumstances. Let's agree to wrap it up for the present. I'll talk to you tomorrow.'

Some of the protestors began to break up and drift away, bored with the daily ritual of dialogue that never seemed to produce any result. A few others stuck to their posts at the foot of the steps, and resumed their chanting.

Sir John half turned on his way up the steps. 'We'll beat this together,' he cried feebly, barely heard above the shouting.

'Never!' replied Tramp-head. 'Not until we have a voice!'

VI

'So what is it they want?'

It was 6 p.m. Mother's face looked tired across the desk. She switched on a shaded lamp that flattered her worn features.

'They want a voice,' shrugged Sir John. 'Representation. A seat at the table.'

The door opened, and Bootles and Sicksmith were ushered in.

'I've asked these boys to join us,' said Mother. 'They have some ideas. Come, come in. Sit down. Tell C what you told me.'

'It seems to us, Sir John,' began Sicksmith, 'that we can channel some of the people's resentment and anger into a more constructive interface.'

'A what?' asked C mildly.

'We suggest appointing two members of the department to act as special liaison officers with the Peace Camp. To hold meetings with them, give them regular briefings on progress, listen to their concerns and feed them back. They would feel included. We would have more influence with them.'

'Shop stewards, eh?' observed Sir John sardonically. 'You could help them organise a strike. If any of them had a job, that is.'

'It doesn't have to be us . . .'

'It's your idea,' put in Mother crisply. 'You run with it. It can't do any harm.'

'Or any good,' C murmured to himself, and aloud, 'No objections.'

As the three men left the office, Bootles tried to detain C with a hand on his arm.

'Could we talk to you about something else, Sir John?' asked Bootles.

C was overdue at his club, and in no mood for office politics.

'Not now, for God's sake. Tomorrow. Lunch. Talk to my secretary.'

VII

The lights were coming on in King's Road as Mars sat in a slow-moving traffic queue. He had collected his Jaguar XJS from the little workshop in a Kensington mews where the car had been serviced, and was driving the short distance home to his Putney flat. The rush-hour traffic made the journey seem interminable. Leashed-in power rumbled quietly beneath his feet, but there was nowhere for him to go. The old Victorian street-lamps in Sloane Square glowed with a pale nostalgia. In his rear-view mirror he could see the red neon sign of the Royal Court, a garish assertion of modernity. The plate-glass bulk of Peter Jones reared up alongside him, closing off the view of Sir Hans Sloane's warm honey-coloured brickwork. All around, the London evening was beginning, edgy with excitement and apprehension. Some soldiers pushed one another through the gates of the Duke of York's barracks, eager for a night on the town. A few cars ahead, a black cab pulled out, executed its agile U-turn, and throbbed off towards Victoria. If only he could do the same: pull out of the traffic, take another direction, break ranks. His life was gridlocked. How long before he could retire? Too long. Put in for a transfer? Where would they send him? Even some fly-blown South American shit-hole would be better than this. He resolved to talk to C about it first thing in the morning.

VIII

'So what have you got for me today?' asked Sir John Mennis of his private secretary, trying to put some enthusiasm into the prospect ahead.

'Lunch, sir,' replied a dapper young man, placing a leather correspondence folder on the desk. 'With Bootles and Sicksmith. Apparently you promised them.'

'Oh God,' groaned Sir John. 'I'd forgotten. How I hate those Tribunes of the People. What do they want?'

'They say they want to talk to you about the review panel. They'd like you to sit on it, *ex officio*. Confer on it some measure of gravitas.'

'Collude in a witch-hunt, more like,' said C despondently. 'They're after Mars, aren't they?'

'Guy Mars is one of their agenda items, yes sir.'

'I'll meet with – what are their names?'

'Bootles and – '

'Yes, yes, I know. Book a table at the restaurant in Bleeding Heart Yard.'

'Very apposite, if I may say so, sir.'

'Yes. In more ways than one.'

Sir John liked to hold his business lunches in the restaurant of Bleeding Heart Yard, the tiny square off Hatton Garden made famous by one of his favourite authors, Charles Dickens. As he stepped from his taxi and entered the cobbled Georgian enclosure, he remembered the vivid portrayal in *Little Dorrit* of a wretchedly poor community, cruelly exploited by unscrupulous landlords. Now the gentrified yard contained nothing but a bistro and an expensive restaurant. He thought it a mildly ironic choice for entertaining Bootles and Sicksmith, who would be sure to wear their own bleeding hearts ostentatiously on their sleeves.

They were waiting for him in the dark basement of the little restaurant, at a tiny table crowded up against the establishment's fabulous wine collection, and carefully set apart from the other diners. Bootles, the younger man, was restlessly chewing bread. Sicksmith rose in greeting, Bootles hesitated, and Sir John waved for them to sit down.

'I'll have the steak,' he said peremptorily to the waiter who materialised at his elbow, 'with Bearnaise sauce. And a bottle of Croz Hermitage.'

The others ordered risotto, the wine was poured, and the little table cleared for business.

'Let's not waste time,' said Sir John, 'as we all know what this is about. I'll sit on your committee. If I die of boredom, you can put my obituary in the minutes. But on one condition.'

Bootles paused with a glass of water half-way to his lips. 'Condition?'

'You leave Guy Mars alone.'

Bootles slowly put his glass back down. Sicksmith looked uneasy. 'Mars is part of the problem, sir,' he said placatingly.

'Why do you have it in for him?' asked Sir John.

'He's no longer one of us. He's a wolf in sheep's clothing.'

'And you're the sheep, I suppose? That fits anyway.'

'Mars is just too arrogant to be a good field operative,' said Sicksmith in a mollifying tone. 'He's made serious mistakes, and taken unnecessary risks.'

'We need to bring him to heel,' added Bootles. 'He should be the people's servant, not their master.'

'You blame Mars for being too proud?'

'We're not the only ones who say it.'

'I don't suppose anything you say is exactly original. But your democratic conceit may be as dangerous as Mars's patrician pride. If we find ourselves in a tight corner again – and we may – we'll have need of men like Mars.'

'But that's all in the past, surely? Old soldiers don't always make good peacetime leaders.'

'Except for Churchill. And Eisenhower. And Khrushchev. Oh, I know the world has changed. Once we fought on battlefields, and our patriotism was written on the body in wounds. To you boys it's all black-and-white newsreels and old men's pub stories. But some wounds never heal.'

And hearts can bleed in secret, thought Sir John to himself.

'So you won't let us touch Mars?'

'I'll agree to send him somewhere quiet. Out of harm's way.'

'I think we can live with that,' said Bootles, looking at Sicksmith for agreement.

'I hope I can,' said Sir John, meditatively sipping at his Hermitage.

IX

The Review Committee was meeting in a room somewhere in the labyrinthine corridors of the Palace of Westminster. Mars had trouble finding it. Eventually he located the room, sat down on a hard chair outside, and waited to be called. Bored already, he glanced at his watch. Only 10.45. He was not sure how much more of this he could stand.

The door opened and a uniformed usher called him in. The committee was ranged along a panelled bench facing into the room, so they looked like a row of judges, or the members of a magistrates' court. The room seemed very drab and public sector, the acoustics harsh and reverberating. Everyone spoke in hushed voices. Mars took the seat offered to him, which faced the tribunal. He felt as if he was in the dock.

Sicksmith, who as Chair sat at the centre, welcomed him and began to explain the committee's brief. On one side of him sat Bootles, on the other Sir John Mennis, who gave Mars a sympathetic but rueful nod of recognition. The two other members of the committee were young female politicians, both strikingly ugly and dowdily dressed. They both stared at him primly over their oversized glasses. *De horribile visu*, thought Mars as he recalled the essential qualification for recruitment as a female scout at Oxford. He wouldn't have fancied being shaken awake by either of the two harpies who confronted him across the floor of the chamber.

'Mr Mars?' said Sicksmith. 'Do we have your attention?' He realised his mind was wandering, and tried to shake his thoughts into clarity. They began to ask him questions about his sphere of responsibility, his operational independence, his understanding of the chain of command. About budgetary control, accountability, risk assessment. About transparency, freedom of information, and public understanding of the service. He answered all their questions cautiously but reasonably. His eyes glazed over, and his mind focused on the large gin and tonic he would order as soon as he escaped from this ordeal. Sir John looked smug and confident, as if he thought Mars was acquitting himself well.

Bootles was growing increasingly restless at the easy ride Mars seemed to be getting. It was his turn to speak.

'Could I ask you, Mr Mars, to look at page 472 in your bundle?'

Mars didn't know he had a bundle, and looked round with mystification. The usher helped him by opening the fat folder in front of him at the relevant page. It contained a set of accounts, relating to one of Mars's covert operations in Paris.

'One of the things we're commissioned to scrutinise,' said Bootles, 'is value for money. Could you help us by explaining some of the entries in these accounts?'

Mars focused on the figures in front of him, which meant virtually nothing.

'For example next to the date 23 October, there is an entry for "subsistence". Total £2,500. Do you recall incurring that expenditure?'

His memory jogged, Mars recalled a memorable dinner in the Champs-Élysées where he had entertained three rather high-class prostitutes with an insatiable taste for champagne. While enjoyable in itself, the orgy had helped him to penetrate a network whose reticulations enfolded the notorious criminal who was his target. But how could be begin to explain all this to the white, acidic face of his interrogator? In the event, there was no need. As he considered his answer, Mars noticed a man slide up behind Sir John and whisper in his ear. Sir John immediately rose, said a brief word to Sicksmith and left the chamber. Mars had no time to wonder what it was all about, when the same man materialised behind him.

'There's an emergency, sir,' he whispered in Mars's ear. 'Mother wants you in her office immediately.'

As he threaded his way back towards the office, the change in the building's atmosphere was manifest. Phones were ringing, people moving about, voices raised in question and hushed in answer. Something was up. Emails were coming in, messages bouncing around the building, people hastily briefing other people. Was this the sign he had been waiting for? His senses quickened, his pulse beating faster, he took the stairs to his superior's office two at a time.

It seemed an eternity waiting for the red light over the big Regency door to go off. Mars sat on the edge of a hard straight chair, every fibre of his being keyed up with anticipation. At last the red light went out, the green one came on, and he stepped quickly over the Wilton carpet to turn the brass handle and open the big panelled door.

She was standing at the window, hands clasped behind her back, looking out over the park. Mars took a seat at the desk, noticing the unobtrusive figure of C in the corner.

'Sit down, Mars,' she said superfluously. The two men exchanged grimaces of covert camaraderie. They had escaped a common ordeal. Then both abruptly sat to attention as Dame Volumnia wheeled round, strode over to her desk, and assumed the chair. Was this indeed the call he had been waiting for: the flare cracking in the sky over no-man's land; the signal to attack? Did she have something for him?

'Have you heard of a man named Amadeo?' she began.

'Yes, of course,' replied Mars. 'Isn't he some European bigwig?'

'He's just become Supreme President of the Council of Europe.'

'Oh. Yes, that's it.' Mars tried to look impressed.

'Do you know anything of his background?' she asked testily.

Mars shrugged his shoulders. The personal history of Eurocrat politicians had never formed part of his jurisdiction.

'He's of northern Italian descent, but as a child was taken to Yugoslavia. Ostensibly he became president of some Eastern European republic,' she continued. 'But in reality he was a warlord during the Balkan conflicts. One of those guerrilla chiefs who carve out a territory and end up being a national leader. Recognised by the UN, and so on. His troops were more like a private army than a regular military force, with some very dodgy Serbian types. Crack soldiers, devastatingly effective in combat. Accused of atrocities and war crimes, but nothing ever stuck. Then suddenly he came out of the Balkans, reinvented himself as an Italian patriot and Europhile, and began to rise through the ranks of the European political elite. It's impossible to conceive that he did this without a massive programme of bribery and corruption. But again, despite floods of rumour and suspicion, nothing ever stuck.'

'It sounds as if he bought and sold protection at every level,' put in Mars.

'Exactly so. But for that very reason we can't get anything on him. Nothing but a continental conspiracy of silence.'

'The problem is not so much his background,' put in C from his shadowy corner, 'as his political programme. He stands for a European super-state, and he's virulently anti-British. Sees himself as restoring the ancient Roman Empire. Portrays us as a troublesome fragment broken off from the Continent. An obvious target for invasion, colonisation, reintegration. There's no better way to unify a state than by defining a common enemy.'

'But Europeans have talked that way ever since we seceded in the 1980s,' observed Mars. 'Nothing ever comes of it.'

'This is different,' said Mother decisively. 'This time, apparently, the political leadership has supreme control of the armed forces.'

'Our intelligence indicates that preparations for invasion,' put in C, 'from the shores of France, Belgium, Holland, are already well advanced. Troops and tanks are massed on the borders, and warships afloat to carry them. Once Amadeo has established control in the European capital – '

' – Rome,' added Mother, as if she was unsure of the depths of Mars's ignorance.

' – Rome, there'll be nothing to stop him. He'll obtain Council approval by whatever means he uses – terrorism, extortion, black-mail – and in a matter of weeks that'll be the end.'

'We could fight,' said Mars doggedly. 'It wouldn't be the first time.'

'Out of the question,' she snapped. 'This time there's no support from the States. No alliance with Russia. The Chinese would be watching and laughing. We'd be on our own. Think of 1066 rather than 1940.'

'Could we take him out? This Amadeo, I mean?'

'Did we succeed in assassinating Hitler? This will be a hundred times harder.'

'What then?'

'We negotiate,' said C. 'We bargain, we cajole, we bend over and take it. Agree to a provisional reintegration, retaining key powers in London. It's the only way.'

'Then if we're not going to fight,' said Mars carefully, 'either overtly or covertly; if we're not going to stand up to him, and we're not going to take him out; if it's all a matter of talk and concessions – then what exactly does if it have to do with me?'

A flash of irritation passed over Mother's face, and she glanced at C as if they shared some common embarrassment.

'Because,' she said, speaking with extreme precision, 'for some reason we don't understand, you are the one person Amadeo has agreed to negotiate with.'

'Me?' gasped Mars. 'Why me?'

'Your guess is as good as ours,' she said, sourly.

'That's why we asked if you knew him,' said C, sliding a photograph across the desk so it came to rest in front of Mars. No one spoke for some time. Mars stared at the photo with incredulity. Then he looked up and said in a strangled voice: 'You really must be joking.'

'Joking? Why?'

'Because ten years ago I drowned this man in the Trevi Fountain.'

X

His imagination raced back to that night in Rome when he had at last come face to face with his mortal enemy. He recalled, as if it were yesterday, how he had chased him through street after hot street, alley after umbrageous alley, past palazzos and monuments and statues of Rome's imperial dead, until finally cornering him in front of the baroque facade of the Trevi Fountain. His name then had

been Perfideo, a name more fitting than the beatific soubriquet he
had since adopted. Mars remembered glimpsing the moonlight
glinting on the blade of a knife as it struck viciously towards his
face, slashing his cheek and leaving a tell-tale scar. He had banged the
knife-hand aside with his forearm, and the blade tinkled harmlessly
on the marble rim of the fountain before splashing into the water.
Then Mars had hurled his whole bulk at Perfideo and smashed into
him, the two bodies bearing one another into the water with an
enormous splash.

The intricate Bernini sculptures, silvered even whiter by moonlight, had frowned down upon them as they grappled knee-deep in
the water, hand to throat, knee against groin, skull battering against
ringing skull. The water boiled around them in the flurry of their
fighting. They were evenly matched; Perfideo's short bulk against
Mars's loftier leanness, the Italian's training in Oriental martial arts
against Mars's commando instruction in ju-jitsu.

At one point Perfideo had his head pressed down against the stone
rim of the fountain, his whole weight crushing down on Mars's
throat, the life pressed almost out of him. The white sculptures of
gods and nymphs looked down on them with indifference. They had
witnessed so much cruelty and violence over the centuries: what was
one more death? But then with an immense surge of survival instinct
Mars kneed the Italian's bulk off him. The next moment his hands
were locked round Perfideo's throat and thrusting his bullet head
beneath the water. The face twisted from side to side, the mouth
contorted in a snarl of rage and fear, thick bubbles of air belching
from the nose. At last the body went limp, and Mars slackened his
grip just as the first police car roared into the piazza, lights flashing,
sirens blaring. Within moments the tiny square was full of shouting
policemen, but Mars had already waded through the fountain, leapt
over the wall and made off into the concealing shadows of Rome's
eternal night.

Before this climax, Mars had spent a year tracking Perfideo's
movements, gathering intelligence and establishing beyond doubt
the full extent of his underground criminal network, based on extortion, terror, and blackmail; his was a network that stretched from
Turkey to Portugal, from Hamburg to Palermo, and embraced the
whole of Europe in its labyrinthine web. At the centre of that web,

like a giant venomous spider, sat the arch-criminal himself, trapping ever more corrupt officials and timid businessmen in the sensitive but deadly interlacings of its myriad strands.

A quiet triumph had accompanied Mars's return to London, though the success of his mission could never be publicised. The death of Perfideo, global master-criminal and arch-enemy of England, passed into the annals of the Secret Service as one of its most notable achievements. At one stroke the head had been severed from an immense serpent. Mars's status as the most celebrated officer in the service was assured. Had he been a regular soldier, he would have been honoured with the highest military decoration. As it was, his reputation as the man who finally disposed of Guiseppe Perfideo was enough.

Now Mars found himself again staring into that dead face, now apparently fully alive, the man sprucely dressed in the Armani uniform of an assured and fashionable Eurocrat. To him the resemblance was unmistakable. The bald, domed skull; the strangely arched eyebrows and the black piercing eyes; the wide, rather feminine mouth, and the square jutting jaw. It could have been mistaken for a photograph of Mussolini. It was understandable that the similarity had not been detected. File photos of Perfideo had been blurry shots taken from a distance. Only Mars had been close enough to that evil face to have it imprinted indelibly on his memory.

Clearly the face had undergone some cosmetic alteration: the eyes were wider, the nose straighter, the mouth fuller. But there was no disguising the ugly shape of that bald head he himself had cracked against the marble rim of the Trevi Fountain; or the jut of that arrogant jaw he had held in the vicelike grip of his suffocating hands. There could be no doubt; this was a portrait of Perfideo, now Amadeo. Part Italian, part Austrian, Perfideo had been a product of Mussolini's fascist regime. Entering the movement as little more than a street thug with a reputation for extreme violence, rather like Mussolini himself, Perfideo had risen to a position of some authority in the *Duce*'s council. He won his military spurs in Abyssinia, showed an immense talent for political organisation, and was acknowledged as one of the architects of fascist Italy. When relations between Hitler and Mussolini soured, Perfideo adopted a low profile and began to play both sides. As Mussolini was being seized at the Swiss frontier by partisans, Perfideo and his men were fighting and bribing their way into Germany. As *Il Duce* was dangling upside down from a lamp-post in Milan, Perfideo was withdrawing towards Berlin in the company of a Wehrmacht division. It was among the smoking ruins of that beleaguered city that Perfideo disappeared. A few years later he surfaced in Rome at the head of a vicious gang of thieves, rapists, and murderers, born out of his wartime black-shirts, who tormented the war-torn city. In the space of a few years he had built a criminal empire that stretched beyond Italy and into the former fascist heartlands of Germany and Eastern Europe, and embarked on a programme of high-profile kidnappings, assassinations, and terrorist bombings that struck fear into the heart of Europe and brought Perfideo to the attention of the British Secret Service. After the summary executions of two British spies and the kidnapping of a British diplomat, MI6 sent Guy Mars to Rome with a simple mission: to find and kill Giuseppe Perfideo.

And now Mars had to come to terms with the facts that his mission had been a failure and his arch-enemy was not only alive, but once again threatening England with a different brand of violence and coercion. As his two superiors pieced together for him the whole story of Perfideo's strange disappearance and even stranger resurrection, he was forced to concede it was all true. Perfideo had been left with a spark of life still in him, enough for the expert resuscitation he received from members of his gang, who, impersonating police officers, smuggled him into a phoney ambulance and drove off into the night. The ambulance never reached a hospital, and Perfideo was never seen again. That part of Mars's reputation proved after all to be built on a lie. Now he had to face the prospect of living with himself as the man who failed to kill Giuseppe Perfideo.

'I thought I'd killed him,' he said softly.

'Yes,' said C, sympathetically. 'He must have survived somehow. Hidden away, reinvented himself and come back to life.'

'Incredible,' said Mother, glancing again at the picture. 'But true. Oh well. He's back now, with a vengeance. He's gone legitimate. And he's an immediate threat to the security of the realm. We have to deal with him. And he's asked for you.'

'He's asked for the man who almost killed him?' said Mars. 'It makes no sense.'

'Who knows?' said C. 'Maybe he wants to let bygones be bygones. Maybe he's mellowed with old age. Or more likely he knows you as one of the few people in the world for whom he has some respect. A kindred spirit, as it were.'

'Forget about the past,' she said brusquely. 'We're sending you. But not to succeed where, it appears, you failed before. Everything's different now. Perfideo was our public enemy number 1. But now we need to make Amadeo our friend.'

'Making friends isn't quite in my line, is it?' said Mars.

'We realise that,' said C. 'But we don't have a choice. Briefing will start immediately. You're to get over there tomorrow. It's a case of *buongiorno Roma.*'

XI

'Ladies and gentlemen, the Captain has switched on the seat-belt signs.'

Mars felt nostalgic for the old days of 'Please extinguish all cigarettes'. He swallowed the last dregs of his Chivas Regal to wash away the cold iron taste of the air-conditioning. Air travel had lost all its romance and become an antiseptic, regulated ritual for inter-national businessmen. As the plane began its descent into Fiumicino Airport, Mars looked gloomily out of the porthole and reviewed his position.

Amadeo had made it clear that that he would engage in diplomatic rapprochement with England only on condition that they send a delegation of one: Guy Mars, officer of the Security Service. Con-fronted by a show of overwhelming force massed on the shores of France, Belgium, and Holland, the English government had little choice but to capitulate to these demands. Boarding his plane at Heathrow, Mars had experienced what was for him the unusual sensation of trooping through Security with all the other passengers, since he had been allowed to carry no weapons, and so there was no need for any special clearance. He felt he was being sent naked into the conference chamber, or like one of the early Christians thrown to the lions in the Coliseum.

As the plane taxied to a halt, he reviewed his schedule of meetings and discussions, provided to him by his own service, but clearly dictated by Rome. Several days of meetings with minor officials, an appearance before a special committee, a speech to the European Parliament, every word written out for him. It all seemed straightforward, apart from the last day, which was mysteriously earmarked for 'Entertainment'. It was not clear when he would meet with Amadeo, whose name did not appear on any of the agendas. Mars wondered what kind of entertainment awaited him at Amadeo's hands.

He pondered for a while on the character of the man he was being sent to deal with. Though he felt all the natural animosity proper to a personal and national enmity, he could not help but admire this mighty opposite. While he himself had been born into a wealthy family, attended Rugby and Oxford, and grown up a member, albeit a wild and unruly one, of the English upper class, Amadeo had been littered in the dark backstreets of Milan by a *putana* who serviced Austrian officers in the north. While Mars had been playing a straight bat on the cricket field, Amadeo had been organising his fellow street urchins into gangs on the streets of Rome. To pull himself up from such a background to become the supreme leader of a European super state was nothing less than miraculous, and testified to quite extraordinary abilities. Mars felt almost guilty in his admiration for Amadeo. And not only admiration, but envy. Amadeo's sphere of operation in its perverse way rewarded talent, while Mars was suffocating in an England that did its best to destroy it. His spirit revived at the thought that he would soon again be grappling, albeit with unfamiliar weapons, with an enemy who was his equal. He felt like the knight in *The Seventh Seal*, laying aside his arms to play chess against Death. If Mars had to choose another identity, it might well be that of Giuseppe Amadeo.

XII

At 5 a.m. the next morning Mars sat at the desk in his hotel room, sipping from a hot espresso, taking bites from a croissant, and leafing through the briefing papers provided for him by London. He was habitually contemptuous of desk-bound pen-pushers, but he had to admit, as he read through the meticulously prepared documents, that they knew their stuff. By the time he stopped reading to shower and dress, he felt fully prepared for the challenging few days that awaited him.

The next few days were filled with a flurry of meetings, held in beautifully appointed rooms in the Palazzo Madama. He met with a succession of ministers, almost all silver-haired, impeccably dressed elderly men, assisted by an army of unnecessarily handsome younger men, all wearing the same dark suits and superfluous sunglasses. Negotiations seemed to proceed with remarkable smoothness, and his adversaries were surprisingly relaxed about England's position. Mars had to pitch a deal which incorporated England into the European economy while keeping her politically and judicially independent. These demands seemed to provoke no resistance, and Mars felt the whole process to be suspiciously easy. There was something going on he did not understand.

At the end of three days Mars felt exhausted, but the deal seemed to be done, needing only final approval from the President. On the evening before his meeting with Amadeo, Mars begged the night off. Glad to be out of the stifling atmosphere of talk-filled rooms, he strolled through the warm night to the Piazza Navona, enjoying a blissful cigarette and examining with curiosity the exquisite Bernini statues in the Fontana dei Quattro Fiumi. Beautiful young people strolled and chattered around him. Romance was in the air. This was the real Rome, and Mars hungered for a taste of its famous *Dolce Vita*.

He sat down at one of the alfresco restaurants and ordered seafood with a bottle of Soave. At the next table sat a strikingly beautiful young woman, with the ample curves, full lips, and dark sultry looks of a young Sophia Loren. She wore a sleeveless white dress that highlighted her tanned limbs. Was she alone? Stood up? A prostitute? Mars did not care. At that moment she represented for him all the *Dolce Vita* of which he had been starved for so long. He picked up his wine-glass and moved confidently over to her table.

Later in his hotel room, the white dress tangled on the floor with his shirt and trousers, Mars buried himself in the soft declivities of that young body, pressing his face between her breasts. She was a nymph from the Fontana dei Quattro Fiumi, and her coral-lined vagina was a fluted shell. But at the critical moment something in him failed, and he was unable to enter her. Urgently she tried to coax him, with soft lips and playful fingers, but nothing helped.

'What's wrong?' she asked.

'Nothing,' he said heavily. 'Too tired. Too old.'

She pursed her lips, shook her head, and pushed him on to his back. She cupped his face in her hands, touching the scar on his cheek left by Amadeo's knife. Then she fell to examining his body, running her fingers down the contours of his chest, until she found, under his ribs, a protruding scar left by a vicious bayonet thrust that had almost killed him in France. She seemed fascinated by this ugly gash with its tough lips folded outwards, this rupture in the otherwise smooth skin. She took his hand in hers, and put it behind her, tracing for him a line down her spine till he encountered an almost identical cicatrice in the exquisite concave curvature of her back.

'What's this?' he asked, feeling the rough raised welt of tissue that disfigured the velvet skin.

'I grew up in a tough neighbourhood,' she said simply. The she kissed him fiercely, pressing his hand on to the scar behind her, banging her teeth against his so violently his head rang with the impact. Shocked by the sensation of her injury, provoked by the violence of her attack, he found himself deep inside her before he realised. He kept his fingertips pressed against her scar as they sobbed their way, almost in pain, to a violent mutual climax.

As he drifted off to sleep, the sensation of touching her scar stayed with him, and in some strange way mingled with the feeling of his thumbs pressing against Amadeo's throat. He had been choked into feeling, wounded into love. He felt whole again, but it was a strange completeness that dwelt with damage, a paradoxical wholeness so intimately twinned with violence.

XIII

The next morning the girl was gone. He had not even paid her. Perhaps she had achieved a similar fulfilment from their violent encounter. He had the impression that she had rifled through his personal effects, but nothing was missing. It didn't matter: he carried no secrets with him. He put her out of his mind, and prepared at last to meet with Amadeo.

At 9 a.m. a limousine collected him from the hotel and slid smoothly along the Corso d'Italia towards the Monte Sacro. Mars had no idea where they were going. Eventually the car pulled off the road and into a broad driveway protected by wrought-iron gates that had been opened by tough-looking guards with shaved heads and black uniforms and carrying automatic weapons. No doubt some of Amadeo's old comrades from the Balkans.

They drove through formal gardens, landscaped in an unmistakably English style, with classical statues posted along the route for decorative rather than ritual effect. At the top of the drive, Mars was surprised to see a huge renaissance palace, clearly little more than a hundred years old, but modelled on some ancient Roman temple. Something caught at his memory: a night of impenetrable blackness, marching troops, searchlights fingering the sky. Then it struck him. He had been here before, carrying a message from the front. This was the Villa Torlonia, Mussolini's official residence, and afterwards the headquarters of the Allied Command. And now it was the private home of President Amadeo! And nobody seemed to think anything of it.

The limo deposited him at the foot of a white marble staircase leading up to the front door. Uniformed servants greeted him and led him into the interior. The place had the contours of a neoclassical palace, the conveniences of a modern residence, and the heavy, gilded vulgarity one associates with the house of a Victorian banker. At the rear of the palace was a grand terrace overlooking the park, and here Mars caught his first glimpse of Amadeo, standing in front of the marble balustrade, hands clasped behind his back and looking outwards. The figure had broadened over the years and so seemed shorter, but the head was still shaved and brown from the sun. Mussolini must have stood in exactly this pose, staring outwards, looking for new lands for Italy to conquer. Hearing Mars's approach, Amadeo turned and greeted him with relaxed affability.

Together they strolled along the terrace, then down into the meticulously maintained gardens of the villa. At first Amadeo talked easily about the house and its history, about Italian food and wine, about the beauty of the women. He seemed anxious to know if Mars liked horses, and if he possessed any skills in their exercise and management.

'You ride, of course. Have you ever handled horses in a team?'

Years ago on an assignment in France, Mars had had to master the art of harness racing, and had even competed in the famous Prix d'Amérique. Amadeo seemed pleased, though not especially surprised.

The villa was impressive enough, and provided a faint echo of Roman splendour. But it was nothing compared to Blenheim or Chatsworth or any number of great English houses. Mars felt that Amadeo was keeping back something special as the climax of this tour. And he was right. As they rounded a corner, Mars found himself inside the courtyard of a large stable block, from which came the knock and clatter of horses against wood. With manifest smugness Amadeo introduced Mars to the best collection of horses he had ever seen. Each one was an Arab thoroughbred of magnificent proportions, long in the fetlock and beautifully arched in the neck.

'They're splendid,' said Mars, who could not resist the attraction of fine horses. He stopped in front of a huge white stallion that seemed to fill the stall it stood in. He looked like an equestrian statue, or a creature from myth.

Amadeo felt his admiration. 'That is Pegasus. He does not run, he flies. In the next stall is his friend, Aldebaran.'

'"The follower",' said Mars.

'Ah, you know Arabic! Exactly. They are a pair. Pegasus has strength and velocity. Aldebaran is the guide, the steadying hand. You see? Speed and precision. A perfect team. But come, we must have something to drink to seal our bargain.'

They returned to the terrace and sat down to an excellent bottle of Montepulciano. It was time for business. Mars was the first to break the ice.

'I hope you don't mind the obvious question. Why me?'

'You get straight to the point!' laughed Amadeo. 'So un-Italian. Let me explain. You know as much of my background as anyone: you know my character, my intellectual powers, my organisational ability. I'm sure you would not be naïve enough to draw a line between criminal and legitimate actions: they are separated only by convention. This world respects only success, and cares little how it is achieved. In my long career I have found very few men I would regard as anywhere near my equal, in cleverness, in strength, in persistence of will. Among those few, Mr Mars, you stand out as *primus inter pares.* The fact that you almost killed me testifies to that. An inferior mind would see that as a ground for animosity. For me it is a basis for respect. And because I hold you in such respect, I have requested your participation in something I have planned.'

'That is all very well,' put in Mars, 'but are we not here to conclude the business between England and Europe?'

'Yes, yes, I have not forgotten. I know you are a gambling man, Mr Mars. I am offering you a wager. The stake is our agreement. If you beat me, the deal is yours, with all concessions granted. If I beat you, then all bets are off. England will capitulate or be crushed. Are the stakes too high for you?'

'And what game are we playing?'

'A chariot race. Here, let me show you something.'

Amadeo led Mars into an ante-room off the terrace, panelled in white stucco and adorned with elaborate gilded mirrors. At its centre stood a table covered by a white-painted balsa-wood architectural model.

'This,' said Amadeo, 'is the Circus Maximus. I have rebuilt it.'

Mars drew nearer to take a look. He recognised the distinctive bagatelle board shape of the old Circus, remembered from his school history books. Everything was in place: the outer walls, the track, the central structure, the thousands of seats. The Circus Maximus, Rome's great hippodrome, arena for the famous chariot races that drew thousands of spectators. Opened as little more than a racetrack by Tarquinius Priscus, developed by Julius and Augustus, it was finally built in stone by Trajan. Mars had noticed, as he was driven from the airport, that the site, a dreary public park, had been surrounded by hoardings concealing some construction work. So now Amadeo had raised the Circus to its former marble splendour. Once again the ancient arena would echo to the thunder of hoof-beats and the squeal of iron wheels; once again the crowd would roar with joy or disappointment as a star driver won or lost; once again the laps would be counted off by the seven bronze dolphins dropping one after another from the old *spina*. It was genius. It had been erected to glorify Italy; to highlight the power and prestige of a new European Roman empire; to establish the supremacy of its new Emperor. And it was for Mars to facilitate Amadeo's triumph, and to taste the dust of defeat, more humiliating than death itself.

'The day after tomorrow the Circus will again be opened to the public. Once again Rome will have its great sporting arena back. The opening will be celebrated with a chariot race between you and me. If you accept my challenge, of course.'

And he has gone completely insane, thought Mars to himself. Yet what devilish brilliance in his madness! Amadeo had brought into politics the terrifying megalomania of the criminal mind. Like one of Shakespeare's tragic heroes, Macbeth or Richard III, his ambition knew no bounds. He was after all another Mussolini, another Stalin, even another Hitler. And what an efficient trap he had sprung on England!

He had chosen Mars, clearly to feed an ancient grudge. But how much sweeter was revenge practised against a whole nation! Mars: a prominent public figure and war hero, naturally selected to represent his country; but one who was also deeply hated by many of his countrymen. To lead him into a situation where the fate of the nation rested on his shoulders, and then to dare him to a contest he could hardly refuse, in which he would have the opportunity of displaying those very characteristics that had made him a hero. If he declined, it was failure for him, and disaster for the nation. If he was beaten, as it was clearly intended he would be, it was humiliation for him, and the end for both. There was no other option but to accept. To call Amadeo's bluff, and to defeat him in this bizarre competition, or die in the attempt.

'You leave me no choice,' said Mars. 'I'll do it.'

Amadeo pursed his lips and acknowledged the admission as a compliment. 'I will lend you my best horses,' he said.

'I'll take Pegasus and Aldebaran.'

'You are no fool, Mr Mars,' said Amadeo with a laugh. 'You will have all day tomorrow to practise in the Circus. On the following day we will stage a grand opening ceremony. Our race will be the main event. The whole world will be watching. I wish you good luck, as one sportsman to another.'

'Thank you,' said Mars. 'May the best man win.'

XIV

There was sweat in Mars's palms as he held the leather reins and gently manoeuvred his horses towards the starting line. The sun was already risen above the great white walls, and even now, in mid September, the heavy Roman heat was beginning to build. Beyond the white flanks of his horses he could see the yellow dust of the track stretching, it seemed, interminably towards the first bend. The stadium was packed with an already noisy crowd. The imperial box, first established by Augustus himself, was filled with dark-suited VIPs, the uncrowned heads of Europe. The world was watching.

On the previous day Mars had taken charge of his chariot and horses and spent the whole day mastering them. The chariot was beautifully designed, made of titanium, modelled to look like ancient bronze, and with light steel wheels edged with hard rubber. His team of horses ran together superbly, with Pegasus setting the pace and Aldebaran steadying his gallop. After a few erratic circuits, Mars had the hang of the business, and by the end of the day had run several of what he considered acceptable laps.

To vociferous cheers from the crowd, Amadeo also edged his chariot to the starting line. The chariots seemed identical, but Amadeo's horses were two huge black stallions, obviously pedigree racehorses, that had not been shown to Mars in the stables of the Villa Torlonia. Mars's spirit quailed at the sight of horses, that looked literally unbeatable.

There was no time for nerves, however, as the preparations for the race were complete. A flood of Italian buzzed from the PA system, and the arena hushed with expectation. Mars tensed his body, holding the reins lightly, and fingered the ivory handle of the long riding crop he would prefer not to use except as a last resort. Amadeo stood in his chariot, squat but straight, leaning back slightly, while Mars was crouching forward. Seconds later Mars realised the prudence of his opponent's stance, since a gun fired loudly, and the spooked horses all shot forward in an uncontrolled rush. Mars was thrown off balance by the sudden velocity, while Amadeo held his position and shot into the lead.

It took a matter of moments for Mars to recover, but it was enough to put Amadeo ahead by almost half a lap. He rounded the bend and disappeared. Mars pulled himself together and shook the reins to urge his horses on. The chariot accelerated and took the curve easily. Amadeo's lead was reduced by a few metres. As the first bronze dolphin dropped in token of a complete lap, Mars had closed the distance and was close behind his rival's spinning wheels.

Through three more laps the chariots kept the same distance. Amadeo leading by a length, Mars tried to overtake on the inside, but Amadeo held him off. Again on the outside, and again Amadeo prevented him. He noticed that Amadeo was slashing his horses mercilessly with a long leather whip. At last on the fifth lap Mars began to gain on his rival. Amadeo's horses were tiring from being ridden too hard, and the superior stamina of Pegasus and Aldebaran was beginning to count. Slowly Mars edged forward so the wheels of the chariots were running in unison. At the first bend Mars swung his chariot outwards, touched Aldebaran's flank lightly with his crop, and swung round the bend to overtake Amadeo.

Now the succession was reversed, and it was Mars's turn to hold the lead, which he managed to do through the first straight of the sixth lap. If he could hold it for another lap, he would be home and dry, his reputation restored, and England would be safe again. He willed his horses forwards, and swept magisterially around and into the penultimate lap.

But now Amadeo was closing with the desperate urgency of a man facing unexpected defeat, lashing his horses into a fury. He drew abreast of Mars's chariot, on the outside, and steered his own wheels so close they were almost touching. Above the thunder of hooves Mars heard a strange metallic click, and automatically glanced downwards at the hub of Amadeo's nearside wheel. A sharp steel blade had protruded from the boss and was edging its way towards the spinning spokes of Mars's left-hand wheel. Mars pulled violently on his right-hand rein and Aldebaran immediately guided the pair away from the deadly probing barb. The chariot was clear, but Mars had lost precious space and Amadeo was once again in the lead.

They were on the final lap now, and it was Mars's last chance. He took it on the first straight, keeping well away on the outside but sweeping ahead till the teams were almost level. Ferociously Amadeo lashed his horses, which were running wildly, their black flanks whitening with dried sweat, their red eyes bulging in terror. Pegasus and Aldebaran were running easily, with a little speed still in reserve. But as the chariots rounded the last bend, Amadeo leaned out over the rim of his chariot and lashed violently at Mars with his heavy whip. A long slash drew blood from his arm, and another stripped flesh from his shoulder.

The whip was cracking towards his face. Instinctively Mars grabbed the lash and pulled with all his strength. Amadeo lost his footing as his horses slewed around the bend, and slid over the rim of his chariot on to the track. Mars felt an impact against his wheel, but had no time to look back. Amadeo's horses, riderless now, slowed down, panting with exhaustion, and Mars's team sped effortlessly past the finish. Heaving on the reins, he stopped the chariot in front of the imperial box. The crowd was silent. This was not the result they had expected.

Dark-suited officials gathered round to congratulate him with a certain degree of embarrassment. With a huge trophy in one hand and a signed copy of the treaty in the other, Mars was ushered quickly from the stadium. A messenger leaned close and whispered in his ear:

'President Amadeo has sustained some slight injuries and is in need of medical attention. He regrets he will not be able to bid you farewell.'

xv

'Welcome home, Guy.'

As Mars walked into the office, Sir John Mennis slapped his hands together in vigorous applause that was taken up with genuine enthusiasm by most of the assembled crowd. 'Ladies and gentlemen,' called C, 'I give you the hero of the hour. England is safe again, thanks to him.'

Mars shook hands briefly with the minister, and found himself facing Mother, who looked very elegant in a black Chanel suit and gleaming white pearls. She leaned forward and offered a cold cheek for him to kiss.

'Welcome back, Guy. We're truly proud of you.'

Champagne corks popped, suited men he hardly knew slapped him on the back, a camera flashed. A tide of relieved enthusiasm eddied round him. Bootles and Sicksmith stood at the back, unwilling to join in, but afraid to reveal any disapprobation.

'Here he comes,' said Bootles bitterly. 'The prodigal son. All the past forgiven and forgotten. Can you smell the fatted calf?'

'I never eat veal,' replied Sicksmith sourly. 'This doesn't change anything. He's done his job in the field, OK. But now he'll be expected to come in from the cold. Let's see how that works out for him.'

As the minister began a long speech, Sir John edged closer to Bootles and Sicksmith, carefully sizing up their body language.

'I'd keep quiet if I were you,' he said.

'Of course,' said Sicksmith. 'We're only thinking about the future.'

The minister droned on. 'He proved himself the best man in the field . . .'

'At least we have a future,' observed Sir John.

'And Mars needs to be part of it,' replied Bootles.

' . . . alone he entered the gates of the city . . .'

'Let's allow him his day of triumph, at least.'

Bootles and Sicksmith lapsed into a gloomy silence. The minister was rounding off his peroration:

' . . . till we called both field and city ours, he never stood to ease his breath with panting.'

The party broke up, and people began to return to their offices. As Mother and C escorted the minister out to his waiting car, a few of the mutinous citizens from the Peace Camp were lounging on the street corner.

'We must do something for him,' the minister pronounced in a loud voice. 'Bring him in. Some promotion perhaps. Do you have a job for him?'

'We'll find something,' she said.

The peaceniks watched the big car slide noiselessly off towards Trafalgar Square.

'Do we have job for him?' Sir John asked her as they re-entered the building.

'Of course,' she replied shortly. 'Yours.'

XVI

Sir John's retirement was announced the following day, and shortly afterwards the rumour leaked that Mars was to be offered the post of Deputy Director. Once again Mars found himself facing Mother across her desk, this time with what was, for him, a far less attractive offer on the table between them.

'Do you think I'm the right man for the job?' he asked. 'I'm a field operative, not an analyst. And certainly not a manager.'

'You'll be my deputy,' she said crisply. 'I'll take care of the managing. Your key duties will be strategy and communications. Including PR.' She pressed a button on her intercom.

'PR?'

'Yes. You'll need to liaise with Bootles and Sicksmith. And of course you'll be speaking regularly to the people via press conferences.'

The door opened, and Bootles and Sicksmith came in.

'Can I request, madam, that part of the job be delegated? I'm not really one for courting public favour, and exhibiting my wounds to the crowd.'

'But the people must be given the opportunity of hearing us, and giving their feedback,' put in Bootles as he took a seat. 'They won't allow any exceptions.'

'You boys can do it,' added Sir John. 'We don't need to press the matter. Take the job, Guy. Take the honour that goes with your form.'

'He'll have to be there,' said Mother decisively. 'But you two can do most of the talking.'

Mars coloured slightly and shifted his position on the chair.

'Just to be clear, madam – and Sir John – there are some things I'm not prepared to do. I won't go before the people and brag about my exploits. I won't tell them I did this and that on the battlefield. I won't exhibit my unaching scars, as if I'd got them in *their* service. I'd rather be a public servant in my own way, than service the public in theirs.'

'Do you see what we mean?' said Sicksmith quietly to Sir John.

'Let's take it offline,' said C. 'You two: you know our position. But to you, Deputy Director: all joy and honour.'

Outside Bootles and Sicksmith descended the marble staircase, heads close together like conspirators. 'You see how he intends to use the people?' protested Bootles hotly. 'To get his promotion by standing on their shoulders, and then to kick them in the face.'

'Well, let's make sure they're fully informed,' said Sicksmith. 'Kindle this dry stubble, and we'll light a blaze that will darken him for ever.'

XVII

A press conference was arranged to announce the appointment of the new deputy director. The room was crowded with media personnel, press photographers, and representatives of popular organisations, including Tramp-head and Trotsky from the Peace Camp.

Mother entered, followed by Mars, Bootles, and Sicksmith, and all took their places on the podium. Mars wore his dress uniform of black tunic with white belt and peaked cap. He towered over the others, looking every inch a soldier. Cameras flashed and microphones bristled from the crowd.

Seated at the back, Trotsky and Tramp-head whispered together.

'You know if he just appeals to his service,' observed Trotsky, 'they won't be able to resist him.'

'Well if he's prepared to incline towards us,' Tramp-head replied, 'we'll accept him. Why not? Let's see. They're starting.'

Dame Volumnia opened the proceedings by announcing Mars's appointment as the new deputy director of the service. Mars thanked her, and promised to do his duty. A smattering of applause greeted his very brief speech of acceptance.

Sir John had planted a couple of conservative journalists who offered tributes to Mars's war service, congratulated him on his victory in Rome, and warmly endorsed his appointment. The room grew restless: this was not what most of the delegates wanted to hear. This was not news.

A woman journalist from the *Mirror* asked how many children Mars had killed during military operations. A *Guardian* columnist asked if Mars was thoroughly committed to the principles of equality and diversity in recruitment to the service. Another interrupted with a question about freedom of information: how much classified data would Mars be making public?

As the cameras flashed and the crowd muttered irritably, Mars's aquiline profile hardened, and a faint touch of anger coloured his face. At last Trotsky stood up and launched into a rambling speech in which he accused Mars of having no love for the people, and demanding that he make a personal statement declaring his commitment to democracy. Mars merely shook his head and looked down at the backs of his hands.

'His scars speak for him,' said Mother.

'Then let him show them!'

She pressed a button, and on a screen behind them flashed up a picture of a man's back, with two livid slashes etched across the shoulder. 'Is that enough for you?'

'No, no. You can't see his face. It could be anybody. Let him strip now, and show his wounds.'

The mood had grown ugly. The majority now swung behind the anti-war protestors, and were vociferous in demanding from Mars a public display of subservience to the people.

Mars rose to his feet and stood for a moment, as if he meant to speak. Then he removed his cap and placed it on the table. He took off his jacket and hung it on the back of his chair. The room was hushed in expectation: he was going to show his scars! But with a slight smile of contempt, Mars turned, walked off the podium, and made his way out of the door.

There was immediate uproar. The journalists all rushed off to file their stories. Bootles and Sicksmith gathered round Mother, who sat stony-faced and silent.

'My office,' she said. 'Now.'

Out in the corridor Mars walked deliberately to his office, collected his coat and briefcase, and made for the exit. C met him at the street door.

'Guy, please. Wait a moment. This is how it's done. Other men like you have managed to swallow it.'

'Not me,' said Mars shortly, and walked through the door and out on to the marble steps.

'She will have no choice but to fire you!' C shouted after him.

'Too late,' said Mars over his shoulder. 'I've fired *her*.'

XVIII

'What do you think?' asked Mother.

'It's just as we predicted,' said Bootles. 'He's a loose cannon, and he's gone rogue. Just walked out of the building.'

'He's an enemy to his people,' added Sicksmith, 'and his country.'

'What do you think he'll do?'

'We think he'll join Amadeo. It's his only option if he wants any kind of revenge.' She looked sceptical. 'We've been keeping tabs on him.'

Bootles produced a file and placed it in front of her. Inside were photographs of Mars and Amadeo, taken from a distance, both looking relaxed and amicable.

'That was his job.'

'Was this part of his job too?' asked Bootles, revealing a photo of Mars at a café table, in close conversation with a beautiful young girl.

'Who's she?'

'One of Amadeo's agents.'

'I expect he fucked her. Wouldn't you? Do you have anything else? Any *hard* evidence?'

'Well,' said Sicksmith, clearing his throat in embarrassment, 'we do have this. Which isn't corroborated. But it's very incriminating.'

He slid a sheet of paper over to her, and she read it quickly. It purported to be the transcript of a telephone conversation in which a voice that sounded like Mars promised to work for Amadeo against England.

'Oh Christ,' she said. 'Is this the best you can do? I suppose you got top marks in the fourth form for writing crap like this.'

She swivelled her chair towards the window and gazed for a while at the waving brown and yellow tree-tops of St James's Park. She seemed to come to a decision.

'All right. What can we do? Pull him in?'

'Not a chance. It would be a national scandal. Make us look ridiculous.'

'Then what?'

'There's only one solution. A final one. Elimination. We'll just make him disappear.'

'Do you have a man up to the job? Mars is the best we have.'

'Not quite. We suggest using Cassio. He trained with Mars. His record is equally good. And he dislikes Mars intensely. Apparently Mars took some woman away from him in Turkey.'

'But Mars will know him.'

'All the better. That will give us an element of surprise. Just long enough to put him off his game.'

'How will he feel about eliminating a fellow agent?'

'We've used him before. He was the one who took out Castle.'

Castle had been a defector, a high-profile agent turned by the Russians. Cassio had pursued him into East Germany and pushed him under a train.

'When?'

'Tonight if possible. It will need your authorisation.'

'Get me the papers and I'll sign them. See if you can think of anything else. Approval of elimination only in the most extreme circumstances. Let's rid ourselves once and for all of this turbulent spy.'

XIX

Mars sat by himself in a small basement bar off Leicester Square. It was 2 a.m. The place smelt of stale smoke. The red plush hangings were threadbare, the gilded mirrors faded and foxed. Behind the bar a morose barman with an immense moustache and sad eyes was cleaning glasses with a grimy towel.

Mars stared into the depths of his whisky, and then lit another cigarette. He felt this was the end for him, but didn't know how it would play out. As he motioned for another drink, he noticed the barman glance up, heard someone else enter the bar, and checked automatically in the mirror. Through the fog of alcohol he felt a stir of recognition. The newcomer was small man in a black belted raincoat and a big trilby hat, with a round baby face and circular glasses. He looked like a cartoon anarchist. Mars watched him in the mirror as he drew up a stool and ordered a Scotch. As he picked up the glass, Mars remembered. Cassio.

The two men had trained together, but Mars had never liked him. Part of this dislike arose from the fact that Cassio always beat him in target practice. But there was also something perverted about Cassio, a certain cruelty and enjoyment of another's pain. He was notoriously brutal towards women, which was one of the reasons Mars had stolen his Anatolian mistress and smuggled her away on the Orient Express. Mars was vaguely aware that Cassio was always being sent on operations in remote places, popping up unexpectedly in Kashmir or the mountains of Bora Bora.

One of the reasons Mars had survived so long in his dangerous profession was that however drunk he became, his instinct for danger never failed him. Everything about the appearance of this man was wrong. The bar used to be a haunt for men in the service, but not for a long time. And Mars hadn't seen Cassio in years.

Cassio glanced across at him shyly, and mimed recognition.

'Mars, isn't it? Haven't seen you for ages. How are you keeping?'

'Well enough. Still with the old firm?'

'In a way, yes. Other duties, you know. Top secret.'

Mars talked with him for a while, deliberately slurring his speech and fumbling with his cigarettes.

'Need a piss,' he said thickly, and heaved his weight off the barstool. He walked slowly and carefully, losing his balance slightly and leaning against the bar to steady himself. He walked up to the door marked Gents, and acted a moment of confusion over which way the door opened.

Once through the door, he darted down the steps that led to the lavatory. He knew the geography of this place intimately. A urinal on the left, toilet stalls on the right. In front of him, against the wall, two sinks, and between them the door of a cupboard he knew was always kept unlocked and which opened outwards. In seconds he was through, crouching in the darkness among the toilet rolls and bottles of bleach, his eye glued to the keyhole.

A few minutes later he saw the door to the Gents open, and a squat black Beretta with a long silencer slide round the edge, followed by Cassio's face. Holding the gun level, Cassio crept in, and looked underneath the cubicle doors. Then he began to walk down the line of cubicles, his movements precise and methodical, pushing at each door gently until he reached the last one. As he neared the end of the row, Mars tensed his muscles. Having eliminated all but one cubicle, Cassio leaned forward to open the last one with the gun pointed and ready. Simultaneously Mars banged at his cupboard door with his shoulder and burst it open. The door slammed into Cassio's arm and unbalanced him. Mars hooked his right foot behind Cassio's leg and with a clenched fist struck at his face. Cassio went down on his back, but his gun hand whipped into position and a bullet punched into the ceiling. But Mars had thrown himself sideways onto the floor, avoiding the shot, grabbed Cassio's shooting arm expertly in a self-defence grip, and with a vicious twisting tug dislocated his shoulder. An elbow to the throat choked Cassio's scream, and Mars snatched the pistol from his nerveless grip.

Cassio pulled himself into a sitting position against the wall. Standing back to avoid the still potentially lethal hands and feet of his fellow assassin, Mars levelled the gun at a point between his eyes, and said softly:

'Who sent you?'

'Piss off.'

Coolly Mars put a bullet into Cassio's left knee. Blood spurted and bone shattered. The other man stifled a howl of pain.

'Again,' said Mars, pointing the gun at the other knee. 'Who sent you?'

Cassio's face contorted with pain. 'You know as well as I do, you bastard.'

Mars shot him in the other knee, and now Cassio could not repress a shriek of agony.

'Stop, stop. Please. No more. It was her. It was Mother – '

Without hesitation Mars put a bullet between his eyes. The contents of Cassio's head painted the wall behind him.

Stuffing the Beretta into his belt, Mars left the Gents, closed the door on the carnage within, kicked open an emergency exit and slipped away into London's perpetually illuminated darkness.

XX

It was a grey morning, and Soho's seedy vitality was just beginning to stir. A homeless man in a sodden fur cap was picking over rubbish from a skip in the gutter. A young uniformed policeman guarded a barrier outside the entrance to the little bar in Old Compton Street. He pulled himself to attention as Sir John flashed his ID and led Dame Volumnia, with Bootles and Sicksmith in train, into the bar. The legs of the dead barman protruded from under an upturned table. One by one they processed down into the Gents' lavatory. Mother looked distastefully around the white-tiled space, sordid with splashed blood, and at the corpse of Cassio sprawled at her feet.

'So he was our best man,' she said with dry derision.

Sir John stood beside her and eyed the scene critically.

'Impressive. Tortured first, to get him to talk. Then execution.'

'What next?' said M of Bootles, who stood in the doorway looking ill.

'We could send someone else,' tried Sicksmith.

'And let Mars work his way through our entire list of specialist agents?' she said with asperity. 'We'd be a laughing stock.'

'But he'll know you sanctioned the hit,' observed Sir John. 'You'll be his first target.'

'Do you think I don't know that?' she said testily. 'We'll have to contact him. Appeal to his better nature.'

'Let's hope he still has one.'

'Face to face. Find him, wherever he is, and we'll follow him there. Start with Rome. Fix it. Will you, C?'

'I take it I have my old job back?' asked Sir John.

'Don't push your luck,' she returned, as with incongruous regality she swept out of the urinal.

XXI

Guy Mars sat alone at a window table in a little restaurant near the Ponte Sant'Angelo. Across the road he could just see the grey waters of the Tiber lapping sluggishly around the piles of the old bridge. In the distance the dome of St Peter's hovered through a fine sunlit mist.

His appearance had altered. His iron-grey hair was black and cropped, making the lean face look younger. The eyes were concealed behind big Tom Ford aviator sunglasses. He wore a black polo shirt with a lightweight black suit and soft leather shoes. In short, he looked Italian, so much so that no one in the restaurant gave him a second glance, or wondered why his unwavering gaze kept such strict watch over the street outside.

He had ordered grilled sole and a carafe of Frascati. The fish tasted muddy and the wine sour. Perhaps it was his own despondency that had stripped all flavour from the food.

He was thinking of those Romans who over the centuries had sat alone, and felt much as he felt now. Of Antony after Actium, all his imperial dreams hanging in tatters in the tangled rigging of Cleopatra's retreating sails. Of Brutus at Philippi, his Republican honour dwindled to the irrefutably self-directed point of his own sword. And he thought of Shakespeare's Coriolanus, that tragic Roman hero who probably only ever existed in the pages of history and on stage; betrayed by his country, abandoned by his friends, choosing a self-imposed exile among strangers and enemies, rather than submit to the unbearable humiliations of democracy. How was it he described himself? 'Like to a lonely dragon, heard and talked of more than seen.' The Tiber waves slapped lazily at the old stones of the Ponte Sant'Angelo, resolutely indifferent to the sufferings they had witnessed over the centuries.

He thought of the world and all its slippery turns. Of people who had been sworn friends, so close they seemed to share a heart, but who had fallen out and become the fellest of foes, kept awake at night by the gnawing passion of revenge. And was not the converse equally a law of human nature? By an alchemy equally perverse, deadly enemies could become dear friends and intertwine their issues. It was so with him. His motherland hated him, and so his love grew crescent for this enemy town. Eternal city; cradle of civilisation; graveyard of ambition. Hard autumn sunlight glanced against Michelangelo's perfect dome; traffic snarled past on the Lungotevere degli Altoviti; and Guy Mars came to the conclusion, as he tossed back the vinegary dregs of his Frascati, that there was nowhere left for him to go.

Except the one place he had never expected to enter: the territory of betrayal, of defection, the unquiet resting place of those who have turned. He would become a traitor to his country, an enemy of the state, eternally an outcast from the peace and protection of England. A lonely dragon. He had crossed a border, and there was no way back. So be it. They had taken everything from him: his dignity, his pride, his self-respect. They had sought to compel him into a conformity that warped his very nature, bruised his essential soul. And they had tried to kill him. She had done it all: the she-wolf, his 'Mother'. He would never forgive her; and he would enter into league with her enemies rather than endure another day of this unbearable separation. Better to reign in Hell, than serve in Heaven.

XXII

Chalk-white moonlight cast fantastic shadows from the poplar trees as Guy Mars slipped over a high wall and into the grounds of the Villa Torlonia. He still wore the same dark suit, but with the addition of a black balaclava helmet, so his face was invisible in the shadows. His right hand grasped the black Beretta with its long silencer, his left, a slim pencil torch.

He crouched in the bushes and listened for sounds of alarm. On the lawn behind the house, statuesque and still in the moonlight, a huge Doberman pricked its sharp ears and snuffed the air. Scenting the man, with a deep low growl it charged towards him. Mars shot the dog between the jaws with the silenced Beretta, and its body skidded to rest at his feet.

A door at the back of the house opened and yellow light spilled over the lawn. The silhouette of a man appeared and looked round for the dog. Hearing nothing, assuming he was off chasing a rabbit, the guard went back in and closed the door behind him.

Remembering the geography from his recent tour of the house, Mars stole through the shrubberies and across the lawn towards the room he knew to be Amadeo's bedroom. Then choosing a window to the left of its big bay, he eased it open with his commando knife, silently raised the sash, and crept through. The dark little room was an ante-chamber to Amadeo's bedroom. Placing his ear to the door, Mars could hear breathing. Two people.

Gathering his senses together, he tried to recall where the light switches were in the bedroom. Just to the left of the door. He was ready. Now or never.

In one fluid movement he kicked open the door, swept his left hand down the wall and flooded the room with light. He could see Amadeo's short tanned body lying naked on the bed, his flaccid penis lolling over his muscled thighs. Beside him lay a woman with harsh blonde hair, smudged red lipstick, and pendulous naked breasts. They had thrown off the sheet after making love in the hot night.

The woman woke first and stifled her scream as she met the cold eyes of the intruder staring at her through the slits of the balaclava. Mars put a finger to his lips, and she gingerly sat up and folded her hands in her lap. Meanwhile Amadeo stirred, sprung awake, and moved to grab something from under his pillow.

'Stop.' Mars's voice cracked through the room, and Amadeo's hand was arrested in its journey. 'Easy. Toss the gun and sit up facing me.' Amadeo's sleepy eyes focused to see the muzzle of the Beretta pointed at his face. He carefully drew an old Luger from under the pillow, and dropped it beside the bed.

Mars let himself down into an armchair and rested the gun on his knee, the barrel trained unwaveringly on Amadeo's chest.

'You'll never get out alive,' said the Italian.

'Granted,' replied Mars. 'But it's you I'll be following down the road to Hell.'

Footsteps were heard from the corridor and there was a light, nervous knocking at the door.

'Everything all right, Signor Presidente?'

Mars signalled to Amadeo to give the all-clear. Amadeo hesitated, then called out. 'It's fine, Guido. A nightmare. Nothing to worry about.'

Footfalls retreated down the corridor.

'Who are you?' asked Amadeo with real curiosity. 'I can see you're a professional. But what do you want with me?'

'I haven't come here to kill you,' Mars replied.

'I assume not, or we wouldn't be having this conversation.'

'Exactly. So listen to me for a few minutes.'

Mars stripped off the balaclava and revealed his face.

'You!' said Amadeo.

'The same. Guy Mars. You know me as someone who's caused considerable damage to your organisation. Twice I've risked extreme danger, and spilled my own blood, in the hope of shedding yours. I've done all this in service to my thankless country, and you should hate me for it. But my name has become even more hateful to my own ungrateful people. They've forsaken me, and let the rabble chase me out of England. It's this extremity that has brought me to your bedroom and disturbed your – rest.'

He glanced at the woman, who stared back at him with eyes of raw sensuality, and squeezed her arms inwards to push out her breasts. 'All right then, your recreation.'

Mars paused for a moment as if to gather his thoughts. 'Mother tried to have me killed.' Amadeo raised an eyebrow in mild surprise. 'This is the last place I'd come to save my life. If I feared death, then I'd give you a wide berth. So I'm here more to spite my banishers than to solicit your protection. It's my turn to make you an offer. Let my misery serve your turn. Harness my resentment to your own benefit. I'll fight against my rotten country with all the hatred of a devil from the bottomless pit. So here I am,' said Mars resignedly, placing his pistol on an elaborate bronze and ormolu table beside him. 'I've always been your enemy. Why should you let me live? Call your guards and they can take me. Or let me join you, and give me a shot at those who hate me more than you do.'

Amadeo rose from the bed, pulling the silk sheet around him like a toga. His eyes were moist and his face shone with that charisma that had drawn so many to follow him.

'Guy,' he said. 'Guy. You noble thing! Your words have dissolved my hate. Let me twine my arms about you.' He stepped towards Mars and seized him in a tight embrace. 'So many times I've tried to break this body,' he murmured, touching Mars's shoulders gently with his fingertips, 'but it always proved too tough. If I'd struck you with Achilles' spear, the splinters would have scarred the moon. You were the anvil to my sword; I honed myself on your hardness. Our fighting souls have been twinned in eternity since the dawn of time. But now hate turns, with equal passion, to love.'

Mars had never been embraced by a man before, and was disturbed by the unfamiliar sensation. Amadeo's hands slipped upwards behind him and caressed his shoulder blades. All the while the woman stared at the two men, her lips parted. It occurred to Mars that she might be hoping to participate in this strange violent passion between two men.

'You see this woman,' said Amadeo. 'My desire for her has burned me like a fire. There are times when I can't get enough of her body. But holding you here in my arms makes my rapt heart dance with a joy I've never felt before.'

Mars disengaged himself slightly from Amadeo's embrace. 'I truly want to be your friend,' he said, 'but your Italian passion is a little too much for me.'

'Of course, of course,' said Amadeo placatingly, and stepped away from him. 'Don't worry, I'm no sodomite. Not with men, anyway.' And he leaned across the bed and rolled the woman over to expose her beautiful rounded rump, which he slapped lasciviously. Seeing Mars eyeing her with evident appreciation, Amadeo nodded towards her and asked: 'Would you like – ?' Mars shook his head with a laugh, and Amadeo shrugged ruefully. 'Another time, maybe.' Then with a salacious camaraderie, 'Now we are friends, we must share everything!'

Then he stripped the sheet from his body and threw it over the woman. Going over to the closet, he pulled out some clothes and began to dress.

'Do you remember when we fought in the Trevi Fountain? You've no idea how often I've replayed that combat in my dreams. In my sleep, we've been down together, fisting each other's throats. A hundred times I've had you down, my foot on your neck, watching you lie helpless at my feet. Then I'd wake each day to the knowledge that there was one man I could never defeat. But enough of the past. Let's breakfast together and plan our future. You,' he said brusquely to the woman, 'Get dressed and make yourself scarce. Go do some shopping. Tell the guards to get breakfast for two. And – ' to her retreating back as she went into the bathroom, fetching on her way a sly smile at Mars, ' – be back tonight. And bring a friend. In fact, bring two.'

He put an arm round Mars's shoulder and led him to the window. In the distance across the park, the rounded hills rose into the lightening sky.

'I tell you Guy, beyond those seven hills there lies an army that will roll England's crown in the dust. I hoped to see you blown to fragments in my first bombardment! But now I'll give you command of half my force, and together we'll advance on England like a flood. We'll take your island as an osprey takes a fish.'

XXIII

A morose silence separated Dame Volumnia and Sir John as they sat together on the chartered jet as it wheeled over the Golfo di Napoli and headed for Fiumicino.

C was leafing through his briefing papers.

'You know they've made Mars Supreme General of the European Army under Amadeo?'

Mother shrugged herself deeper into her coat, and didn't reply. They had had to pull many strings and call in old favours to get clearance for their entry. Security was visibly tightening up throughout Europe, and England's diplomatic credit seemed virtually bankrupt. She was under the impression that their free passage was brokered by the Foreign Office, but C guessed only Amadeo himself would possess the authority to let them through. He wondered what kind of trap they were flying into.

XXIV

President Amadeo stood on the bonnet of an OF-40 tank, parked in front of the Arch of Titus in the shadow of the Coliseum, and addressed his troops. His resemblance to Mussolini had now entered the phase of outright imitation, since he wore a black fascist cap, baggy trousers, and high leather boots. Even his gestures, the arms flung outwards and then folded in, the rebarbative jut of the jaw, even the pose on top of the tank, irresistibly recalled *Il Duce*. Beneath him the big Fiat engine growled with subdued anger.

In the open turret of the tank, his face concealed by a padded helmet and goggles, stood Guy Mars. In his early years of service he had been a tank commander, and had been among the first Allied vehicles to enter Rome at the liberation. He felt elated to be back where he belonged, a soldier, under orders but in command of his own destiny, dedicated to his mission.

The tank's blunt snout faced an apparently infinite recession of ranked infantry, all dressed in black uniforms and steel helmets, all listening intently to their commander's words. This mobilisation before the ancient ruins of the Forum was more symbolic than necessary, since the forces arraigned to invade England were already in position along the entire length of the Channel, from Dieppe to Hamburg. The strategy was to attack simultaneously at so many points that England's defences would be hopelessly overstretched.

Amadeo finished his oration with the clenched fist salute he had reintroduced. A thousand men responded in kind. They were ready to roll. Out through the old gates of the city; north along the Via Appia; across France, as the German armies had marched in 1940; an inexorable advance designed to terrorise little England into abject submission.

Mars's head ducked down into the turret of the tank and the iron door clanged shut behind him. But as he slipped the tank into gear and eased it slowly forward, some commotion in the front rank opposite prompted him to brake and stop his advance. Some of Amadeo's senior officers were disputing about something. An old man was trying to push his way past them to reach the President . . . suddenly as he peered through the tank's observation slit, Mars recognised the dapper figure of Sir John Mennis being roughly seized and held back. All the while his voice was remonstrating angrily about diplomatic privilege and the Geneva Convention.

'I tell you, when your General hears of this your lives won't be worth living. I've been like a father to him, he's my beloved son ... Let me through! Let me through!'

Amadeo jumped down from the bonnet of the tank, strode up to Sir John, and stared him in the face. 'Let him go.'

The old man's arms were suddenly released. C carefully straightened his tie and returned Amadeo's stare with the unabashed confidence of an old man.

'Sir John Mennis, senior representative of the Government of England,' he stated formally.

'You're English, then?' asked Amadeo.

'I am, as your General is.'

'Why then,' laughed Amadeo, 'you should hate England as much as he does! Is this the best your country can do: send a decrepit old man to defend her? I suppose you're all that's left, when you've pushed out of your gates the very man who would have defended them! Given your enemy your shield! Do you think your feeble breath can blow out the fire your country is destined to flame in? Get back to England. Prepare for your execution.'

'If General Mars were here now he'd listen to me. He'd treat me with respect.'

Amadeo's face took on a look of cunning. 'You think so? Suppose I told you that he is here? And that he's heard every word you've said?'

Sir John fell silent, and stared around for some sign of Mars's presence. The door of the tank opened and Mars stood up in the turret. He removed his helmet and goggles and revealed himself.

'There he is!' cried Sir John, lurching towards the tank and placing his hands on the bonnet. 'O my son, my son. Guy! You're preparing fire for us. Let my tears quench it. Hear me, please, Guy. Hear me.'

'He knows no father,' said Amadeo. 'He's become a perfect man, a kind of nothing. He has no title, till he can forge himself a name in England's burning ruins.'

'Is this true, Guy? Have you turned so far against us?'

'You're no father to me,' said Mars harshly, 'and I'm not your son. My loyalty lies elsewhere. Be gone. My ears are stronger against your pleas than your gates against my force. Away with you!'

Sir John bowed his head as if in mourning, and then stepped back from the tank. He seemed to be waiting for something. Amadeo looked critically at Mars, as if gauging how deeply Sir John's words had affected him. Mars's face remained expressionless until suddenly he spotted someone coming forward through the ranks, the soldiers stepping aside as if in respect. Mars's mouth opened in surprise as he saw approaching him an old woman, her elderly face pale in the bright sunshine. Her clothes were as smart as ever, but her white hair was in some disarray. Without cosmetic assistance her face revealed to him its true geography of wrinkles and lines. Her bones seemed thin. Above all, she appeared to Mars as he had never seen her before, frail. That was it: frail. And it was that weakness that made his seated heart knock at his ribs, and his eyes blur with unaccustomed tears. Frailty, thy name is woman.

Dame Volumnia approached the tank, stood under the huge 105 mm cannon, and looked up at him. He fought back his emotions and looked sternly back at her. So my heart can melt too, he thought to himself, after all. Damn it. Am I a sheep to follow the instincts of the herd? I'll stand alone, as if a man were author of himself, and knew no other kin.

'Don't ask,' he said aloud, his voice forced and harsh. 'Don't ask me to disband my troops, or capitulate again to your bureaucracy. And don't tell me my behaviour is unnatural. This is my nature now.'

'You were always the best of them, Guy,' said M in a clear voice. 'My best agent, my best officer. I was always proud of you, even when you disappointed me. I treated you as a son. I loved you like a mother.'

'Is that why you tried to have me killed? Mother?' he replied bitterly.

'I had no choice, Guy, I swear. You must know that. Any mother would rather see her son dead at her feet than see him live in shame. Now you've left me nothing to love, nothing to believe in. How could I rejoice again in your victory, when it would mean defeat for my own country? How can I defend my country's good, when her success would mean your death? What a choice! To have you captured and executed as an enemy of England; or to cheer at your triumph as you tread on England's ruin.'

She shivered as if from cold, though the day was already warm. 'I've said what I came to say. You've already denied me the one thing I'm here to ask. I'll go back home and wait for you there.'

Mars was silent for some time. Then he heaved himself out of the tank, strode across the bonnet and jumped down to stand in front of her. He took one of her leaflike hands in his, and gazed at her in silence. Almost in a whisper, he said: 'O Mother! Mother! What have you done? You've won a happy victory for England. But for your son – believe it, O believe it – most dangerously you have provided.'

Then still holding her hand, he spoke aloud: 'Amadeo, I cannot proceed with this war. But I can negotiate,' he looked to Dame Volumnia, who nodded in consent, 'a convenient peace. Would you not do the same if you were me?'

Amadeo shrugged, as if the matter were of some indifference to him. Privately he was delighted at the outcome. To observe Mars's compassion conflicting with his duty refreshed his hopes. 'Out of this,' he said to himself, 'I'll revive my former fortunes, and set my foot on Mars's neck.'

XXV

It was the following day, Mars had delivered to Amadeo a treaty conceding England's sovereignty to Europe, and all military operations had been suspended. Amadeo sat on the terrace of the Villa Torlonia with three senior officers of his army, a lieutenant general, a major general, and a brigadier. They were discussing what to do with Guy Mars.

'So what's your reaction?' the lieutenant general asked Amadeo.

'I'm like a man poisoned by his own charity. I've nurtured a viper in my own bosom. And he's stung me half to death.'

'If I read you correctly,' said the major, 'we can deliver you from your present danger.'

'But he's a hero of the people now,' remonstrated Amadeo. 'They see him as a saviour, the winner of a bloodless victory.'

'As long as there is tension between you and him,' said the brigadier, 'the people will remain uncertain. But if one of you falls, the survivor becomes heir to his loyalty.'

'I know it,' said Amadeo bitterly, 'I've got every reason to strike at him. He came begging to my door, and I took him in, made him a partner. Gave him all his own way. Helped to build his reputation, till I seemed his follower, not his equal.'

'So you did, Signor Presidente,' said the major. 'We couldn't believe it.'

'And now he's betrayed me,' said Amadeo. 'He's sold us down the river, pawned our labour, spilled our blood. Therefore he shall die. And I'll renew me in his fall.'

Instinctively they all raised their glasses in a silent toast.

XXVI

'Mr President! Heads of the European nations! Elected representatives of the European states!'

Mars was addressing the European Parliament. He stood at a lectern, while Amadeo as President sat on a raised dais behind him next to the elderly leader of the house.

'I stand here still your soldier,' Mars continued. 'I feel no more love for my own country than I did when I accepted your commission. Still I serve under your great command. Let me advise you that I led your armies to a costly confrontation, yet returned a victor, with no drop of blood spilled in the enterprise. I have brought you home a prize worth infinitely more than the cost of its acquisition. We have made peace with honour. A treaty signed, with all your requisitions duly delivered, lies before you!'

'Don't bother to read it,' cut in the harsh insulting tone of Amadeo's voice from behind. 'But tell the traitor in the strongest terms how he's abused your powers.'

'Traitor,' gasped Mars, turning round. 'How?'

'Ay, traitor. Sovereign Heads of State, he has betrayed your business and given your city, Rome, to his "Mother"! He's shredded his loyalty like a piece of rotten silk. Smashed his oath like a baby's rattle. Then whined and roared away your victory.'

'Ye gods!' shouted Mars.

'Don't mention them, you big cry-baby!'

'Liar! Slave! Call me a baby? I appeal to you: do you hear his manifest lies? Remember when I beat him in the chariot race, and left my wounds upon him? Who do you believe?'

'Order, order. No more of this,' cried the querulous elderly voice of the leader. 'I will clear the chamber.'

'God strike me dead,' cursed Mars. 'Baby! Bloody your swords upon me, men and lads. Baby! Lying bastard. Look to your own history, if you've written it truly. How like an eagle in a dove-cote I fluttered your Romans in the Circus! Alone I did it! Baby!'

'Have you not heard enough?' cried Amadeo. Boos and jeers began to rise from the assembly.

'Let him die for it!'

'Tear him to pieces!'

'He killed my father!'

'Gentlemen, gentlemen,' cried the Leader, 'no more outrage, I beg you. The man is noble, and must have a fair hearing. Mr President, step aside. Keep the peace.'

'I'll show you peace,' shouted Amadeo. 'I'll hack him to pieces. Let me at him.'

'Villain!' shouted Mars, clenching his fists. 'Traitor!'

'Kill him!' yelled Amadeo.

A volley of shots rang out simultaneously and echoed thunderously around the walls of the old chamber. Mars clutched at his chest, crashed forward on to the lectern and fell to the floor. Immediately Amadeo stepped over to him, placed one of his feet on Mars's chest, and shot him in the head with a 9 mm pistol. A shocked silence gave way to hubbub.

'For God's sake ... in the Senate House! ... no one has the right ... arrest them ... arrest them.'

'Senators!' cried Amadeo, holding up his hands in a gesture of conciliation. 'Hear me speak.'

'This chamber is for speaking, not for execution! How dare you?'

'Senators, Heads of State, representatives of the people,' Amadeo shouted above the tumult. 'If you only knew the danger this man represented, you'd rejoice to see him cut down. If I am to blame, let me endure your heaviest censure. But let me declare myself your loyal servant, and explain why this man had to die.'

'You will answer for this,' cried the Leader, but his voice quailed as the tall figures of Mars's three murderers came and stood in front of him, their pistols in their hands.

'Arms in the Senate! Peace, for God's sake, peace!'

'Take up the body,' shouted the Leader, 'and bear it hence. We must mourn for him.'

'If he is innocent,' Amadeo cried disarmingly, 'we will mourn for him.'

'And if he is guilty,' added the Leader, 'let's say he sinned with honour.'

Ripples of opinion swept through the assembly, but fear and uncertainty robbed them of decision.

'Murder in the house! Which of us is safe? ... If he was a danger, Amadeo was right to kill him ... We'll have to make the best of it.'

'Mr President,' the Leader appealed to Amadeo. 'We must restore order.'

Amadeo was staring at the corpse of Guy Mars, as if transfixed.

'I am struck with sorrow,' he said, in a hollow voice of disbelief. 'Take him up, Comrades. Bear him in solemn procession. Trail your rifle-butts. Though he harmed me, and my injuries are still fresh, yet shall he have a noble memory. Here, let me help.'

Together the killers of Guy Mars picked up his lifeless body, and between them bore it slowly through the hall. As they passed, some members of the assembly crossed themselves, some bowed their heads, some even reached out to touch the nerveless fingers of a trailing hand that dangled lifelessly from the bier.

XXVII

And so Guy Mars, who made himself a nameless nothing, denied all kinship, and acted as if a man were author of himself, attained at last, at least, a kind of popularity.

PART IV

CHAPTER 7

Shakespeare and 9/11

Shakespeare's encounter with the world-changing events of 9/11, when Islamic terrorists piloted two planes into New York's World Trade Center, killing some 3,000 innocent people, could be described as a secondary collision following the primary impact of that tremendous and terrible atrocity. The attacks of 9/11 soon came to represent an extensive typology of collisions: the 'clash of civilisations' between East and West; the unstable boundaries between war and peace in our contemporary world; the destructive violence that potentially underlies western values of liberty and peaceful co-existence. In the aftermath of the attacks, people turned to Shakespeare's poetry for general reflections and observations on violence, or revenge, or the meanings of tragedy. But these were little more than symptomatic cultural reflexes. On the face of it, 9/11 seemed to have little to do with Shakespeare, and Shakespeare seemed to have little to say about 9/11.

A few years later, in 2005, a group of American Shakespeareans, led by the late Douglas Brookes, began to take forward a project designed to address two major questions: does Shakespeare have anything of value to tell us about events such as 9/11? And has 9/11 changed the way in which we read, see, and interpret Shakespeare? Eventually this initiative bore fruit in the form of special issue of *Shakespeare Yearbook*, with the title *Shakespeare After 9/11: How a Social Trauma Reshapes Interpretation.*[1] The diverse critical and creative responses included in this volume, from critics and philosophers, theatre practitioners and poets, suggest that Shakespeare may have anything or nothing to do with 9/11. As one contributor, Christopher Pye, puts it, the call on scholars to engineer a collision between Shakespeare and 9/11 seemed both inevitable and random:

'Shakespeare after 9/11': it is difficult to imagine a call to engagement for Shakespeareans more urgent, unrefusable even, and more perfectly gauged to induce paralysis. I am thinking of the status of the event itself, suspended as it is at this point in the middle distance between trauma and narratability. At that awkward interval, it is hard to escape the sense that any entry to the question will be a forced one. How can we forge a correspondence here, get text to answer to event, event to text? This is the difficult condition of any occasional criticism (and in the end what criticism is not occasional?). But the problem of rhetorical force is obviously heightened in relation to a circumstance so charged with the ongoing consequence of repercussive violence. So one feels compelled and one hesitates. (p. 171)

It is less a matter of inviting Shakespeare to observe along with us, as in a timeless theatre or a protracted rerun, the slow and terrible collision that was 9/11, as it is a matter of introducing two different sets of particles to one another in the Large Hadron Collider of the literary imagination. The project of *Shakespeare After 9/11* was an experiment in the true scientific sense: it tested and analysed, objectively and rigor-ously, the data derived from the exercise of placing together two entities that need not necessarily ever have had anything much to do with one another.

I

In Robert Louis and Fanny Stevenson's burlesque novel *The Dyna-miter*, a terrorist plot is hatched to plant a bomb in Leicester Square. The objective of the terrorists is carnage and fatality: 'the seats in the immediate neighbourhood are often thronged by children, errand-boys, unfortunate young ladies of the poorer class and infirm old men – all classes making a direct appeal to public pity, and therefore suitable with our designs'. The choice of target, over any other crowded spot in London, is determined by the fact that the square contained (as it still contains) a statue of Shakespeare: 'Our objective was the effigy of Shakespeare in Leicester Square: a spot, I think, admirably chosen ... for the sake of the dramatist, still very foolishly claimed as a glory by the English race, in spite of his disgusting political opinions.'[2] The statue is a stone copy of the marble effigy, commissioned by public subscription, executed by Peter Scheemakers, and erected in Westmin-ster Abbey in 1741. In its original time and place it functioned to commemorate the pre-eminent genius of English culture. But it was also a signalling of Shakespeare's official reception into the structures of national authority and power, constituted by church, state, and monarchy.[3] A suitable target, therefore, even in its displaced locus of London's West End, for a terrorist bent on symbolically assaulting the imagery of British imperial power; and killing a few innocent people in the process.

The American equivalent of the Leicester Square statue of Shakespeare stands in New York's Central Park. This bronze effigy was partly funded by a historic benefit performance of Shakespeare's *Julius Caesar* at the Winter Gardens Theatre on 25 November 1864, in which Cassius, Brutus, and Antony were played by the three sons of actor Junius Brutus Booth. The performance was interrupted by an unsuccessful attempt on the part of Confederate conspirators to set fire to New York by igniting several hotels, one of which was next to the theatre. A few months later John Wilkes Booth assassinated President Abraham Lincoln in his box at Ford's Theatre in Washington, DC, shouting, clearly in memory of Julius Caesar, '*Sic semper tyrannis*'.

In both fact and fiction, the smoke and flames of terrorism have often lapped close to Shakespeare, who seems to wear in alternation two masks, that of the smiling tyrant, and that of the saturnine conspirator; with one hand inviting the terrorist's bomb, with the other inspiring the political assassin. Whose side is he on? On 19 March 2005 an Islamist terrorist drove a car bomb into the Doha Players Theatre in Qatar, killing himself and the play's director, Jonathan Adams, during a performance of Shakespeare's *Twelfth Night*. Here Shakespeare was attacked in fact, not fiction. But since we cannot enter the mind of the terrorist, except imaginatively, we can only guess at what exactly it was that was being attacked.[4]

There is abundant evidence of Shakespeare being deployed in the interests of state violence, an enlistment that endorses the idea that his work is implicated with global capitalism, and potentially plays into the hands of insurgents. Mackubin T. Owens, Professor of Strategy and Force Planning at the US Naval War College, suggested that Henry V's speech of threatening before Harfleur should have been used in Iraq as propaganda to discourage support for Saddam Hussein: 'This speech should be printed in Arabic on leaflets and dropped on Baghdad, Basra, and especially Tikrit.'[5] This is the context in which Shakespeare's *Henry V* is distributed free to US troops in the Middle East as one of the revived 'Armed Services Editions' of pocketbook classic texts that were initially distributed to soldiers during the Second World War.[6]

Shakespeare can also be invoked as an authority in the dropping of more than leaflets. In a famous advert in the *Armed Forces Journal*, Royal Ordnance, world-renowned British supplier of defence systems, claimed to have 'helped protect The Globe [theatre] in 1588' against the Spanish Armada. Today Elizabethan nationalism is very much a thing of the past, and the company's remit is the global theatre of international conflict. Like the Arms Dealer in Sulayman Al-Bassam's *The Al-Hamlet Summit*, Royal Ordnance supplies weapons to anyone who will buy.[7] In the year this advert appeared, the company was exhibiting, despite an ostensible arms embargo against Iraq, at the Baghdad Arms Fair.[8]

In the world of terror Shakespeare seems to be a double agent, a man 'to double business bound' (*Hamlet* 3.3.41).[9] When British Muslim Moazzam Begg was incarcerated in Guantanamo Bay, from whence he was released without charge, he was given Shakespeare to read, as an alternative he thought to the Qu'ran, and as a substitute for the clearly unacceptable Bible.[10] But Ismael Beah relates how, when serving as an enslaved boy soldier in Sierre Leone, engaging in unthinkable acts of terror and atrocity, his kindly lieutenant would read to him from Shakespeare passages deemed supportive of their bloody cause.[11]

We might consider these examples marginal to mainstream criticism and reception of Shakespeare, perverse expropriations from which no literature is ever immune. But there are grounds for arguing that Shakespeare could be a natural target of terrorism, since Shakespeare is a constitutive element of the 'culture of violence' that helps to sustain state power (and which of course, in the eyes of those against whom it is directed, amounts to 'terror'). If Shakespeare is used as a front for state violence and terror, then is he not in the front line of the war against terror? If that equation exists, then we should seek to understand it. The question raised here is not whether terrorism involving innocents is ever morally justifiable (it is not), but whether or not a better understanding of what motivates terrorists might help to identify and eradicate the sources of terror. In other words we can try, wrote Rowan Williams after 9/11, 'to act so that something might possibly change, as opposed to acting so as to persuade ourselves that we're not powerless'.[12] Or as Noam Chomsky observed of the same events, we can react to such 'major atrocities' in two ways: 'we have a choice. We can express justified horror; we can seek to understand what may have led to the crimes, which means making an effort to enter the minds of the likely perpetrators'.[13] Getting into the minds of terrorists might seem a daunting task, and one that many would justifiably repudiate. After all, the terrorist has made no attempt to get into the minds of his (or her) victims. In a much quoted article on 9/11, Ian McEwan argued that such empathy with the intended victim would render terrorism impossible.

It is hard to be cruel once you permit yourself to enter the mind of your victim. Imagining what it is like to be someone other than oneself is at the core of our humanity. It is the essence of compassion, and it is the beginning of morality. The hijackers used fanatical certainty, misplaced religious faith, and dehumanizing hatred to purge themselves of the human instinct for empathy. Among their crimes was a failure of the imagination.[14]

The 9/11 hijackers were instructed to kill their preliminary targets, members of the aircrew, as cleanly as possible so as to avoid the distraction of another's pain. 'If you slaughter, do not cause the discomfort of those you are killing, because this is one of the practices of the prophet.'[15]

But what choice do we have in the face of monstrous 'atrocity'? We can live with terrorism, seeking to protect ourselves; we can declare war on it and hope to defeat it by violence; or we can try to reach a better understanding of it, as a necessary part of the long and difficult process of finding peaceful co-existence in a common world.

II

Terrorism is of course a contested term, which eludes definition, and tends to be applied indiscriminately to very different manifestations of violence.[16] The US State Department, Department of Defense, and FBI use three different definitions; and terrorism has been used as a label for the poisoning of food in supermarkets; aggressive currency speculation; obscene phone calls; pornography and rape. Terrorism can be understood as political violence: 'Terrorism, in the most widely accepted contemporary usage of the term, is fundamentally and inherently political.'[17] But this is also disputed in contexts where there seems to be little direct connection between the violence and any constructive political programme it purports to serve (late nineteenth- and early twentieth-century anarchism for instance, or the Oklahoma City bombing). Many would assert that terrorism is not a form, but a failure, of politics.

When the late Osama bin Laden called America a 'Christian crusader terrorist state', he was not simply inverting the derogatory. The modern understanding of terror as a political weapon derives from examples of state terrorism, initially the Reign of Terror in revolutionary France: violence used by the government against its own citizens. The revolutionary state sees this as necessary action against counter-revolution: Robespierre justified terror not just as an unavoidable expedient, but as a form of justice.[18] But by the later nineteenth century, when Russian populists assassinated Tsar Alexander II, terror had become the name for political violence used by dissident groups against the state. This could be violence against the state's representatives, as in targeted assassination (the extreme right-wing Russian group Narodnaya Volya tried to avoid civilian casualties); or indiscriminate violence against innocent people, as in Irish Fenian and anarchist bombings. The objective might be a simple *coup d'état* or regime change: Narodnaya Volya wanted to establish a constitutional government. Or it might be a more general intention to disrupt, subvert, and disorganise the state: to expose its weakness, show its true colours, provoke its 'latent fascism'. In these latter cases it is often particularly difficult to see the link between the act of violence and what its perpetrators hope to achieve, between the putatively justifiable means and the desired end.

The only constant is the eponymous ingredient of terror. Terrorist methods have always entailed 'the deliberate evocation of dread'.[19] The term can be misapplied, but it is not inappropriate. Terrorists set out to cause fear: fear within the civilian population, the armed forces, the officials of the state itself. Fear is the primary message of terrorism. This has been the case since the origins of terrorism with the Hindu Thugees, the Muslim Assassins, and the Jewish Sicarii, all terrorists *avant la lettre*. The production of terror may involve deliberate provocation of fear in the victim: we see this in recorded and broadcast threats and enactments of ritual murder, where the manifest dread of the victim facing decapitation is intended to exhibit the power of the captors, and to exert the pressure of compassion on those capable of influencing policy (for example, by releasing prisoners, withdrawing troops, and so on). The Thugees valued their victims' fear, and offered it as a sacrament to Kali. Or the victims may simply be targeted for death. Here the objective is to kill rather than frighten: one example would be the Lockerbie bombing, which seems to have been an act of revenge aimed at the death, not the terror, of the victims. Perhaps even 9/11 itself, motivated as it was by revenge, and aimed at a high casualty count, maximum destruction, and the predictable campaign of reprisal. Strategically 9/11 may have been designed simply to draw America into Afghanistan, from which inhospitable terrain the Mujahideen had successfully expelled the Soviet Union, and in which our troops are still dying. But fear is still involved, even if momentarily among the victims, and certainly more permanently in those who witness the terror. Terrorism is, as Jurgensmeyer puts it, 'the public performance of violent power';[20] power that can be measured by the dread the terrorist can make his victim feel. Words can mean what they say: fear is the primary message of terrorism.

When modern terrorism began as state terror, the term was adopted by leaders of the revolutionary state. Terrorism now is a name we give to dissident groups and individuals, not a name they accept themselves. When terrorism was widely used by nationalist and anti-colonial movements after the Second World War, its perpetrators called themselves freedom fighters, liberationists, guerrillas, not terrorists. IRA captives demanded to be classed as prisoners of war, not common criminals. Only the Jewish Stern Gang in Israel accepted (and then only informally) the nomenclature of terrorists. But all these groups used terrorism as a political weapon, often successfully, in Algeria, Kenya, Cyprus, Palestine. They were terrorists to the British or French colonial powers, but freedom fighters to themselves and their supporters. The state claims the monopoly of violence and moral authority; the terrorist appropriates the one, and tries to reclaim the other.

No liberal democratic state would admit its actions to be terrorism, although in extreme circumstances such states have performed acts that have been called 'terrorist'. States that are based on terror, such as Nazi Germany, declare their own illegitimacy by the embrace of such methods of rule. But suppose, as some have argued, the strategic Allied bombings of Cologne and Hamburg and Dresden, and the atomic explosions over Hiroshima and Nagasaki, were uses of illegitimate violence (in other words, prohibited by international convention), in the absence of legitimate power (ground forces capable of taking Berlin or Tokyo), against innocent civilians, and designed to provoke dread and horror. The charge is mitigated, but not dispersed, by the unscrupulous illegality of the Axis powers.

Terrorism is normally understood as political violence used against the state, since the state is viewed as sole custodian of the monopoly of legitimate violence. But clearly there are overlaps here. The difference between terrorism and war is that war is bound by rules on civilian immunity, the treatment of prisoners and so on (rules disregarded during the Second World War by Germany and Japan). Terrorists systematically violate those rules, while simultaneously claiming to be at war. On the other hand liberal democratic states have been known to transgress international law. Was the invasion of Iraq in itself legal? In doing so they trespass on the dangerous ground of terror. The US military responses to 9/11 against Afghanistan and Iraq adopted the tactic known as 'shock and awe' from the book by Harlan K. Ullman and James P. Wade, Junior, *Shock and Awe: Achieving Rapid Dominance*, which recommends for rapid military success the infliction of 'a level of national shock akin to the effect that dropping nuclear weapons on Hiroshima and Nagasaki had on the Japanese'.[21] 'The battle plan,' said a Pentagon spokesman, 'is based on a concept developed at the National Defense University ... it focuses on the psychological destruction of the enemy's will to fight rather than the physical destruction of his military forces.' 'We want them to quit. We want them not to fight,' adds Harlan Ullman, 'rather like the nuclear weapons at Hiroshima, not taking days or weeks but minutes.'[22] The term 'Ground Zero', previously a technical term for the effects of an explosion above ground level, first entered common currency to define the impact of the atomic bomb on Hiroshima.[23]

The other important consideration when reflecting on contemporary terrorism is the relationship between terror and religion. The terror born in France in 1793 was the secular terrorism of state violence that formed the underside of the Enlightenment. But 'before the nineteenth century, religion provided the only acceptable justification for terror'.[24] Dissident terrorism also embraced predominantly secular political goals throughout the nineteenth and most of the twentieth centuries, up to about

1970, even where religion had some part to play (as it did and does in Ireland, Israel, Palestine). Today terrorism is thought of as inseparable from religion.[25] The Thugees, Assassins, and Zealots were religious terrorists, engaged in holy terror. The Thugees killed their victims as sacrifices. The Assassins often carried out their murders at holy sites on feast days; they too saw their operations as sacrificial, and as admitting them to Paradise. The aim of the Zealots was a Jewish theocracy purified of Roman rule. Today's terrorism has come full circle in returning to the religious roots from which it originally sprang. Religious terrorism is not only very dangerous, since its perpetrators consider themselves directly answerable in the last instance only to God, and regularly court martyrdom; it is also very 'difficult to comprehend'[26] for a secular political culture. Destructiveness on the scale of 9/11, we might say, requires the apocalyptic scope of a religious imagination. 'Today's terrorists don't want a seat at the table,' R. James Woolsey put it, 'they want to destroy the table and everyone sitting at it.'[27]

III

In general, Shakespeare scholars have touched upon links between Shakespeare and terrorism indirectly, while engaged in exploring the more general theme of 'Shakespeare and violence'. In R. A. Foakes's book of that name,[28] the prevalence of violence in the modern world is not hard to explain: violence is 'natural to men' (*Shakespeare and Violence*, p. 1). 'The horrific acts of terrorism on 11 September 2001' simply demonstrate an age-old genetic, biological and cultural 'addiction to violence' (p. 1) on the part of humanity in general and the male gender in particular: 'part of what constitutes the nature of human beings' (p. 3). In responding to the attacks with violence, Americans were responding to 'instinctual drives that prompt us to defend ourselves when attacked' (p. 1). Violence is deeper however than self-defence, which presupposes a prior assault: and here Foakes posits what he calls a 'primal scene' (p. 8) of violence in the form of a sudden, random, unmotivated attack on an innocent victim. His example is Cain, according to the Old Testament the first human being to be born, and the first murderer. Cain's killing of Abel is 'apparently spontaneous' and has no 'adequate motive'. Shakespeare, argues Foakes, was especially interested in this kind of violence.

[T]he urge to violence is deeply embedded in the human psyche ... Shakespeare was much more deeply interested in what I call the primary act of violence, or primal scene, especially violence that may appear to arise spontaneously and to be essentially meaningless, until meaning is attributed to it after the event. (p. 16)

Thus biblical commentators such as Philo and St Augustine tried to attribute to Cain motives beyond those explicit in the Old Testament story, where the fratricide is presented simply as 'an act of wanton violence for which no motive is given' (p. 25).

It is true, notwithstanding the rationalisations of the church fathers, that there is something troubling about God's apparently arbitrary preference of Abel over Cain. But the motivation that remains mysterious there is God's, not man's. 'God doesn't give his reasons', as Derrida observes.[29] Faced with such arbitrary preference, the human impulse to anger springs not from instinctual violence, but from a sense of injustice. Cain makes the existential choice not to accept God's advice to manage his anger (Foakes misreads this sentence of Genesis), but to follow its prompting towards fratricidal violence. God places Cain in this dilemma, just as he tests Abraham and Job, and we may find this experimentation cruel, preferring perhaps an Equal Opportunities deity who would divide his partiality exactly in two. But the Bible is an attempt to explain the world as it is, in the light of faith. Shit happens. We will encounter difficulty, misfortune, injustice, and we will experience anger, often with justification. God is ultimately responsible for all this. But He also gives us the choice to decide who will be the master; anger or love. Cain should have been master of his rage, and his brother's keeper.

Cain for his crime is cursed and exiled, a wanderer and a fugitive, embodiment of otherness. But in his remorse he is pitiable – 'My punishment is greater than I can bear!' (Genesis 4.13) – and God marks him with a sign of protection. Cain, the master criminal, then marries, builds a city, and fathers a significant portion of the human race. For Foakes this shows violence as coterminous with the origins of mankind and the birth of civilisation. But the biblical account also shows that there is a life beyond violence and vengeance; that yesterday's criminal (yesterday's terrorist, perhaps) can be tomorrow's founding father; and that divine forgiveness is potentially infinite. God's question to Cain was double-edged: even though my brother wrongs me, am I not still – exiled, guilty, branded as he is – his keeper? Who are my brethren? Who is my neighbour?

In the Old English epic *Beowulf* the monster Grendel is described as a descendant of Cain, whose monstrous act makes him ancestor of all evil beings, all enemies of God and mankind.[30] The action of the poem is driven, like most heroic literature, by the principle of revenge. Grendel's attack on the hall is unmotivated; but Beowulf avenges it. Grendel's mother avenges the killing of her son, Beowulf revenges the second attack. The dragon in the second part is taking revenge for what's been stolen from him; Beowulf avenges the destruction the dragon has caused. But Robert Zemeckis' film version of *Beowulf*[31] tells an entirely different story. Whereas in the poem Grendel is a kind of featureless monster, giant, demon, in the film he is much more humanised. In the poem there is no room for pity for the monster, who is just the enemy. In the film the monster's fear and pain are pitiful. We discover why this is so when Beowulf invades the monsters' lair. It appears that Grendel's mother is in fact a seductive demoness no hero could possibly resist (Angelina Jolie). Her son Grendel is also the son of King Hrothgar. In the poem the fight with Grendel's mother is narrated by Beowulf himself on his return. In the film Beowulf becomes an unreliable narrator: in fact he didn't kill her at all, but fell for her charms just as Hrothgar had done. The fruit of their union is the dragon who later terrorises Beowulf's kingdom.

So men and monsters are not separate species at all, but linked together by kinship. The jealousy, enmity, hatred, vindictiveness that ravage the world are all conflicts within the same family. The moral of the poem is that monsters are evil and must be destroyed. The moral of the film is that the monsters are part of us, and we are in some way responsible for them.

In its revision of the Old English epic, *Beowulf* the film enacts theoretical debates on alterity that have given new currency to notions of the monstrous. In Richard Kearney's *Strangers, Gods and Monsters* our encounters with the alien stranger tell us about ourselves. Monsters are 'tokens of fracture within the human psyche': 'They speak to us of how we are split between conscious and unconscious, familiar and unfamiliar, same and other.'[32] In regarding the stranger as an alien or monster we are, according to Kearney, refusing to acknowledge alterity within ourselves, and declining to accept the other as truly other. 'Rather than acknowledge that we are deep down answer-able to an alterity which unsettles us, we devise all kinds of evasion strategies', which include scapegoating and fetishism. Either way, 'We refuse to recognise the stranger before us as a singular other who responds, in turn, to the singular otherness in each of us. We refuse to acknowledge ourselves-as-others' (*Strangers, Gods*, p. 5). Kearney offers a critique of deconstructionist alterity (Levinas and Derrida) which separates self and other 'so schismatically that no relation at all is possible', and proposes the construction of 'hermen-eutic bridges' between the 'poles of sameness and strangeness' (p. 10). Hence he rejects both Levinas's 'radical alterity' ('the unthinkable-impossible-unutterable beyond Being and Logos') and Derrida's 'infinite hospitality' (p. 16), since some strangers are just not welcome, and some monsters really are bent on destruction:

Faced with such putative indetermination, how could we tell the difference between one kind of other and another – between (a) those aliens and strangers that need our care and hospitality, no matter how monstrous they might at first appear, and (b) those others that really do seek to destroy and exterminate (as evidenced in genocidal slaughters from Belsen to Bosnia where certain 'enemies' are indeed murderous adversaries). Or to take one of the most ancient examples of ethical discernment, how are we to differentiate between the voice that bade Abraham kill Isaac and the voice that forbade him to do so? (p. 10)

We will return to Abraham and Isaac. Kearney's definition of the monstrous, though allowing for the irredeemable, is fundamentally at odds with that of Foakes. Foakes regards violence as 'natural' to humanity, not only in the form of a reactive or defensive lashing out, but in what he calls the 'primal scene' of random, unmotivated brutality. Mapping these categories on to 9/11, the attack on New York would fall into the latter category, and the American response into the former. Kearney's method requires a serious and patient analysis of the monstrous. Is this alien invader an implacable enemy who threatens our very survival? Or is he rather a repressed aspect of ourselves, or a kindred spirit exiled and returning in pain to seek a justifiable retribution? Foakes's take on the monstrous is closer to the original *Beowulf*, where men don't pause to speculate about the origins or motivations of the monsters who attack them, but follow their natural protective instincts by returning violence for violence.

Kearney's analysis occupies the same territory as the *Beowulf* film, advocating that we must consider the possibility of relationship, affinity, kinship with those who appear to us as monstrous. The problem of course is exactly the one identified by Kearney: what do you do when the monster bursts through your door, and the smoke and flames of violence lap greedily around your tall towers? For then it's already too late for philosophy.

Matt Reeves's film *Cloverfield*[33] brings together 9/11 and the monstrous in a remarkably interesting conjuncture. The film reprises 9/11 both in terms of is action and its technology of representation. The whole film purports to be a camcorder record of the destruction of Manhattan, found by the US military in 'the area formerly known as Central Park'. Hence the visual style echoes the abrupt, jerky, interrupted images of the hand-held recorders that filmed the collapse of the World Trade Center. The mobile and fragmentary reconstruction of falling towers, clouds of dust billowing through Manhattan streets, people running aimlessly or walking like ghosts, inexplicable sounds and awesome silences, is visually exact and emotionally harrowing to watch. The destruction is caused by an immense and amorphous monster, which seems indestructible and inexhaustibly self-regenerating. Nowhere in the film is there any hint of what it might be, or where it might have come from. A 'shock and awe' military response completes the destruction of the city, but does not seem to be capable of eradicating the creature. The device of the lost and discovered camcorder allows for the survival of the testimony despite the deaths of the witnesses, who are killed either by the monster, or by friendly fire. The deeper reverberations of the film are encapsulated in a key image where the severed head of the Statue of Liberty crashes down into the street, as if more is going on here than random and meaningless destruction (the model of a decapitated Liberty was displayed by Paramount as part of the film's marketing campaign).

The *Beowulf* poet was no deconstructionist, but he understood with typical Old English fatalism how the serpent of violence was twined about every act of creation, every song of joy, every constructed edifice. Hrothgar's great hall Heorot towers in the air, high and horn-gabled, visible for miles, inviting admiration and envy. Grendel's enmity is awakened in the outer darkness by the sound of rejoicing he hears from the hall. Civilisation creates the wilderness;

Heorot's towers arouse the enmity of the surrounding dark. The destruction of the hall is linguistically bound in with its construction (a poetic feature accessible only in the original Old English): even as its walls rise, they are said to be waiting for the fury of fire and the whelming of war. And it is the song of Creation that torments the monster of destruction, Cain's kin, by his ancestry exiled in darkness, with everything he has lost. The poem incorporates, to use Slavoj Žižek's terminology, an awareness of the systemic, 'objective' violence implicit in civilisation, as well as the isolated 'subjective' violence represented in Grendel's attack.[34] The poem sings of the society that turns the surrounding countryside into wilderness; the community that both embraces and excludes; the hall that enfolds within its own magnificent construction the seeds of its ultimate destruction.

When Jean Baudrillard responded to 9/11 it was very much along these lines. In an earlier essay,[35] Baudrillard had defined the Twin Towers in New York as epitomising the postmodern condition of capital. Historically capitalism developed from open competition into monopoly, and thence to duopoly, 'a tactical doubling of monopoly'. Postmodern capitalism needs the tense equilibrium of binary opposition, 'couples of simultaneous opposition', symbolised by the two towers of the World Trade Center. Baudrillard pointed out that this doubling was new, since the modernist architecture of New York typically invested in 'competitive verticality', single buildings ever taller than the last. The new post-monopoly architecture of the World Trade Center 'incarnates a system that is no longer competitive, but compatible'. The two towers represented 'the visible sign of the closure of the system in a vertigo of duplication'.

They ignore the other buildings, they are not of the same race, they no longer challenge them, nor compare themselves to them, they look one into the mirror of the other and culminate in this prestige of similitude.

In 'L'Esprit du terrorisme', his controversial reflections on 9/11, Baudrillard offered remarkably similar thoughts.[36] The collapse of the Twin Towers was the supreme suicidal act not just of the terrorists, but of western global capitalism itself. Inwardly contemplating their own power, the two towers did not see the two planes approaching, but stood silent in a mute binary mirroring of their own self-destruction. Baudrillard acknowledges and shares the general moral condemnation of the act ('Terrorism is immoral'), but insists on identifying another parallel reaction, a secret 'prodigious jubilation felt at having seen this global superpower destroyed'. Everyone, claims Baudrillard, is possessed of a 'terrorist imagination', and the terrorists were able to rely on this 'unconfessable complicity'. It is essential to Baudrillard's analysis that the deadly threat came after all not from outside, but from within, from 'the very heart of the culture' under attack, from apparently ordinary Americans, educated and trained in the US, generously offered the freedom of the skies. Ian McEwan spoke of the first plane slipping into its target 'as cleanly as a posted letter':[37] a cruel message, but one delivered via the state's own efficient machinery; perhaps even in Žižek's words, 'a catastrophic consequence of the smooth functioning of our economic and political systems'.[38] For Baudrillard, terrorism is the inverse side of American power, its invisible shadow: 'the visible fracture (and the hatred) that pits the exploited and underdeveloped nations of the world against the West masks the dominant system's internal fractures'.

IV

Shakespeare's *Macbeth* is of all his plays the one closest to terrorism, closest indeed to what Foakes calls 'the most spectacular act of terrorism in his time, the Gunpowder Plot'.[39] Though the plot failed, where 9/11 spectacularly succeeded, its cultural and political impact was equivalent: it possessed official policy-making, haunted the popular imagination, and justified a 'war on terror' conducted against Roman Catholics.

Alan Sinfield states that in *Macbeth* and in the play's critical reception, a clear distinction is visible between 'the violence the state considers legitimate and that it does not'. According to this ideological perspective 'violence is good . . . when it is in the service of the prevailing dispositions of power; when it disrupts them, it is evil' (*Faultlines*, p. 94). This 'qualitative' distinction between kinds of violence otherwise indistinguishable seems 'natural' only because we are ideologically trained not to think of state violence as violence at all. This distinction parallels Žižek's contrast between 'subjective' and 'systemic' violence. We notice the former, 'acts of crime and terror', and are blind to the latter, which provides our standard of a normal 'non-violent zero': 'Systemic violence is something like the "dark matter" of physics, that counterpart to an all-too-visible subjective violence.'[40] Sinfield's argument is that the play can be read either conventionally – as implicitly endorsing state violence, and condemning the violence of disruption and insurrection – or oppositionally, as equating the two. The play contains both possibilities, and the 'qualitative' difference lies in the chosen strategy of reading.

Francis Barker's reading of *Macbeth* in *The Culture of Violence* distinguishes between illegitimate and legitimate violence, between 'the transgressive deed' and 'violence in the name of the restitution of legitimacy'.[41] He concedes that these forms of violence are remarkably similar in the play, even twinned with one another, as the play invests its poetry both in authority and in the energies that seek to overthrow it. Barker concludes however that ultimately *Macbeth* 'exists precisely to warn against such an alteration in the sovereign order' (p. 64). The play shares in the tendency of culture to collude with violence.

When Macbeth is described as confronting the rebel Cawdor on the battlefield with 'self-comparisons' (1.2.56), the audience is made aware of likeness as well as difference. This, together with Macbeth's rapid alternation of titles, indicates that identity here is not fixed, but dispersed among patterns of similarity (54). The violent killing of Macdonald thus prepares us for the murder of Duncan, and ultimately for Macbeth's own death, which parallels both his initial repression of rebellion, and his act of regicide. Although Duncan's sacred kingship can produce an ideological language of organicism, social totality, kinship, and family, the play makes absolutely explicit the bloody violence that underpins it:

> he faced the slave
> Which ne'er shook hands, nor bade farewell to him,
> Till he unseamed him from the nave to th'chaps
> And fixed his head upon our battlements.
>
> 1.2.21–4[42]

Royal authority, whether it be gracious Duncan's or canny Malcolm's, requires as its legitimising totem the severed head of a defeated enemy, Macdonald or Macbeth. Thus the text reveals the unmistakable similarity between 'subjective' and 'systemic' violence, the 'demonic complicity'[43] between war on terror and terror itself, and simultaneously represents and demystifies state power. For Barker, *Macbeth* is 'the tragedy that comes closest to dramatising the monarch in presence', but also comes closest to 'dramatising, only just in the wings, the violent overthrow of that same sovereignty' (*Culture of Violence*, p. 59). The play is able 'both to confirm the ideology of kingship in an unassailable positivity, and also to heighten and intensify the assault on that sovereignty which inheres in the act of political murder and "social" violation at the centre of the play' (p. 60). Ultimately, however, for Barker *Macbeth* presents 'violence in the name of restitution of legitimacy' as 'wholly to be sanctioned', while the 'transgressive deed' of dissident violence is 'punished savagely' (p. 66). Thus the play ends with 'a crushing victory for reparation' (p. 70).

These readings stand as typical New Historicist and cultural materialist takes on *Macbeth*. The play presents both state violence and terrorist violence, but colludes with state violence in a tribute to legitimacy. Sinfield and Barker both see the play in this way, as Sinfield admits that it has to be read 'against the grain' to produce a radical reading. Here, then, where 'power is constituted through theatrical celebrations of royal glory and theatrical violence visited upon enemies of that glory', Shakespearean tragedy is 'one of power's essential modes'.[44] Here we see the 'family resemblance between authority and its Other'.[45] The context of the play could hardly be more conducive to this collusion of culture with power if, as some scholars suggest, Macbeth was played before James I at Hampton Court in August 1606, possibly before the first such assembly of state officials gathered since the discovery of the Gunpowder Plot. Jonathan Goldberg notes that the play begins and ends with severed heads,[46] and Leonard Tennenhouse suggests that those severed heads represent a historical reversal of fortune parallel to November 1605. The assassin's head is served up to the King in an inversion of terror that offers violence to the sovereign as a gift: 'The play's tribute to James comes as Shakespeare signals the reversal of Macbeth's reversal ... by having Macduff hold up the severed head of a tyrant'.[47] Just as at the beginning Macbeth plays the hangman in enacting a ritual disembowelling and decapitation of Macdonald, so at the end Macduff echoes the executioner's cry: 'Behold where stands / Th'usurper's cursed head' (5.9.21–2). Both killings point unmistakably towards Tyburn, and the ritual slaughtering not only of the Gunpowder Plotters, but of many other Catholics. The answer to terror is war on terror: 'blood will have blood' (3.4.122). But because in a war on terror the innocent suffer along with the guilty, such violence shows, in Richard Wilson's words, 'the history of terror humanist culture shares with the tyranny it opposes'.[48]

One severed head, after a while, looks much like another. The gruesome iconography of such trophies, publicly exhibited as they were in Shakespeare's London, was both particular and general. Each example called attention to one individual traitor's justly deserved fate. But each also provided an anonymous mirror in which the potential traitor could view his own features. In a context where piety itself is treason, you don't have to be a conspirator to feel the monitory shudder the young Shakespeare might have felt, if he did view the spiked heads of his mother's Catholic relations, Edward Arden and John Sommerville, executed in 1583 for plotting to assassinate Elizabeth on behalf of Mary Queen of Scots.[49]

But what exactly did James I himself see in that glass held up by the witches to display for Macbeth a vision of the future Stuart monarchy? Did he glimpse the shadow of the missing Scottish monarch whose shameful botched decapitation facilitated his own succession, that of his own mother Mary?[50] Did he see the reflection of his own head, which had come so close to destruction in the Gunpowder Plot? He cannot surely have been prescient enough to see the severed head of his son Charles in that mirror of futurity; but he cannot have been immune from the fear of such possibilities. 'Show his eyes' the stage witches may have whispered before James at Hampton Court, 'and grieve his heart' (4.1.109).

with its two invasions, two Cawdors, two feasts, two doctors, two kings, and two kingdoms, the 'equivocation' of this tragedy – which 'palters with us in a double sense', 'in every point twice done, and then done double', duplicating 'double trouble' in such mutual incrimination – mirrors insurgency with counter-insurgency, victims and violators, so insistently that it cannot simply be a demonstration of his 'war on terror' designed to delight King James.[51]

The plotters and the establishment they sought to destroy were of course members of one Christian faith, and were closely interrelated by kinship. But as the Reformation facilitated civil war between Protestant and Catholic, so the reciprocal violence of persecution and terrorism placed certain dissidents beyond the pale. They became the enemy, aliens, others. Lancelot Andrewes in his first 'Powder Sermon' lamented that 'this land should foster or breed such monsters!'[52] But as we have seen, if the monster is in fact kin, even perhaps the King's bastard offspring, then should he not acknowledge some responsibility for his son's violence of resistance? Macbeth too is a monster, brutal and demonic, a 'hellhound' (5.8.3), according to Macduff, one of the 'rarer monsters' (25). What does the play have to tell us about monstrosity, about the mind of the terrorist, about what it was like to be Cain?

V

Scholars argue about the date of Macbeth, and whether or not the single Folio text we have may incorporate several different versions of the play. But it can hardly be disputed that Macbeth *is* himself the Gunpowder Plot:

> If th'assassination
> Could trammel up the consequence and catch
> With his surcease, success, that but this blow
> Might be the be-all and the end-all – here,
> But here, upon this bank and shoal of time,
> We'd jump the life to come.

1.7.2–7

'Blow' was the word James claimed to have understood (as 'explosion' rather than 'impact') from the Monteagle letter, when he alone 'did upon the instant interpret and apprehend some dark phrases therein' in a manner contrary to any imaginable customary or rational elucidation.[53] Later Sir Edward Coke alluded to 'those dark words of the letter concerning a terrible blow'.[54] Gary Wills observes that in the aftermath of the Plot, words like 'train' and 'blow' could never have been innocently deployed, any more than 'sneak attack' after Pearl Harbor, or 'grassy knoll' after the assassination of JFK (*Witches and Jesuits*, p. 27). The words would always invoke that unimaginable, unspeakable crime, both terrifying and sublime:

> O horror, horror, horror!
> Tongue nor heart cannot conceive, nor name thee.
>
>   2.3.56–7

That of course was the official, authorised response to the Plot, a response mandated by the state propaganda that set out to 'blow the horrid deed in very eye / That tears shall drown the wind' (1.7.24–5). William Barlow, in the sermon preached a few days after the discovery, like Macbeth used the word 'blow' in these two senses. The conspirators were like Caligula, who 'wished that all the Citizens of Rome, had but one neck, that at one blow he might cut it off'. If successful, the 'horrid deed' of the Plot would have had unlimited consequences: 'this lawless fury had, with this blowing up, bin blown in and over the whole nation'.[55] For the plotters themselves, and for those who felt affinity with them (and who clearly outnumbered the very few who became actively involved), the prospect of 'this terrible blow' that might be 'the be-all and the end-all' was fatally attractive: a catastrophic destruction of the ruling elite; a liberation of the realm from tyranny and oppression; the apocalyptic advent of a new age of religious liberty, jumping the life to come.

There is ample scope for drawing parallels. But I want to focus on the 'terrorist imagination' that possesses Macbeth, and of which he is possessed. This play does not, like *Julius Caesar*, explore political assassination in terms of a multiplicity of motivations, some good, some bad. It does not reflect on the shortcomings of the current state, explore the dilemmas of republican virtue, or envisage the possibilities of a new order. There is in *Macbeth* no notion of effecting political change, destroying tyranny, bringing about an improved state of affairs. Macbeth doesn't actually have any reservations about the kingdom, except that he is not king of it; nor does he want to be king to actually do anything with the acquired political power. Everything then is in the desire, the hunger, the passion to pit the self against power, and by destroying power, to authenticate the potency of the self, the force of desire, the triumph of the will.

All this involves immense determination, suicidal bravery, the kind of reckless heroism displayed by Macbeth on the battlefield. But at its root lies terror: 'why do you start and seem to fear / Things that do seem so fair?'

> why do I yield to that suggestion,
> Whose horrid image doth unfix my hair
> And make my seated heart knock at my ribs
> Against the use of nature?

1.3.133–6

The moment of temptation is a rapture of desire and fear. The explosive knocking of Macbeth's violently beating heart figures the breaking loose within him of a monstrous desire. Later it becomes indistinguishable from the famous knocking at the gate which is the external summons of morality and law, perhaps even, as the Porter has turned the castle into a devil's domain, the *Tollite Portas* of the Harrowing of Hell. In between the two appellations, Macbeth has 'broke ope / The Lord's anointed temple' (2.3.60–1), and the gashes of Duncan's death wounds lie gaping like 'a breach in nature' (2.3.106). The monstrous erupts into the world from the self, not from outside. And fear, terror, abjection, belong to the monster as well as to the victims of the monster's violence.

This takes us to the heart of terrorism. If we think of terrorism subjectively, simply as that which afflicts 'us', then we are unable to grasp the terror that lies on the other side of difference. Because of course the alien has his monsters too, and he is terrified of them. What makes this for us so 'difficult to comprehend' is that his monsters are 'us'.

Macbeth kills Duncan out of fear, envy, a kind of quiet rage. These emotions are quite impersonal, and barely connected to the King himself as a man. What Macbeth fears above all else is the promotion of others: that others will be preferred above him. Just as God arbitrarily accepted Abel's animal sacrifice, and rejected Cain's vegetarian offering, so Duncan equally arbitrarily elects as king the candid youngster, rather than the blood-boltered warrior. Like Cain, Macbeth can conceive of another's success only as his own diminishment. 'Fear is a great form of worship', says the 9/11 hijackers' spiritual manual: 'and the only one worthy of it is God.'[56] The suicide terrorist is literary frightened to death.

Macbeth responds to a call, a promise, a summons, that we hear from the witches, but is whispering everywhere in the shadows of Macbeth's world. Abraham heard such a call, such a summons, which he heard as the voice of promise, the word of God. The voice told him to sacrifice his own son. The classic modern interpretation of this story is of course Kierkegaard's *Fear and Trembling*, named after St Paul's phrase that now seems inseparable from discussions of contemporary violence and terrorism.[57] This contingency is in itself interesting, as the fear at issue here is not fear of violence, fear of attack, fear for one's own safety. It is the existential terror of decision. Fear and trembling are about risk, throwing yourself into the unknown, jumping futurity. Killing a king, piloting a plane into the World Trade Centre or the Pentagon, driving a car bomb into a packed theatre playing Shakespeare, would seem to be textbook examples of such a response to the strange violent mandate of otherness.

In Kierkegaard it is the trembling of Abraham, as fearfully he prepares to obey that terrible summons, which is nothing less than an imperative to violate his highest moral beliefs. But Kierkegaard says that such faith entails a teleological suspension of the ethical, and is quite irrational and indefensible on moral grounds. It has been suggested that the terrorist does exactly this when he commits himself to an act of suicidal and murderous violence. Those who send the terrorist to his death stand in for Abraham, sacrificing their own sons to what they believe to be the requirements of God. The terrorists themselves are rather in the position of Isaac, bound in subjugation to the altar of sacrifice. In the Qu'ran the boy (Ishmael, not Isaac) is asked his opinion, and concurs with Abraham that the command must be obeyed. 'O my father! Do that which you are commanded, *Insha Allah* [God willing] you shall find me *As-Sabirun* [obedient]' (37.102).[58]

VI

The terrorist imagination is apocalyptic, possessed of an irrational hope that the annihilation of one's own body and the bodies of others can effect a kind of cleansing purgation of the world, sweeping away its corruption, blowing away its power, clearing a space for the incursion of the divine. 'Tame your soul, purify it', the 9/11 hijackers were instructed. 'Fight them until there is no more *Fitnah* [unbelief]', says the Qu'ran: 'and the worship will all be for Allah (alone in the whole of the world)' (8.39). The Gunpowder Plot was obviously seen as an averted apocalypse from which the kingdom was mercifully delivered: James told Parliament that his kingship had been saved from two trials, a flood of spilled blood and a fire (the Gowrie Conspiracy and the Gunpowder Plot), which could have been 'two great and fearful Doomsdays'.[59] By the same token, the hope of destroying 'the whole body of the state' at one blow was an aspiration of apocalyptic proportions. But not everyone could have seen James as Noah, or as the Son of Man from Revelation. If Baudrillard is right, and we are all endowed with a 'terrorist imagination', then many (including Shakespeare) must have felt the breath of the conspiracy with a frisson of Kierkegaardian fear and trembling, rather than just with a sigh of relief.

Macbeth is of course full of apocalyptic language and symbolism, often generalised but often also specifically eschatological: Duncan's murder is in itself 'the great Doom's image' (2.3.72). The strongest apocalyptic feeling in the play is that of time growing short, running out: the kingdom is at hand. That which has always been about to come, is suddenly on its way. 'The time between you and your marriage in heaven is very short.'[60] Lady Macbeth, on receiving her husband's letter, feels immediately 'transported' 'beyond / This ignorant present', and able to feel futurity bursting through the immediate. 'I feel now / The future in the instant' (1.5.54–6). Barker says of this speech that it betrays an 'aspiration which is prepared dynamically to reshape time in a quasi-modernist, if not almost revolutionary apprehension of the present "instant" as a constellation pregnant, shot through with a desired future' (*Culture of Violence*, p. 63). In his analysis, this hope is the embryonic revolutionary content of *Macbeth*, that messianic hope for change in 'the entire order of things' which the play's ultimately legitimist ideology cannot countenance.

But in *Macbeth* what hope lies beyond the change? Freedom, justice, democracy? Anything that Francis Barker would have wanted to see? No: only death. 'When the hour of reality approaches, the zero hour . . . wholeheartedly welcome death for the sake of God'.[61] There will be a future, those men must have been assured, in which the *dar al Islam* covers the whole world, and their actions would contribute to its eventual victory. But the suicide bomber will not see it. No matter: he already has his reward. They were brought to believe, and presumably must have believed, that they would step

off tarmac and into heaven. 'Afterwards begins the happy life.' This is
what it really means to 'jump the life to come', to 'jump the gap
between word and deed',[62] to accomplish with one catastrophic
action the immediate collapsing of the boundaries between present
and future, between this world and the next. There are only two
places in which such a sublime transfiguration is conceivable: one is
in suicidal terrorism, like 9/11; the other is in art. And there is an
'unconfessable complicity' between the two.

We can see this complicity, as Terry Eagleton has recently reminded
us, in Conrad's novel *The Secret Agent*, 'the first suicide-bomber novel
of English literature'.[63] Conrad depicts a corrupt world which he
himself would like to see swept away: so he cannot avoid an imaginative sympathy with his own creation, the Professor. 'What's wanted'
states the anarchist suicide bomber, 'is a clean sweep and a clear start
of a new conception of life'.[64] Eagleton points out that this is also
'the familiar cry of the avant-gardist who rather than submit to the
messiness of history and material process seeks to leap at a bound
from present to future, actual to desirable, finite to infinite' (*Holy
Terror*, p. 123). To feel, one might say, 'the future in the instant' of
self-destructive cataclysm.

Karlheinz Stockhausen provoked outrage when he confounded art
and reality over 9/11, calling it 'the greatest work of art imaginable for
the whole cosmos'.[65] 9/11 created on a grand scale '*the leap out of
security*, out of what is usually taken for granted, *out of life*, that
sometimes happens to a small extent in art'.

Minds achieving something in an act that we couldn't even dream of in
music, people rehearsing like mad for 10 years, preparing fanatically for a
concert, and then dying, just imagine what happened there. You have
people who are that focused on a performance and then 5,000 people are
dispatched to the afterlife, in a single moment. I couldn't do that. By
comparison, we composers are nothing. Artists, too, sometimes try to go
beyond the limits of what is feasible and conceivable, so that we wake up, so
that we open ourselves to another world.

The fortuitous correspondences with the vocabulary of *Macbeth* are
eerily repetitive: 'act', 'dream', 'dispatched', 'wake'. Attempting later
to distance himself from his own words ('It's a crime because those
involved didn't consent. They didn't come to the "concert".'), Stockhausen came even closer to the language of terrorism in *Macbeth*.

What happened spiritually, *this jump out of security*, out of the self-evident, this sometimes also happens in art ... or it is worthless.[66]

Stockhausen and Macbeth share the same word, 'jump' (*Sprung*), and bring together in a common vocabulary the shared fantasies of aesthetic transcendence and suicidal martyrdom.

Macbeth lives beyond the moment of his transcendence in a world devoid of meaning, where there is 'nothing serious in mortality' (2.3.84). Asked if the terrorism of Al-Qaeda could be identified as 'a quintessential expression of founding violence', the kind of revolutionary violence that lies at the root of every state, Derrida said that such terrorist violence differs from political violence in that its actions '*open onto no future*', it leaves '*nothing good to be hoped for*'.[67] So in Macbeth the millennial rapture of feeling the future in the instant is replaced by the weary fatalism of 'tomorrow and tomorrow and tomorrow'. Everything can be done tomorrow: tomorrow, perhaps, they will finally feel 'safe'. Notwithstanding, they remain stranded 'here upon this bank and shoal of time', where tomorrow never comes, since there is '*nothing good to be hoped for*'.

We see then why Shakespeare is such an interesting subject for reflections on terrorism, and why his work is routinely colonised by politically inimical appropriations. This latter phenomenon is facilitated, not caused, by Shakespeare's global currency as the world's canonical author: he is interpreted in such incompatible ways simply because he is there to be interpreted, a common property. Political appropriations are obliged to be single-minded, without any room for nuances and reservations. If you see Shakespeare as an Anglo-American cultural superhero, then you can't also see him as a friend to the oppressed. If you see him as representing a kind of Christian crusader capitalism, then you're unlikely to find him tolerant and inclusive and fair-minded. And if you see Shakespeare as a kind of ideological front for state violence and terror, then you're unlikely to use him in defence of tyrannicide or violent insurgency against state power.

But the reverse of all these distinctions also holds true, and Shakespeare has been used to prove and defend anything and everything. Shakespeare the double agent; the man 'to double business bound' (*Hamlet* 3.3.47).

Perhaps he was a double agent. As a man, if Wilson, Stephen Greenblatt,[68] and others are right in their speculations about Shakespeare's crypto-Catholicism, Shakespeare could have made the choice to enlist under the banner of religious martyrdom. Perhaps that's why he was able to dramatise those forbidden desires, that secret jubilation, that messianic hope that seems so much clearer about the coming terrors (which as we know are within our power to bring about), than about the kingdom to come. But if Catholic martyrdom was an option for Shakespeare, it's one he didn't take. So simultaneously he was able to depict the reality of that nothingness that would inevitably follow on such violent destruction, and to compare it honestly, if ruefully, with the imperfections of the status quo. Better Malcolm than Macbeth, Shakespeare probably would have said; better James I than Thomas Percy. Better even Bush than bin Laden.

Both state violence and dissident terrorism came very close to Shakespeare and his work, touching his personal life, shaping the context in which he worked, colouring his work itself. As scholars like Richard Wilson have shown, Shakespeare was much closer in kinship (and probably sympathy) to the Gunpowder plotters than to the King whose authority performed a terrible violence on those Catholics convicted of conspiracy. The idea that *Macbeth* could have been played as a courtly compliment to James I, justifying his anti-Catholic 'war on terror', is haunted by the manifest fascination the play shows for the terrorist imagination. The poetry of the play appeals directly, as Baudrillard said of 9/11, to the secret jubilation many would have felt if the Plot had succeeded, and if that apocalyptic vision of the monarchy destroyed had been performed in reality as it could be imagined in art. A clean sweep, a new start, a new conception of life.

Despite their family resemblances, art and terrorism are not analogous; they are diametrically opposed to one another. The cynicism of Baudrillard's 'terrorist imagination', or the feverish excitement of Stockhausen's catastrophic 'concert', give access to an element of the truth about 9/11. Tragedy began with the violence of Dionysian ecstasy, and with sacrifice. But the violence was ritualised and framed, and the human sacrifices, Pentheus or Oedipus, were slaughtered only in imitation. 'Philosophical and artistic works', says Kearney, 'are ... capable of furnishing some extra, because indirect, insights into the enigma of horror. For both proffer an *unnatural*

perspective on things – by virtue of style, genre and language.'[69]
Abraham heard a voice that told him to kill; but the whole story,
whether in the Bible or the Qu'ran, shows God releasing his servant
from the responsibility of sacrifice, and the human offering com-
muted to the slaughter of an animal. 'The sacrifice of Isaac,' Derrida
points out, 'belongs to what one might just dare call the common
treasure, the terrifying secret of the *mysterium tremendum* that is a
property of all the so-called religions of the Book, the religions of the
races of Abraham.' And the supposed site of this event is the
common location of Solomon's Temple, the grand Mosque of
Jerusalem, the Dome of the Rock, the Way of the Cross: 'It is
therefore a holy place but also a place that is in dispute, radically
and rabidly, fought over by all the monotheisms, by all the religions
of the unique and transcendent God, of the absolute other . . . they
make war with fire and blood' (*Gift of Death*, pp. 64 and 70). 'Isaac's
sacrifice continues every day', he concludes (p. 70). But in the Bible
it never occurred in the first place. Derrida is scornful of any 'wide-
eyed ecumenism' that would seek common ground in the 'common
treasure' (p. 70). But we can only hear and respond to the first voice,
in any of the three Scriptures, by not reading the written account
that includes the second. The human being is not turned into an
animal or monster to facilitate his slaughter; he is one of us, our
dearly beloved son. It is a story of redemption, not sacrifice.
Terrorism can occur only when the violence of the believer's fear
and trembling, the noise of the seated heart knocking at the ribs,
drowns the kind of carefully orchestrated composition we find in
scriptural religion, or in the tragic art of Shakespeare.

VII

The chapter that follows is a critical-creative consideration of the
meanings and energies released when Shakespeare is brought into
collision with terrorism. It is a critical and cultural discussion of the
issues entailed in the 2005 bombing of the Doha Players Theatre in
Qatar, during a performance of Shakespeare's *Twelfth Night*. But
interpolated into it is an imaginative attempt to reach the 'inside
story' of the atrocity, by dramatising the event from the terrorist's
point of view. Both strands of the piece draw on substantial research

into Middle Eastern politics and culture, and extensive fieldwork in the region,[70] as well as a deep critical-creative engagement with the cultural politics of contemporary Shakespeare. This strange, and perhaps unpredictable, encounter between Shakespeare and the sharp end of modern politics generates new meanings in both directions. There is now more to discern in *Twelfth Night* than there was before; and equally, we can arrive at a different understanding of the contemporary world via the harsh light cast upon it by this Shakespearean detonation.

CHAPTER 8

'Rudely interrupted'

I

On Saturday, 19 March 2005, Omar Ahmed Abdullah Ali tidied his workstation at Qatar Petroleum and shut down his computer for the last time.

There were very few people in the office that day, and none of them noticed anything unusual about his behaviour. They recalled him afterwards as 'a decent man', a family man whose wife had, only a month before, given birth to their third child.

Earlier that morning the thirty-eight-year-old Egyptian computer programmer had said goodbye to Umm Abdullah and his three children quite normally, as if nothing unusual were about to occur. *I am not what I am.*[1] Now he left the office quietly, unassumingly, attracting no attention, and went to collect his black Land Cruiser from the company car park. Driving slowly and carefully, he pulled the car on to the road and headed towards the Doha suburb of Fariq Kalaib.[2]

II

That same Saturday the Doha Players were putting on *Twelfth Night* in their own theatre in Fariq Kalaib. The production was playing to an audience of around seventy people, including western expatriates, Palestinians and Lebanese, Eritreans and Somalis, and local Qataris. Previous performances had been praised by the local press as 'lively' and 'fresh'. The production featured a Caribbean setting, and the stage backdrop vibrated with tropical colour. The show was in full swing.

One year before, the Doha Players had celebrated their fiftieth anniversary as an amateur theatrical group. The tiny Gulf state of

Qatar (population 840,000, mostly expatriate) is a hive of theatrical activity, owing to the diverse population and to strong support from the state, with at least four functioning theatre groups, including a national theatre. The facilities afforded to theatre in the country, all based initially on grants from the ruling royal family, are probably the best in the Middle East. The Doha Players is a largely British and Commonwealth group, which enjoys the support of the local community, including Arab expatriates, as well as the British Ambassador.[3]

The theatre building in which *Twelfth Night* was being performed was built in 1979. It stood close to the Doha English-Speaking School. Initially the theatre was an out-of-town venue, like Shakespeare's Globe, but the suburbs have grown around it. Adjacent to the theatre stood a hall known as the West End, in nostalgic memory of London's theatre district, and which was used as a tea and coffee bar at intermissions. On the main door of the theatre were carved conventional masks of tragedy and comedy, recognised emblems of theatre throughout the world, and a familiar sight in London's own West End.

III

In the name of Allah, Most Gracious, Most Merciful, Sawd Al-Jihad presents 'A Letter to the Mujahideen in Iraq'.

O defenders of the religion, brave lions who support words with actions; O those who have fulfilled their promise and given up everything for the sake of Allah: continue in your path of honour. We will not let the crusaders set foot in any place in the land of the prophet Mohammed.

I also command all the brave lions of jihad in Qatar, Bahrain, Oman, the United Arab Emirates and all the countries surrounding Iraq to support you. If every bee stings the pig from a different direction, then he will die from his wounds. O guardians of Islam, stand firm alongside your brothers so that Allah will stand firm next to you.[4]

IV

The intermission was drawing to a close and the second half of the play was due to start (the performance had been rescheduled by one hour to allow for an earlier finish). The animated and excited audience were ushered into the auditorium to take their seats.

Enter Viola, and Clown with a tabour

VIOLA: Save thee, friend, and thy music: dost thou live by thy tabour?
CLOWN: No, sir, I live by the church.
VIOLA: Art thou a churchman?
CLOWN: No such matter, sir: I do live by the church; for I do live at my
    house, and my house doth stand by the church.
VIOLA: So thou mayst say, the king lies by a beggar, if a beggar dwell near him;
    or, the church stands by thy tabour, if thy tabour stand by the church.
CLOWN: You have said, sir. To see this age! A sentence is but a cheveril
    glove to a good wit: how quickly the wrong side may be turned
    outward!

3.I.I–13

V

Omar Ahmed Abdullah Ali stopped his car within view of the theatre.
He could see the building, the theatre and its annex, the breeze-block
perimeter wall and cars parked in a defensive circle around it. He
could see the steps leading up to the door of the theatre. There were
no sentries or guards, no additional security, no locked doors. There
was a gap in the ring of cars wide enough for him to get through.[5]

Throughout the long slow drive he had felt numb, detached, a man
sidelined by the enormity of his own mission. Even the thought of the
explosives with which the car was packed had caused him no particular concern. Now, as the moment approached, he began to feel
anxious. His palms sweated on the steering wheel. Unwelcome images
came to mind, pictures of his wife and children, distractions. He
focused, as he had been trained to do, on the objective of the action.
*We will not let the crusaders set foot. There will not be any safe
passage. We promise to introduce them to the word terror over and
over again, and they will try and translate it into all their languages.*[6]

He eased the car into forward gear. *Allah made us promise.
Forsake everything in his cause, and for the sake of your victory.*[7]
His grip tightened on the wheel. He floored the accelerator and sped
towards the breeze-block wall. The big car crashed through the wall,
scattering dust and debris, and roared towards the steps of the theatre
entrance. *God is great. God is great. Brave lions of jihad.*

The car hit the steps with a bang, and the chassis grounded on the
concrete. Desperately Omar tried to accelerate forward to drive into
the building, but the wheels spun helplessly. The engine screamed.

***

The play's director, teacher and amateur actor Jonathan Adams, was sitting in the control room at the back of the theatre watching the performance. From outside he heard a bang and the sound of an engine running at high speed. Something going on in the car park. The noise would disturb the performance. He went to the door to see what the commotion was all about.

***

Omar saw Jonathan appear at the top of the steps. The mission was in jeopardy. *Be clamorous, and leap all civil bounds / Rather than make unprofited return.*[8] God is great. He triggered his explosives.

***

Jonathan took the full force of the blast and was blown back into the theatre, probably killed instantly. The suicide bomber also died. Twelve other people were injured, including six Qataris, a Briton, an Eritrean, and a Somali, none seriously.

The impact of the 'massive explosion'[9] was heard and felt inside the auditorium. Kerry Ruek, playing Feste, was blown from the stage in mid-speech. He remembers, with characteristic understatement, the performance being 'rudely interrupted'.[10] The sound and lighting engineers were blown out of the control room. Everything went dark. There was smoke everywhere, things were flying through the air. It was pandemonium.[11]

A gas explosion was suspected. Members of the Players quickly gathered children together to evacuate them. People streamed from the building.

Outside, what had happened was all too obvious. Nearby buildings had been extensively damaged. The windows of the school were all shattered. Cars were burning in the car park. People had been blown off their feet and were seen lying on the ground.[12]

The body of Jonathan Adams lay inside the ruined theatre entrance. His wife Rosemarie was the first to reach him. Kerry Ruek tried desperately to revive him, but to no avail.[13]

As the car had been tilted at an angle on the steps, the force of the explosion blew backwards and demolished the theatre annex. If the play had not been rescheduled, the annex would have been filled with members of the audience enjoying their interval tea and coffee.[14] Had the mission gone according to plan, casualties would have been much higher. Instead, by luck and misjudgement, the terrorist succeeded in inflicting a few non-fatal wounds, and killing only himself and Jonathan Adams.

In an instant, comedy had turned to tragedy. The theatre doors, with their comic and tragic masks, lay where they had been hurled among the building's wreckage. *How quickly the wrong side may be turned outward.*

VI

Qatar is a relative stranger to terrorism, though there are many reasons why it could be ranked as a prime Al-Qaeda target. Qatar hosted the US Central Command's operational headquarters from early 2003, after it was shifted from Saudi Arabia, thus forming a bridgehead for the occupation of Iraq. The Al Saliya camp on the outskirts of Doha, only twelve miles from the theatre, houses 2,000 American troops. The US Embassy was formerly located in the area occupied by the theatre, but now stands some six miles away. On 14 March 2005, days before the bombing, the US State Department had issued a general warning to all Americans travelling in the Gulf that 'extremists may be planning to carry out attacks against Westerners and oil workers' in the region. The Doha atrocity occurred on the second anniversary of the invasion of Iraq (launched on 20 March 2003).

Conversations with the survivors of the attack indicate that at the time there was no particular awareness on the part of the Doha Players or their audience of any serious or imminent terrorist threat. Qatar had not seen this kind of violence before, and was thought of as very safe. No one had even noticed the significance of the date.

More significantly, the players could see no rationale for an attack on them, their audience, and their theatre. It is difficult for them to see what they do as in any way controversial. They are not a military or political organisation, and did not think of themselves as having any high-profile symbolic value. They see themselves as a diverse Qatari expatriate community, not an outpost of western civilisation. They have no strong American affiliation. They do nothing to antagonise local sentiments, serve no alcohol, and conform obediently to the state's byzantine censorship regulations. They are sceptical about any anti-theatrical motivation deriving from Islamic dislike of drama, since there are also local theatre groups (Qatari Group Theatre and Gulf Group Theatre) as well as a national theatre.[15]

But targeted they were, and allegedly by Jund al-Sham, the group which claimed responsibility for the attack. Only a few days before, an audio recording posted on an Islamist website, purporting to contain the voice of Saleh Mohammed al-Aoofi, Al-Qaeda's commander in Saudi Arabia, suggested to intelligence analysts that a new phase of global terrorist organisation might well be in the process of formation. Al-Aoofi was paying homage to Musab al-Zarqawi as the heir apparent to Osama bin Laden. Jund al-Sham was the name of al-Zarqawi's Jordanian terrorist militia, and the implication was that its operations would be extended from insurgency in Iraq to Al-Qaeda's territory of global jihad. Former French defence official Alexis Debat writes:

Last week's bombing in Doha may signal the beginning of that phase. Even though very little is know at this point about the Egyptian computer expert who exploded his car next to the Doha English-Speaking School, Jund Al-Sham's comeback on the global scene in a country so remote from its initial area of operation seems to validate a number of developments recently picked up by US and Iraqi intelligence services. This information is increasingly interpreted as indicating that Zarqawi has emerged as the most important operational leader of the global jihad and even a possible replacement to bin Laden as the figurehead of the movement.[16]

Shakespeare and Jihad no longer appear such improbable bedfellows. The Doha Players may have served as a soft civilian target, like the Soho nightclub threatened by a failed car bomb in London (2007). They may have represented a random gathering of westerners and their associates, like the occupants of Glasgow Airport, who in 2007 narrowly escaped violence from another grounded car bomb. But it is far more likely, surely, that they represented what Jürgen Habermas calls a 'symbolically suffused' objective[17], one that brought together a loaded matrix of meanings: the English language; western culture; Christian civilisation. These familiar terms, for the fundamentalist, translate as the foreigner; the infidel; the crusader. And in this instance all these figures were represented by the name of Shakespeare.

VII

The Doha Players responded to this event with shocked innocence. Such candour may seem in retrospective analysis naïve, but God forbid that we should ever lose the capability of innocence, or the right of innocence to be shocked. Derrida was grasping at some such imperative when he spoke of 9/11, insisting on the absolute necessity of

compassion for the victims and indignation over the killings. Our sadness and condemnation should be without limits, unconditional, unimpeachable ... they respond with what might be called the heart and they go straight to the heart of the event.[18]

But Shakespeare is clearly inseparable from, indeed almost synonymous with, the Anglo-American western culture that is identified (and not only by fundamentalists) with the Israel–Palestine problem, with the invasions of Afghanistan and Iraq, and with a global cultural dominance inimical to Islam. Derrida again:

The world order ... targeted through this violence is dominated by the Anglo-American idiom, an idiom that is indissolubly linked to the political discourse that dominates the world stage, to international law, to diplomatic institutions, the media, and the greatest technoscientific, capitalist and military power.[19]

The Shakespeare of post-colonial criticism is often presented as an instrument of oppression. Post-colonial critics have shown how, over the previous two centuries, Anglo-American criticism consolidated an imperial Shakespeare, one whose works testified to the superiority of the civilised races, and could be used to establish and maintain colonial authority.[20] Shakespeare represents the crowning glory of the English language, but the history of how that language was extended from a parochial island tongue into the world language of 1,000 million masks a much more violent process involving subjugation of native peoples, extirpation or annexation of native cultures, and the imposition through administrative and educational systems of Anglocentric norms and ideologies.

The various forms of colonial response have been well studied and well documented. Some subjugated cultures engaged in imitation and mimicry, assisting the domestication of the foreign power. Elsewhere native intellectuals challenged colonial culture in favour of their own native literatures, initially by exposing the conscious or unconscious racist content of imperial fictions, as when Chinua Achebe declared that Joseph Conrad was 'a bloody racist'.[21] Dramatists in the former colonies began to reread Shakespeare from a colonised viewpoint. Post-colonial criticism also re-evaluated the early modern period in which empire had its origins, and demonstrated that colonial discourse was no mere passive backdrop to Shakespearean drama but rather one of its key discursive contexts.[22] In other words, these plays were immersed in the formation of empire before they became its tools, 'entangled from the beginning with the projects of nation-building, empire and colonization'.[23]

This is the Shakespeare referred to by United Press International editor Martin Walker, writing of the Doha bombing; the Shakespeare who

stands for the Western invasion of Islam's holy peninsula. He is the symbol of the English language that he helped perfect, and thus he also symbolizes its steady advance into the mouths and sensibilities of a generation of educated Arabs.[24]

VIII

In discussing Shakespeare and terrorism in the previous chapter, I have dwelt naturally on tragedy. Tragedy takes us to the heart of violence, and to the violence of the heart. In *Macbeth* we can discover both the motivation for, and the horror of, terrorism. But when an Al-Qaeda militant attacked Shakespeare in Doha, his target was a comedy.

In *Twelfth Night* innocence is constitutive and foundational: the play 'dallies with the innocence of love, / Like the old age' (2.4.47–8). But in the context described above it becomes harder to view a performance of *Twelfth Night*, in Qatar, on the second anniversary of the invasion of Iraq, as harmlessly innocent. It was of course exactly that, within the values of the liberal democratic culture the play itself embodies, and the Doha Players espouse. But to Omar Ahmed Abdullah Ali, and to those who trained and equipped him, it must have represented something much more inimical and provocative: a flagrant display of western cultural power. It is still possible to recall, though only as a faint echo from an 'old age', that celebration of *Twelfth Night* as a kind of prelapsarian festivity:

Twelfth Night ... is filled to the brim and overflowing with the spirit that seeks to enjoy this world without one thought or aspiration beyond. It jumps the hereafter entirely.[25]

A strict Muslim like Omar, taught from the very beginning of the Holy Qu'ran to 'have faith in the Hereafter',[26] would have had no illusions about being able to jump the life to come, and no sympathy for anyone who thought they could.

There are those who do think, because they are virtuous, 'there shall be no more cakes and ale' (2.3.114–15). But if the play were nothing but cakes and ale, we too would be seeking elsewhere for the location of the virtuous. But it is not. *Twelfth Night* is not known to modern criticism as a simple celebration of fun-filled Epicureanism. In fact it has been understood in completely the opposite way, as a wry reflection on the shallowness of irresponsible gaiety. W. H. Auden saw Shakespeare here in a mood of 'puritanical aversion' from the 'pleasing illusions of life'; and Jan Kott thought it a 'bitter comedy about the Elizabethan *dolce vita*'.[27] To these critics, and to many others, the undertones of sadness, nostalgia, disillusion that haunt the play suggest an atmosphere of disenchantment and distaste for thoughtless pleasure. Sir Toby is 'sure care's an enemy to life', but the play does not for one moment fall into the illusion that responsibility, 'care', can be ignored or set aside. In interpretations such as these, Malvolio becomes a serious witness to the conscience of the age, and a precursor of the Puritan Commonwealth.

Malvolio, 'a kind of Puritan' (2.3.140), rejects the epicurean *dolce vita* as vehemently as did Jawad Akbar and Omar Khyam, who plotted to blow up London's Ministry of Sound nightclub.[28] Malvolio sees himself as the natural heir to the household authority, and longs to be in a position where he can extirpate what he sees as riotous behaviour. He is tricked into making a fool of himself, and detained as a madman. He is 'propertied' (4.2.94), treated as an object without human rights. He is imprisoned in a dark cell ('they have laid me here in hideous darkness' (4.2.30)), and subjected to forms of torture such as sensory deprivation ('They ... keep me in darkness ... and do all they can to face me out of my wits' (4.2.94–6)).[29] He feels that he has been 'abused' ('there was never man so notoriously abused' (4.2.90)), and his employer Olivia, having heard his story, is bound to agree: 'he hath been most notoriously abused' (5.1.380).[30]

To those who trick and torment him, all this is legitimate amusement. Olivia apologises to Malvolio, and the Duke commands Fabian to 'pursue him, and entreat him to a peace' (5.1.379). But the last words uttered by Malvolio on stage suggest that he will not be so easily entreated to a 'peace' on others' terms:

> I'll be revenged on the whole pack of you! (5.1.377)

These are not words calculated, like the fake letter of challenge, to 'breed no terror' (3.4.190). They were never spoken on stage on 19 March 2005, as Omar Ahmed Abdullah Ali had successfully brought home his revenge against the whole pack of them. Terror was already breeding, already bred.

IX

Twelfth Night ends with restoration, reconciliation, and unity. The lost are found. Misunderstanding is cleared up, identity restored: 'Cesario' can turn her assumed masculine disguise inside out to reveal her true feminine self. The comic subplot is disclosed, and Malvolio released from his bondage. The members of the cast are largely organised into heterosexual couples (Viola–Orsino, Olivia–Sebastian, Sir Toby–Maria), so the convention of marriage is employed to realign the characters into an orderly configuration, free from disguise, transsexual relationship, and misapprehension:

> When . . . golden time convents,
> A solemn combination shall be made
> Of our dear souls.
>
> 5.1.381–3

But the play does not actually end with this 'solemn combination', but with an isolated individual, and with a song. Feste's valedictory ballad is a melancholy little reflection on the intrinsic unhappiness of endings. Looking back to childhood, he recalls a time when 'play' was innocent and unproblematic: when pranks and folly needed no justification, being acceptable as innocuous fun appropriate to the status of a child – 'A foolish thing was but a toy' (5.1.388). For the adult however, all that has changed: the irresponsibility of folly in a grown man is regarded as unacceptable, threatening, and subversive;

the adult who wants to continue playing games is regarded as a criminal, and excluded by authority from civilised society, displaced to the margins of social life – 'Gainst knaves and thieves men shut their gates' (5.1.392). Adulthood marks an end to the liberated irresponsibility of play.

'I am sure,' Sir Toby affirms, 'care's an enemy to life' (1.3.2). Yet the song with which the play closes seems to confirm that 'care' is the very condition of 'life'; and that to be 'careless' is not to be 'carefree', but to be engaged in a continual hopeless effort to keep the inevitability of anxiety at a distance. Is life then its own enemy, self-divided against its own deepest and most passionate needs? Are play and pleasure locked into an irreconcilable antagonism with the anxiety that threatens them?

The one character who professes belief in the necessity of anxiety is the one character who is excluded from the otherwise universal harmony of the play's conclusion. Malvolio, bitterly disillusioned and 'notoriously abused' (5.1.376), has excluded himself from the compact of cheerfulness and gaiety secured by the rest of the cast. Possessed by a vindictive rage, he unites both those who have fooled him and those to whom his own folly has been exposed, in a comprehensive passion of indignation: 'I'll be revenged on the whole pack of you!' (5.1.375). He places himself outside the newly integrated community of the play, and casts a shadow over its delicately achieved balance of concord and reconciliation, which, we recognise, has been attained only at the cost of ejecting an inassimilable fragment. Even in his absence, his painful alienation and his oath of vengeance brood ominously over the play's closure; and there at the margins of the drama, his bitter and disappointed presence seems to meet the chastened resignation of the Clown, stranded alone with his own melancholy music, evidently no more a part of the collective celebrations than is Malvolio himself.[31]

But if care truly is both life's implacable enemy and life's inescapable antagonist, then Malvolio can be regarded as a central figure in the play. His fate is to be duped with false hopes and tempted with illusory aspirations; to experience disillusion and disenchantment, and finally to be diagnosed as mad, bound, confined, and eventually released to endure the open mockery of his captors and the suppressed amusement of his superiors.[32] In the light of Feste's song, and of the ambivalent nature of the play's 'happy ending', Malvolio can obviously stand as a representative figure in that inhospitable world where even innocent folly is punished and excluded. He is of course a victim of poetic justice, since he was a self-appointed instrument of that universal anxiety, dedicated to the identification of folly in others and the systematic denial of folly in himself. Yet although foolishness, irresponsibility, and the hopeless pursuit of perpetual pleasure are all common characteristics – they are certainly central to the character of Orsino, and Olivia is not free from them – Malvolio is the only character to be punished for his participation in a common destiny. He is the scapegoat, the victim who bears away with him the sins of the community.

Perhaps the ritual is only a game, and Malvolio may be entreated back to join the party. Or perhaps not. As the Clown stands alone, outside the official revelling of a united court, looking towards a disenchanted world where the rain rains every day, Malvolio's threat of revenge may begin to assume a shadowy substance and a menacing shape, haunting the western secular dream of materialist freedom. Those who invest their existence in the expectation of perpetual pleasure, guaranteed happiness, the uninterrupted continuance of the game, will always be exposed to the resentment and resistance of those acquainted with anxiety. Although Malvolio is no historical portrait of a puritan, it remains a tempting possibility (pursued by some stage productions) that his banishment and threatened revenge may correspond to the marginalisation and eventual victory of the puritans, who were later to fight against the King in the civil war.

The fact that on that night in Doha Malvolio did not get the chance to utter his desire for vengeance in words, since another vengeance had already been taken in deed, measures the real cultural damage done by Omar's suicide bomb. For Malvolio *is* inside the play, and his voice is there to be heard alongside the voices of those who abuse him. The harsh discordance of his cry for revenge, and the long shadow he casts over the play's final reconciliation, are left as characteristically jarring notes in Shakespeare's sweet but polyphonic music. The difficulty of maintaining community in such circumstances is not shirked, but confronted and handed over to the audience as a problem of interpretation. *Twelfth Night* is not a childlike celebration of innocuous play, but a mature and complex drama which explores the conflict between a playfulness that can offend, and a carefulness that can threaten play. Malvolio's anguish must be heard; but equally the community of the play's world must find some road to peaceful coexistence. Ultimately the play appeals to justice via a simple notion of fairness which can go very deep, and can form a ground of truth and reconciliation between people who have all suffered enough:

> If that the injuries be justly weigh'd,
> That have on both sides pass'd.

5.1.366–7

X

How far had *Twelfth Night* travelled to reach its Caribbean setting in the Doha Players Theatre? Not very far at all, in fact. Traditional nationalistic and newer historicist interpretations locate it somewhere between the paradigmatic 'English country house' and the nowhere of romance. That the play belongs on some kind of borderline is often acknowledged, but this is not thought of geographically, but rather as the border between reality and fantasy, or 'the borders of wonder and madness'.[33]

'Illyria' is usually either nowhere in particular, or the Adriatic coast of Greece. Thus the play is often thought to combine its Englishness with a Graeco-Roman ambience. Illyria was in fact somewhere in the western regions of the Balkan peninsula, on the coastline now occupied by Croatia, Montenegro, and Albania. In the eastern regions of Europe, then, and on a significant borderline between West and East. In Shakespeare's time this region was a critical border, since it hinged Christian Europe to the Islamic Ottoman Empire.[34] In one of the play's sources, Barnabe Riche's *Riche His Farewell to Militarie Profession* (1581), the Duke has 'spent a yeres service in the warres against the Turke'.[35] In *Twelfth Night*, there are references to the Shah of Persia: Fabian talks of a pension 'from the Sophy' (2.5.181), and Sir Toby pretends that Viola has 'been a fencer to the Sophy' (3.4.284). These references probably derived from published accounts of Sir John Shirley's travels and adventures in the Levant. Shirley acted as a kind of ambassador to the Shah in visits to Moscow, Prague, and Rome. Maria describes Malvolio's smile as containing 'more lines than is in the new map with the augmentation of the Indies'. (3.2.75–7) The reference is to a map published in 1599 that gave greater prominence to the East Indies. And just as Othello associates himself both with the 'turbaned Turk' and the loyal Venetian who kills him, so Orsino, preparing to sacrifice Viola on the altar of his jealous passion, presents himself as a legendary 'Egyptian thief' (5.1.116) who tried to kill the thing he loved.

The world of the play is then at some considerable distance from England, and is large enough to encompass allusions to the Islamic world, to Persia, and the Ottoman Empire. We may think of Shakespeare as almost synonymous with an anglophone culture of empire, as Michael Neill puts it: 'Our ways of thinking about such basic issues as nationality, gender and racial difference are inescapably inflected by his writing'.[36] Yet here we see Shakespeare setting his play on the border between West and East, Christianity and Islam, and opening doors to both. Today it is manifest that the Shakespeare once dispersed by linguistic imperialism around the globe is also a Shakespeare wholly or partially 'hybridised' by contact with other languages and cultures. As Dennis Kennedy puts it, 'almost from the start of his importance as the idealized English dramatist there have been other Shakespeares, Shakespeares not dependent on English and often at odds with it'.[37] Shakespeare in short 'goes native' every time he crosses a geographic or national border, and 'may thus be construed as the repositioned product of a complex of social, cultural and political factors that variously combine under the pressure of colonial, postcolonial and more narrowly national imperatives'.[38]

XI

The objective of terrorism is to terrorise. In the case of the Doha bombing, the point seems to have been to scare expatriate workers into leaving Qatar.[39] The Doha Players were certainly frightened by the attack, and they testify to a sense of anxiety and suspicion not previously present in their everyday lives. But they have no intention of leaving Qatar, or of abandoning their interest in theatre. On the contrary, the atrocity has brought them closer together into a self-help group dedicated to rebuilding the ruined theatre as a testament to Jonathan Adams. The campaign to raise the funding took some time to build momentum, but took off when students of the Qatar Academy raised 152,000 Qatari Riyal (QR) in memory of their admired and much missed teacher by means of a cultural festival. This was supplemented by a grant of more than 8 million QR from

His Highness the Emir Sheik Hamad bin Khalifa al-Thani. Qatar Foundation Vice-President for Education Dr Abdulla al-Thani celebrated the way in which students 'channelled their shock and grief into a fundraising effort in memory of their teacher'.

They will defend our society against intolerance, and they will be the guardians of our nation's civilised values.[40]

My words are ... full of peace.[41] Chair of the Doha Players, Kerry Ruek said:

The rebuilding of the theatre will leave a lasting legacy for the community in memory of Jon. The new theatre will stand as a message of peace and understanding among all peoples of the world.

Dave Garrod, a member of the theatre board, is quoted as saying that the new theatre would be named 'The Phoenix'.[42] If so, the name is beautifully appropriate. The legend of the Phoenix is Egyptian in origin, the sacred firebird of ancient mythology, but it was adopted by Christians and became a figure for the self-immolation and resurrection of Christ. Shakespeare's poem 'The Phoenix and the Turtle' locates the scene in Arabia:

> Let the bird of loudest lay
> On the sole Arabian tree ...

Thus eastern and western traditions in this emblem lie reciprocally enfolded in a 'mutual flame'. Jonathan Adams and the theatre he loved perished together. But a new theatre will rise from the ashes of the old, and preserve his memory, let us hope, 'to eternity'.[43]

Afterword: 'Tales from Shakespeare'

My title is of course taken from the famous anthology of Shakespeare stories, *Tales from Shakespeare*, written jointly by Charles and Mary Lamb, and first published in 1807, which represented my first acquaintance with Shakespeare.[1] These prose narratives, as they explained in their 'Preface', were extrapolated from the plays in order to introduce children to Shakespeare: 'The following Tales are meant to be submitted to the young reader as an introduction to the study of Shakespeare' (p. iii). In the stories, Shakespeare's dramatic poetry is rendered into prose, and the intricate theatrical plots simplified into linear narrative 'to give them the regular form of a connected story' (p. iii). The tales are not, however, composed as synopses, or plot summaries, since the writers took care to incorporate into them as much of Shakespeare's own poetic language as the prose narrative form permitted:

his words are used whenever it seemed possible to bring them in; and in whatever has been added diligent care has been taken to select such words as might least interrupt the effect of the beautiful English tongue in which he wrote: therefore, words introduced into our language since his time have been as far as possible avoided. (p. iii)

Hence the Lambs' stories consist of quotation as well as paraphrase. They simultaneously reproduce Shakespeare, imitate him, and translate him into a modern and accessible idiom. They are both Shakespeare and not-Shakespeare.

Apparently, then, a genuine and enduring engagement with Shakespeare may commence with something as inauthentic as the Lambs' *Tales from Shakespeare*. Nor was the context of the book's incursion into my life without significance. It was my eleventh birthday, August 1958. It was very early, still dark, the curtains in the front window of our council house closed. My father would have been due to start his shift at six o'clock, and wanted to see me before he left for work. There, on the table, stood a cardboard bookcase containing ten volumes, cased in bright primary colours, red, green, blue. They shone like jewels in the early morning darkness. Ten classics of English literature, whose titles I can still reel off without thinking: *Gulliver's Travels*, Charles Kingsley's *The Heroes*, *Alice in Wonderland*, Andersen's *Fairy Tales*, *Black Beauty*, *Children of the New Forest*, *Robinson Crusoe*, *A Christmas Carol*, Palgrave's *Golden Treasury*, and *Tales from Shakespeare*. The books were published under the title 'Presentation Library' by Beaverbrook Newspapers, and had been acquired no doubt from our daily newspaper, the rabidly reactionary popular broadsheet *Daily Express*. The gift was in recognition of my having just taken, and passed, the 11+, the selective examination that determined the next stage of schooling. I was due to start grammar school the following September.

These books were certainly the most influential gift of my life, and I read all of them, over and over again. They not only inspired, but formed the very shape of my literacy. They introduced me to the principal kinds of literature, novel, drama, and poetry, and to some major authors such as Dickens, Swift, Shakespeare, the Romantic poets. They provoked in me an insatiable appetite for all literary forms, for adventure, and fantasy, and tragedy, and satire, and lyric, and history, and fairy-tale; and for the richness and beauty of poetic and fictional language. There was only one dud in the box, *Black Beauty*: I never really cared for horses.

Only one of the ten books in the original collection survives today, *A Christmas Carol*, but I have picked up a few more at car-boot fairs, and hope eventually, like Isis searching for the fragments of the lost Osiris, to reassemble the whole set. Still the books have stayed with me. In the relaxed scholarly environment of the 1970s, I unashamedly used my 1957 childhood copy of *A Christmas Carol* to write an article on Dickens for a learned journal. *Gulliver's Travels* inspired the fable 'A Voyage to Bardolo' in *Nine Lives of William Shakespeare*. And in 'The Voyage of the *Red Dragon*' in this book, there are easily detectable echoes of *Treasure Island*.

The canon of classic literature embodied in the 'Presentation Library' belongs, no doubt rightly, to the past, and differs utterly from anything that would be assembled for an eleven-year-old today. It was nationalistic, and imperialist, and insular, and conservative, and male-dominated. But for a working-class child in the 1950s, it brought into my possession the inestimable gift of literacy: the passion for reading, the love of writing. After all, I was only eleven. All the rest could wait.

The Lambs targeted their work particularly at young girls, whose need for access to literature was much greater than that of boys: 'For young ladies ... it has been the intention chiefly to write; because boys being generally permitted the use of their fathers' libraries at a much earlier age than girls are, they frequently have the best scenes of Shakespeare by heart, before their sisters are permitted to look into this manly book' (p. v). I certainly was permitted the use of my father's library, though it contained only a history of the Great War, a dog-eared dictionary, and a book on motor-cycle maintenance. People of my class scarcely owned books before the 1960s. But they were by no means illiterate. Despite having left school at twelve, my father was a voracious reader; but his books came from the public lending library. In 1958 he gave me something he himself had never had: a library of my own.

In their 'Preface', the Lambs presented the tales as shadows to the Shakespearean substance, as inauthentic imitations deriving their value second-hand from the grandeur of their source. The tales are 'small and valueless coins' extracted from a horde of 'rich treasures': 'pretending to no other merit than as faint and imperfect stamps of Shakespeare's matchless image' (p. iv). I don't know how much my parents paid for the 'Presentation Library', but the cost must have been significant when deducted from the wages of an unskilled labourer. The price paid was probably more commensurate with the rich cultural 'treasures' represented by the books themselves, and with the inestimable personal value of the gift, then the 'small and valueless' estimation set by the Lambs on their appropriations of Shakespeare.

But the metaphor in the preface is about authenticity as well as value. It concerns the relationship between the 'stamp' and the 'image'. The comparison derives from the postal stamp that reproduced the head of the sovereign. Shakespeare's work represents the real, the Platonic form, the Aristotelean substance; while the 'stamp' is a reflection, an idol of the cave, a walking shadow. Shakespeare's *Hamlet* is the original, Charles Lamb's version a transitory adumbration. And yet it was the Lambs' *Tales* that began my long conversation with Shakespeare, begun in the 1950s, formalised into a research commitment in the 1980s, and still active today. In practice that hard-and-fast distinction between the substance and the shadow does not hold. That which is not Shakespeare has an uncanny way of becoming Shakespeare, and vice versa; or rather there is a continual reciprocal traffic of exchange and transformation between the two.

It is clearly a matter of some importance for this study that my first encounter with Shakespeare was not directly with the plays at all, but with an appropriation: with a text that combines the characteristics of an imitation and a pastiche; uses the critical techniques of selective quotation and paraphrase; and stands, in formal terms, somewhere between a revision and an adaptation. This was a text that, even in the word-play of its title, claimed derivation – the stories are *'ex libris'*, 'from Shakespeare' – and yet simultaneously implied aberration – the stories oblige the reader to travel away 'from' Shakespeare, even as they direct him/her towards the plays themselves.

Their lasting effect on this reader endures and abides. Continually drawn or driven away from, persistently pulled or pressurised back towards, Shakespeare. Or not-Shakespeare. Or maybe there's no difference between the two. Or there is a difference, but I just can't see what it is any more.

I hope this book will go some way towards answering some of these questions.

Notes

PREFACE

1 Graham Holderness, *Textual Shakespeare: Writing and the Word* (Hatfield: University of Hertfordshire Press, 2003), p. 14. Quotation from Hélène Cixous, *Three Steps on the Ladder of Writing*, translated by Sarah Cornell and Susan Sellers (New York: Columbia University Press, 1993), p. 21.

2 Graham Holderness, *Nine Lives of William Shakespeare* (London: Bloomsbury/Arden, 2011), p. 20.

INTRODUCTION: FROM APPROPRIATION TO COLLISION

1 Sonnet 76. References to Shakespeare's sonnets are from *The Sonnets of William Shakespeare* (London: Shepheard-Walwyn, 1974).

2 The edition cited above is based on Thomas Thorpe's 1609 Quarto edition, but the text of this poem includes the Capell emendation of 'fel' to 'tell'.

3 D. C. Greetham, *Theories of the Text* (Oxford: Clarendon Press, 1999), p. 22.

4 Ibid., pp. 370–1, and also p. 406: 'McGann, like Marx, determines that "conceiving" and "thinking ... appear as the direct efflux of [the] material". That is we can read back into spirit and thought the primary evidence to be obtained from materiality, which is, for McGann, text's "only condition".'

5 Jerome McGann, *The Textual Condition* (Princeton University Press, 1991), p. 9.

6 Michel Foucault, 'What is an Author?', in *The Foucault Reader*, edited by Paul Rabinow (New York: Pantheon Books, 1984), p. 108.

7 *The Appropriation of Shakespeare: The Works and the Myth*, edited by Jean I. Marsden (Hemel Hempstead: Harvester Wheatsheaf, 1991), p. 8.

8 Terence Hawkes, 'Introduction' to his edition, *Alternative Shakespeares Volume 2* (London: Routledge, 1996), p. 8.

9 Gary Taylor, *Reinventing Shakespeare: A Cultural History from the Restoration to the Present* (London: Hogarth Press, 1990; London: Vintage, 1991), p. 411.

10 From Giambattista Vico: 'what is true, and what is made by man, are one and the same'. See Terence Hawkes, *Structuralism and Semiotics* (London: Routledge, 1977; 2nd edn, 2003), p. 3.

11 *Hamlet* 2.2.239–40. All references in this chapter are to the New Cambridge Shakespeare edition, edited by Philip Edwards (Cambridge University Press, 1985).

12 See H. O. White, *Plagiarism and Imitation During the English Renaissance: A Study of Critical Distinctions* (Cambridge, Mass.: Harvard University Press, 1935), p. 16.

13 *Shakespeare and Appropriation*, edited by Christy Desmet and Robert Sawyer (London: Routledge, 1999), p. 12.

14 Evidently suggested by Michael Bristol, *Big-time Shakespeare* (London: Routledge, 1996).

15 *Philosophical Shakespeares*, edited by John Joughin (London: Routledge, 2000), p. 16.

16 The reference is to Terence Hawkes, *Meaning by Shakespeare* (London: Routledge 1992), p. 3.

17 See for example Harold Bloom, *Shakespeare: The Invention of the Human* (London: Fourth Estate, 1999). Bloom has also published a book *Hamlet: Poem Unlimited* (New York: Canongate, 2003).

18 Matthew Arnold, 'Shakespeare', in *The Poetical Works of Matthew Arnold*, edited by C. B. Tinker and H. F. Carey (Oxford University Press, 1950), p. 2.

19 Ralph Waldo Emerson, *Representative Men: Seven Lectures* (London: George Routledge & Sons, 1883), pp. 201–2. John Joughin notes that for Emerson 'the playwright's singularity is a striking blend of the familiar and the "hitherto unthought"'. *Philosophical Shakespeares*, p. 4.

20 Henry James, *Selected Literary Criticism*, edited by Morris Shapira (Cambridge University Press, 1981), p. 310.

21 See for example Stanley Cavell on James, in Joughin, *Philosophical Shakespeares*, pp. xv–xvi; and John Joughin on Emerson, ibid., pp. 3–4. See also Graham Holderness, *Textual Shakespeare: Writing and the Word* (Hatfield: University of Hertfordshire Press, 2003), pp. 247–8.

22 Terry Eagleton, *William Shakespeare* (Oxford: Blackwell, 1986), p. x. See also John Joughin in *Philosophical Shakespeares*: 'the dramatist's open-ended resistance to conceptual control might finally turn out to be a far more crucial resource for critical thought' (p. 11).

23 René Descartes, 'Second Meditation', in *Discourse on Method and the Meditations*, translated by F. E. Sutcliffe (Harmondsworth: Penguin, 1968).

24 Martin Scofield, *The Ghosts of 'Hamlet': The Play and Modern Writers* (Cambridge University Press, 1980), p. 3.

25 Stephen Greenblatt, 'General Introduction', in *The Norton Shakespeare: Based on the Oxford Edition*, edited by Stephen Greenblatt, Walter Cohen, Jean E. Howard, and Katherine Eisaman Maus (New York: W. W. Norton, 1997), p. 1.

26 The analogy can be pursued by observing that while Shakespeare's *Hamlet* remains malleable, subsequent rewritings of the play do not share the same flexibility. When mixed with other elements, as in an alloy, elemental metals lose their flexibility by the introduction of 'grain boundaries' across which atoms find it much harder to move. The carbon atoms in steel present an external force with much more resistance than the atoms of iron, so the crystals are more likely to dislocate than 'slip'. We remain surrounded by appropriations of *Hamlet*, but not with appropriations of appropriations. Appropriations are more like alloys than elemental metals. For a discussion of a range of *Hamlet* appropriations, see my *Textual Shakespeare*, pp. 178–212.

27 Homer, *The Odyssey*, translated by E. V. Rieu (Harmondsworth: Penguin, 1946), p. 75.

28 Francis Bacon, *De Sapientia Veterum Liber* (London: Robert Barker, 1609). Quotations from *The Wisedome of the Ancients, Done into English by Sir Arthur Gorges Knight* (London: John Bill, 1619). Bacon's scientific interpretations of ancient myths are extraordinarily advanced as well as acute, though earlier commentators saw him as attributing rather than extrapolating meaning: 'the sages of former times are rendered more wise than it may be they were by so dexterous an interpreter of their fables' (Thomas Tenison, quoted in Benjamin Farrington, *Francis Bacon: Philosopher of Industrial Science* (London: Macmillan, 1973), p. 77). Yet the ancient Greeks obviously thought of Proteus as a model for primary matter. The twenty-fifth Orphic hymn invokes Proteus as first-born, transmuting matter and possessing all knowledge. See *The Book of the Orphic Hymns* (London: J. Hibbert, 1827), p. 16. A fascinating passage in Ovid's *Fasti* identifies Proteus along these lines: 'Aristaeus wept, when he saw his bees killed / And honeycombs abandoned incomplete.' 'Proteus will . . . tell you how to regain what is gone.' The advice is to sacrifice a bullock and bury its carcase. 'From the putrid ox / Swarms bubble. One life axed bred a thousand.' *Fasti*, translated by A. J. Boyle and R. D. Woodard (Harmondsworth: Penguin, 2000), lines 364–5 and 379–80.

29 Proteins achieve this iterability by a process scientists call 'folding'. In order to carry out a particular function as an enzyme or antibody, proteins must take on a particular shape or 'fold'. When proteins fold incorrectly, they may be the cause of diseases such as Alzheimer's and BSE. Many biological terms similarly derive from the Greek word

protos, meaning primary; for example the 'protists', the generic term for single-cell beings, from viruses to larger organisms such as the amoeba (full name *Amoeba proteus*). 'Proteus' has proved to be a useful brand name for a range of products in biosciences and information technology. Wadsworth's *Proteus Classics* provides a large database of writing with tools for customising individual anthologies. A bioscience company named 'Proteus' 'discovers and develops molecules of primary importance and turns them to any form that meets the needs of the near future'. 'Protean 292X', a portable video signal generator, is (ironically) manufactured by a company called 'Hamlet'. All these examples entail an appropriation of Proteus' metamorphic capabilities. For modern science, the god is firmly bound, and singing like a canary.

30 Linda Charnes, 'We were never Early Modern', in Joughin, *Philosophical Shakespeares*, pp. 51–67, quotes taken from pages 65 and 66.

31 T. S. Eliot, 'Burnt Norton', in *Collected Poems* (London: Faber, 1936), p. 187.

32 Many literary applications have been made of this phenomenon. D. H. Lawrence in 1914 used it to explain his approach to character in 'The Sisters' (later to become the novels *The Rainbow* and *Women in Love*): 'There is another ego, according to whose action the individual is unrecognizable, and passes through, as it were, allotropic states which it needs a deeper sense than any we've been used to exercise to discover are states of the same single radically unchanged element (like as diamond and coal are the same pure single element of carbon).' *The Letters of D. H. Lawrence*, vol. II, edited by George Z. Zytaruk and James T. Boulton (Cambridge University Press, 1981), pp. 182–4. G. M. Hopkins used the principle to reconcile the mutability of nature with the permanence of resurrection in 'That Nature is a Hericlatean Fire and of the Comfort of the Resurrection': 'This Jack, joke, poor potsherd, patch, matchwood, immortal diamond / Is immortal diamond' (*Poetry and Prose*, edited by W. H. Gardner (Harmondsworth: Penguin, 1953), p. 66). Today it is possible to have the cremated remains of a loved one reconstituted into a diamond ring.

33 Gary Taylor, 'Afterword: The Incredible Shrinking Bard', in Desmet and Sawyer, *Shakespeare and Appropriation*, p. 205.

34 Stephen Hawking, *The Universe in a Nutshell* (London: Transworld, 2001).

35 Sonnet 15. From *The Sonnets* (1974).

1 THE VOYAGE OF THE *RED DRAGON*

1 Thomas Rundall, *Narratives of Voyages Towards the North West* (London: Hakluyt Society, 1849), p. 231.

2 *The East India Company Journals of Captain William Keeling and Master Thomas Bonner, 1615–1617*, edited by Michael Strachan and Boies Penrose (Minneapolis: University of Minnesota Press, 1971), p. 31.

3 Richmond Barbour, *The Third Voyage Journals: Writing and Performance in the London East India Company, 1607–10* (Basingstoke: Palgrave, 2009).

4 Samuel Purchas, *Hakluytus Posthumus or Purchas His Pilgrimes* (1625).

5 Both extracts quoted from Barbour, *Journals*, p. 244.

6 William Benchley Rye, *England as Seen by Foreigners in the Days of Elizabeth and James the First* (London: John Russell Smith, 1865), p. cxi.

7 *The Voyages of Sir James Lancaster Knight to the East Indies*, edited by Clements R. Markham (London: Hakluyt Society, 1877).

8 Sidney Lee, *A Life of William Shakespeare, with Portraits and Facsimiles* (London: Smith, Elder, 1898), p. 369.

9 Frederick S. Boas, *Shakespeare and the Universities and Other Studies in Elizabethan Drama* (New York: Appleton, 1923), p. 95.

10 E. K. Chambers, *William Shakespeare: A Study of Facts and Problems* (Oxford: Clarendon Press, 1930), vol. ii, p. 334.

11 Cited in G. Blakemore Evans, 'The Authenticity of the Keeling Journal Entries Re-asserted', *Notes & Queries*, 197 (15 March 1952), pp. 127–8.

12 For instance *Hamlet*, edited by Ann Thompson and Neil Taylor, Arden Shakespeare 3rd series (London: Bloomsbury, 2006), pp. 53–5.

13 Gary Taylor, in *Travel Knowledge: European Discoveries in the Early Modern Period*, edited by Ivo Kamps and Jyotsna G. Singh (Basingstoke: Palgrave, 2001), pp. 211–22.

14 Boas, *Shakespeare and the Universities*, p. 95.

15 Ania Loomba, 'Shakespearean Transformations', in *Shakespeare and National Culture*, edited by John Joughin (Manchester University Press, 1997), p. 114.

16 Though there is a suggestive reference in Markham: 'On the 18th of June … we had a great feast and a play playd'. According to Sir William Foster, who defended Rundall against Sir Sidney Lee, another journal kept during the sixth voyage of the East India Company by one Benjamin Greene of the *Darling*, included a fragment listing the names of characters and the opening lines of a play. See Loomba in Joughin, *National Culture*, p. 112. Gary Taylor also cites other corroborative circumstantial evidence in Kamps and Singh, *Travel Knowledge*, pp. 230–2.

17 Bernice Kliman, 'At Sea about *Hamlet*: A Detective Story', *Shakespeare Quarterly*, 2:2 (summer 2001).

18 Kliman dismisses the allusion cited in note 16 above to 'a play playd' as more likely to refer to some sport or pastime.

19 See for instance Laurie Maguire and Emma Smith, *30 Great Myths about Shakespeare* (London: Wiley-Blackwell, 2013).

3 SHAKESPEARE AND THE KING JAMES BIBLE

1 Louis Marder, *His Exits and His Entrances: The Story of Shakespeare's Reputation* (Philadelphia: Lippincott 1963), p. 362.

2 The programme was broadcast on BBC2, Saturday, 12 March 2011.

3 William Barlow, 'The Sum and Substance of the Conference', in *Constitutional Documents of the Reign of James I*, edited by J. R. Tanner (Cambridge University Press, 1961), p. 63.

4 *Th'overthrow of Stage-Playes, by the way of a controversy betwixt D. Gager and D. Rainoldes* (Middleburgh: R. Schilders, 1599).

5 John Drakakis, 'Theatre, Ideology and Institution', in *The Shakespeare Myth*, edited by Graham Holderness (Manchester University Press, 1987), pp. 24–5.

6 'His Highness wished that some especial pains should be taken in that behalf.' See Barlow in Tanner, *Documents*, p. 63.

7 *The Bible: Authorised King James Version*, edited by Robert Carroll and Stephen Prickett (Oxford University Press, 1997), p. lxxi.

8 *The First Folio of Shakespeare*, prepared by Charlton Hinman (London and New York: W. W. Norton/Paul Hamlyn, 1968; reissued with an additional introduction by Peter Blayney, 1996), p. 5.

9 See Frank Kermode, 'The Canon', in *The Literary Guide to the Bible*, edited by R. Alter and F. Kermode (London: Collins, 1987), p. 606.

10 Carroll and Prickett, *Bible*, p. lix.

11 *First Folio* (Norton Facsimile, 1968), p. 7.

12 Carroll and Prickett, *Bible*, p. xxvi. For the 'Bishops' Bible', see 'English Versions of the Bible', in *The Cambridge History of the Bible*, edited by Peter Ackroyd and Christopher F. Evans (Cambridge University Press, 1970), vol. II, pp. 159–61.

13 See Gustavus S. Paine, *The Men Behind the KJV* (Grand Rapids, Mich.: Baker Book House, 1959), pp. 136–9.

14 Adam Nicolson, *When God Spoke English: The Making of the King James Bible* (London: HarperCollins, 2003), p. xv.

15 'The rules to be obserued in translation', manuscript, Cambridge University Library, quoted from Nicolson, *God Spoke*, p. 79.

16 Lambeth Palace Library, MS 98.

17 British Library, Harley MS 7368, fo. 9.

18 See James Shapiro, *1599: A Year in the Life of William Shakespeare* (New York: Harper Perennial, 2006), p. 175.

19 Rudyard Kipling's story 'Proofs of Holy Writ' was published in *Strand Magazine* in April 1934. It was republished in the magazine's December 1947 issue, with a note by Roger Lancelyn Green describing the quoted conversation.

20 Anthony Burgess, 'Will and Testament', in *Enderby's Dark Lady, or No End to Enderby* (London: Hutchinson, 1984), pp. 9–34. See also Paul Frannsen, 'The Bard, the Bible and the Desert Island', in *The Author as Character: Representing Historical Writers*, edited by Paul Frannsen and Ton Hoenselaars (Hackensack, NJ: Fairleigh Dickinson University Press, 1999).

5 THE *CORIOLANUS* MYTH

1 See *Coriolanus*, edited by Peter Holland (London: Bloomsbury, 2013), p. 134.
2 John Osborne, *A Place Calling Itself Rome* (1973). Published in *Four Plays* (London: Oberon Books, 2000).
3 Titus Lartius is played by Serbian actor Dragan Mićanović, who has drawn an explicit parallel between the Serbian general Ratko Mladić, and Coriolanus: 'if he read *Coriolanus* he could find his story in it'. Quoted in Zoe Dare Hall, '*Coriolanus* echoes the war in Serbia', *Telegraph*, 20 January 2012.
4 Slavoj Žižek, 'Sing of a new invasion', *New Statesman*, 12 December 2011.
5 All quotations are taken from Holland's *Coriolanus*.
6 *Coriolanus*, directed by Ralph Fiennes (Icon Entertainment International/BBC Films, 2011).
7 I find these displays irritatingly conventional, as does Stephen Greenblatt, who describes the Citizens in the film as 'young ideologues mouthing slogans, marching under banners'. 'A Man of Principle', *New York Review of Books* (8 March 2012).
8 'A mechanized human, incapable of thought beyond the boundaries prescribed by his programming from birth'. Holland, *Coriolanus*, p. 136.
9 Ibid., p. 134.
10 Philip French, review of *Coriolanus*, *Observer*, 22 January 2012; Greenblatt, 'A Man of Principle'.
11 *The Hurt Locker*, directed by Kathryn Bigelow (First Light Productions, 2009).
12 A. O. Scott, 'Soldiers between peril and protocol', *New York Times*, 25 June 2009.
13 Brian Turner, 'The Hurt Locker', in *Here, Bullet* (Farmington, ME: Alice James Books, 2005).
14 *Skyfall*, directed by Sam Mendes (Eon Productions, 2012).
15 I am thinking of Alec Leamas in John le Carré's *The Spy Who Came In From the Cold* (London: Gollancz, 1963) or Maurice Castle in Graham Greene's *The Human Factor* (London: Bodley Head, 1978). Compare the conclusion to Ian Fleming's *You Only Live Twice* (London: Jonathan Cape, 1964), where Bond remains AWOL on a similarly prolonged vacation, but only because he has lost his memory.

7 SHAKESPEARE AND 9/11

1 *Shakespeare After 9/11: How a Social Trauma Reshapes Interpretation* (New York: Edwin Mellen Press, 2011) features essays by Slavoj Žižek, Linda Charnes, Hugh Grady, Christopher Pye, and Jonathan Gil Harris, and poems by Tom Sleigh, Robert Polito, and Graham Holderness, among others.

2 R. L. Stevenson and Fanny Van der Grift Stevenson, *More New Arabian Nights: The Dynamiter* (London: Longmans, Green & Co., 1885), p. 189.

3 See Graham Holderness and Bryan Loughrey, 'Shakespearean Features', in *The Appropriation of Shakespeare: The Works and the Myth*, edited by Jean I. Marsden (Hemel Hempstead: Harvester Wheatsheaf, 1991), pp. 183–201.

4 Notwithstanding, the attempt is made in the creative-critical essay that follows this chapter.

5 Mackubin T. Owens, 'Shakespeare was no Pacifist', Ashbrook Centre for Public Affairs at Ashland University, November 2002. www.ashbrook.org/publicat/oped/owens/02/shakespeare.html [accessed 20 September 2013].

6 The Dover Thrift Edition of *Henry V*. For the original Armed Services Editions, see Christopher P. Loss, 'Reading between Enemy Lines: Armed Services Editions and World War II', *Journal of Military History*, 67:3 (July 2003), pp. 811–34; for the revived initiative, see the Legacy Project at www.warletters.com/ases/index.html [accessed 20 September 2013].

7 Sulayman Al-Bassam, *The Al-Hamlet Summit* (English/Arabic) (Hatfield: University of Hertfordshire Press, 2006).

8 See Alan Sinfield, *Faultlines: Cultural Materialism and the Politics of Dissident Reading* (Oxford: Clarendon Press, 1992), pp. 1–7; Graham Holderness, *Cultural Shakespeare: Essays in the Shakespeare Myth* (Hatfield: University of Hertfordshire Press, 2001), pp. 180–3.

9 Quotations from *Hamlet* are from Ann Thompson and Neil Taylor's Arden Shakespeare 3rd series edition (London: Bloomsbury, 2006).

10 Moazzam Begg, speaking at the symposium 'Shakespeare: Violence and Terror', Shakespeare's Globe, 5 August 2006.

11 Ismael Beah, *A Long Way Gone: Memoirs of a Boy Soldier* (New York: Farrar, Straus, and Giroux, 2007).

12 Rowan Williams, *Writing in the Dust: Reflections on September 11 and its Aftermath* (London: Hodder & Stoughton, 2002), p. 26.

13 Noam Chomsky, quoted in Richard Kearney, *Strangers, Gods and Monsters: Interpreting Otherness* (London: Routledge, 2002), p. 135.

14 Ian McEwan, 'Only love and then oblivion. Love was all they had to set against their murderers', *Guardian*, 15 September 2001.

15 'Last words of a terrorist', *Observer*, 30 September 2001. The document has been published in *The 9/11 Handbook: Arabic Text, Annotated*

Translation and Interpretation of the Attacker's Spiritual Manual, edited by H. G. Kippenberg and Tilman Seidensticker (London: Equinox, 2006). See also Hans G. Kippenberg, '"Consider that it is a raid on the path of God": The Spiritual Manual of the Attackers of 9/11', *Numen*, 52:1 (2005), pp. 29–58.

16 Walter Laqueur, *The Age of Terrorism* (Boston: Little, Brown, 1987), pp. 149–50.

17 Bruce Hoffman, *Inside Terrorism* (New York: Columbia University Press, 1988), p. 14.

18 Terry Eagleton, *Holy Terror* (Oxford University Press, 2005), pp. 1–2; Alan Badiou, 'Philosophy and the "War against Terrorism"', in *Infinite Thought: Truth and the Return of Philosophy*, translated by Oliver Feltham and Justin Clemens (London: Continuum, 2003), pp. 42–67.

19 Jessica Stern, *The Ultimate Terrorists* (Cambridge, Mass.: Harvard University Press, 2001), p. 11.

20 Mark Jurgensmeyer, 'Terror Mandated by God', *Terrorism and Political Violence*, 9:2 (summer 1997), p. 17.

21 Harlan K. Ullman and James P. Wade, Jr, *Shock and Awe: Achieving Rapid Dominance* (Washington, DC: National Defense University, 1996), p. 26.

22 'Iraq faces massive US missile barrage', CBS News, 24 January 2003.

23 The *Oxford English Dictionary* cites its definition of 'Ground Zero' as 'that part of the ground situated immediately under an exploding bomb, especially an atomic one' from a 1946 *New York Times* report on the bombing of Hiroshima.

24 David Rappaport, '"Fear and Trembling": Terrorism in Three Religious Traditions', *Political Science Review*, 78:3 (September 1984), pp. 668–72.

25 See David G. Kibble, 'The Attacks of 9/11: Evidence of a Clash of Religions?', *Religion*, 35:1 (January 2005), pp. 1–11.

26 Jurgensmeyer, 'Terror Mandated by God', p. 22.

27 Quoted in *Countering the Changing Threat of International Terrorism* (Washington, DC: National Commission on Terrorism, 2000), p. 2.

28 R. A. Foakes, *Shakespeare and Violence* (Cambridge University Press, 2003).

29 Jacques Derrida, *The Gift of Death*, translated by David Willis (University of Chicago Press, 1995), p. 57.

30 Seamus Heaney, *Beowulf: A Verse Translation*, edited by Dennis Donoghue (New York: W. W. Norton, 2003), lines 106–14.

31 *Beowulf*, directed by Robert Zemeckis (Imagemovers, 2007).

32 Kearney, *Strangers, Gods and Monsters*, p. 4.

33 *Cloverfield*, directed by Matt Reeves (Bad Robot, 2008).

34 Slavoj Žižek, *On Violence: Six Sideways Reflections* (London: Profile Books, 2008), p. 2.

35 Jean Baudrillard, 'Simulations', in *Continental Aesthetics*, edited by Richard Kearney and David Rasmussen (Oxford: Blackwell, 2001), p. 423.

36 Jean Baudrillard, 'L'Esprit du terrorisme', translated by Donovan Hohn, *Harper's Magazine* (February 2002), pp. 13–18. First published in *Le Monde*, 2 November 2001.

37 McEwan, 'Only love and then oblivion'.

38 Žižek, *On Violence*, p. 1.

39 Foakes, *Shakespeare and Violence*, p. 1.

40 Žižek, *On Violence*, p. 2.

41 Francis Barker, *The Culture of Violence: Tragedy and History* (Manchester University Press, 1993), pp. 65–6.

42 Quotations from *Macbeth* are taken from the New Cambridge Shakespeare edition, edited by A. R. Braunmuller (2nd edn; Cambridge University Press, 2008).

43 Christopher Pye, 'The Sovereign, the Theatre, and the Kingdome of Darknesse: Hobbes and the Spectacle of Power', in *Representing the English Renaissance*, edited by Stephen Greenblatt (Berkeley: University of California Press, 1988), p. 299. 'The authoritarian preserves a secret compact with the anarchist'. Eagleton, *Holy Terror*, p. 9.

44 Stephen Greenblatt, '"Invisible bullets": Renaissance Authority and its Subversion', in *Political Shakespeare: New Essays in Cultural Materialism*, edited by Alan Sinfield and Jonathan Dollimore (Manchester University Press, 1985), p. 33.

45 Steven Mullaney, *The Place of the Stage: Licence, Play and Power in Renaissance England* (University of Chicago Press, 1988), p. 126.

46 Jonathan Goldberg, '*Macbeth* and Source', in *Shakespeare Reproduced: The Text in History and Ideology*, edited by Jean E. Howard and Marion F. O'Connor (London: Methuen, 1987), p. 249.

47 Leonard Tennenhouse, *Power on Display: The Politics of Shakespeare's Genres* (London: Methuen, 1986), p. 15.

48 Richard Wilson, '"Blood will have blood": Regime Change in Macbeth', *Deutsche-Shakespeare-Gesellschaft-West Jahrbuch*, 143 (2007), p. 16.

49 Michael Wood, *In Search of Shakespeare* (London: BBC Books, 2003), p. 95.

50 Goldberg, '*Macbeth* and Source', p. 259.

51 Wilson, '"Blood will have blood"', p. 30.

52 Lancelot Andrewes, *Selected Sermons and Lectures*, edited by Peter McCullough (Oxford University Press, 2005), p. 152.

53 Quoted in Gary Wills, *Witches and Jesuits: Shakespeare's 'Macbeth'* (Oxford University Press, 1995), p. 19.

54 Ibid., p. 123.

55 Quoted ibid., p. 21.

56 'Last words of a terrorist'.

57 Søren Kierkegaard, *Fear and Trembling,* translated by Alistair Hannay (Harmondsworth: Penguin, 2003).

58 Quotations from *The Noble Qu'ran*, translated by Taqi-ud-Din al-Hilali and Muhammad Muhsin Khan (Madinah: King Fahd Press, n.d.).

59 Quoted Wills, *Witches and Jesuits*, p. 19.

60 'Last words of a terrorist'.

61 Ibid.

62 Frank Lentricchia and Jody McAuliffe, *Crimes of Art and Terror* (University of Chicago Press, 2003), p. 8.

63 Eagleton, *Holy Terror*, p. 121.

64 Quoted ibid., p. 123.

65 Quoted in Julia Spinola, 'Monstrous art', *Frankfurter Allgemeine Zeitung*, 25 September 2001.

66 Stockhausen, quoted Lentricchia and McAuliffe, *Crimes of Art and Terror*, pp. 9–10; my italics.

67 Derrida quoted in Giovanni Borradori, *Philosophy in a Time of Terror: Dialogues with Jürgen Habermas and Jacques Derrida* (University of Chicago Press, 2003), p. 167 and p. 113.

68 Stephen Greenblatt, *Will to the World: How Shakespeare became Shakespeare* (London: Jonathan Cape, 2004), pp. 108–10.

69 Kearney, *Strangers, Gods and Monsters*, p. 134.

70 Fieldwork in Qatar undertaken by Bryan Loughrey, to whom Part IV is deeply indebted.

8 'RUDELY INTERRUPTED'

1 *Twelfth Night*, 3.1.143. All references are taken from the Arden Shakespeare edition, edited by J. M. Lothian and T. W. Craik (London: Methuen, 2007).

2 Reconstruction based on the known facts. See 'Bomber identified as Egyptian', *The Peninsula* (newspaper), 21 March 2005; 'Egyptian bomber blamed for Qatar attack', *Breaking News*, 20 March 2005; 'Protest rally over Qatar bombing', *BBC News*, 21 March 2005.

3 Details derived from conversations between Bryan Loughrey and members of the Doha Players, March 2007.

4 Extracts from Saleh Mohammed Al-Aoofi, 'Audio statement from Al-Qa'eda in Saudi Arabia to Abu Musab Al-Zarqawi in Iraq'. This taped speech 'according to US intelligence officials, gave a green light to the Doha bombing'. Alexis Debat, 'The new head of Jihad Inc.?', *CBS News*, 17 March 2005.

5 Based on recollections from Kerry Ruek, chair of the Doha Players, in conversation with Bryan Loughrey, March 2007.

6 Extracts from Al-Aoofi, 'Audio statement'.

7 Ibid.

8 *Twelfth Night*, 1.4.21–2.
9 US Army Captain Eric Clark, quoted from 'Egyptian bomber blamed for Qatar attack'.
10 Kerry Ruek in conversation with Bryan Loughrey.
11 The words of Julie Hirst, quoted from 'Protest rally over Qatar bombing'.
12 Ahmed Goudah, quoted from 'Egyptian bomber blamed for Qatar attack'.
13 Details derived from conversations between Bryan Loughrey and members of the Doha Players, March 2007.
14 Gerard Kennedy, quoted in 'Bomber identified as Egyptian'.
15 Details derived from conversations between Bryan Loughrey and members of the Doha Players, March 2007.
16 Debat, 'New head of Jihad Inc.?'
17 Jürgen Habermas, quoted from Giovanni Borradori, *Philosophy in a Time of Terror: Dialogues with Jürgen Habermas and Jacques Derrida* (University of Chicago Press, 2003), p. 25.
18 Jacques Derrida, quoted from Borradori, *Philosophy in a Time of Terror*, p. 87.
19 Derrida quoted ibid., p. 100.
20 *Post-colonial Shakespeares*, edited by Ania Loomba and Martin Orkin (London: Routledge, 1998), p. 1.
21 Chinua Achebe, 'An Image of Africa: Racism in Conrad's *Heart of Darkness*', in *Hopes and Impediments: Selected Essays 1965–1987* (Oxford: Heinemann, 1988), p. 8.
22 Francis Barker and Peter Hulme, '"Nymphs and Reapers heavily vanish": The Discursive Con-texts of *The Tempest*', in *Alternative Shakespeares*, edited by John Drakakis (London: Methuen, 1985), p. 198.
23 Michael Neill, 'Postcolonial Shakespeare? Writing away from the Centre', in *Post-colonial Shakespeares*, ed. Loomba and Orkin, p. 168.
24 Martin Walker, 'Why they Bomb Shakespeare', *UPI Business News*, 21 March 2005, www.upi.com/Business_News/Security-Industry/2005/03/21/Walkers-World-Why-they-bomb-Shakespeare/UPI-52131111404108/ [accessed 20 September 2013].
25 H. J. Ruggles, quoted in Lothian and Craik, *Twelfth Night*, p. lii.
26 *The Koran*, translated by Arthur J. Arberry (Oxford University Press, 1983), p. 2.
27 Auden and Kott, quoted in Lothian and Craik, *Twelfth Night*, p. liv.
28 Akbar said they would not be blamed for killing innocent people at the club, as they were targeting only 'slags dancing around'. 'Gang "planned to blow up London nightclub"', *Guardian*, 25 May 2006.
29 See David Carnegie, '"Maluolio within": Performance Perspectives on the Dark House', *Shakespeare Quarterly*, 52:3 (autumn 2001), pp. 393–414.

30 'Abuse' is the term commonly used to describe the torture and humiliation of detainees in the notorious Abu Ghraib military prison in Iraq.

31 See Yu Jin Ko, 'The Comic Close of *Twelfth Night* and Viola's *Noli Me Tangere*', *Shakespeare Quarterly*, 48:4 (winter 1997), pp. 391–405.

32 See Allison P. Hobgood, '*Twelfth Night*'s "notorious abuse" of Malvolio: Shame, Humorality and Early Modern Spectatorship', *Shakespeare Bulletin*, 24:3 (September 2006), pp. 1–22.

33 Frank Kermode, quoted in Lothian and Craik, *Twelfth Night*, p. lv.

34 In the 1590s the Turks were launching major campaigns in Hungary.

35 Quoted in Lothian and Craik, *Twelfth Night*, p. 157.

36 Neill, 'Postcolonial Shakespeare?', p. 184.

37 Dennis Kennedy, *Foreign Shakespeare* (Cambridge University Press, 1993), p. 2.

38 Thomas Cartelli, *Repositioning Shakespeare: National Formations, Postcolonial Appropriations* (London: Routledge, 1999), p. 1.

39 'The bombing appeared to be directed against Qatar's pro-western policies and at frightening expatriate workers.' *Guardian*, 21 March 2005.

40 *Qatar Foundation News*, 11 October 2006.

41 *Twelfth Night*, 1.5.213.

42 'Tributes to man who took full force of blast', *The Times*, 21 March 2005.

43 Shakespeare, 'The Phoenix and the Turtle'. *William Shakespeare: The Complete Works*, edited by Stanley Wells and Gary Taylor with John Jowett and William Montgomery (Oxford University Press, 1988), p. 782. In *Twelfth Night* (5.1.159), a play in which more than one new person rises from the ashes of the old, the vessel stolen by Antonio is called the *Phoenix*.

AFTERWORD

1 Charles [and Mary] Lamb, *Tales from Shakespeare: Designed for the Use of Young People* (London: George Routledge & Sons, 1807).

Index